Confronting Globalization

Confronting Globalization

Economic Integration and Popular Resistance in Mexico

Editors
Timothy A. Wise
Hilda Salazar
Laura Carlsen

Kumarian
Press, Inc.

#51389259

Confronting Globalization: Economic Integration and Popular Resistance in Mexico
Published 2003 in the United States of America by Kumarian Press, Inc.
1294 Blue Hills Avenue, Bloomfield, CT 06002 USA

Production and design by Rosanne Pignone, Pro Production
Index by Robert Swanson, ARC Films, Inc.
Copyedited by Beth Richards
Proofread by Phil Trahan, The Icon Corner

The text for Confronting Globalization is set in Times Roman 10/12.
Printed in the United States of America on acid-free paper by Thomson-Shore, Inc.
Text printed with vegetable oil-based ink.

⊚ The paper used in this publication meets the minimum requirements of the American National Standard for Information Sciences—Permanence of Paper for Printed Library Materials, ANSI Z39.48–1948.

Library of Congress Cataloging-in-Publication Data
    Confronting globalization : economic integration and popular resistance
in Mexico / editors, Timothy A. Wise, Laura Carlsen, Hilda Salazar.
       p. cm.
    Includes bibliographical references and index.
    ISBN 1-56549-163-7 (pbk)—ISBN 1-56549-166-1 (hc)
    1. Mexico—Economic conditions. 2. Free trade—Mexico. 3. Free
trade—United States. 4. North America—Economic integration. I. Wise,
Timothy A., 1955– II. Carlsen, Laura, 1957– III. Salazar, Hilda, 1953–
HC133.C66 2003
330.972—dc21

                                     2002156661

11 10 09 08 07 06 05 04 03 02   10 9 8 7 6 5 4 3 2 1 First Printing 2003

Contents

Acknowledgements

THIS BOOK IS THE PRODUCT OF AN EFFORT BETWEEN UNITED STATES AND MEX-
ican researchers and activists, in itself a small example of the growing
cross-border collaboration between the two countries. It sprang from an
appreciation for the rich and creative responses to globalization on the part
of Mexican civil society organizations. Those organizations and movements, large and small, deserve first mention: peasant groups, trade
unions, migrant clubs, indigenous communities, environmental organizations, and human rights groups. Without their creativity and tenacity, a
project like this would not have been possible.

During a year and a half of work, the authors of the case studies contributed not only as writers, but also as part of a collective process of discussion, reflection, and analysis about the new realities in globalized
Mexico. We are grateful for their participation in this dialogue. We also
thank the participants at our August 2001 conference, "Social and Environmental Impacts of NAFTA: Grassroots Responses to Economic Inte-
gration:w" Alejandro Nadal, Victor Suárez, Luís Hernández Navarro,
Adriana Estévez López, Silvia Ribeiro, Armando Bartra, Luís Nava, Juan
Manuel Sandoval, and Alberto Arroyo. We also thank El Colegio de Mexico and its Program on Science, Technology, and Development for hosting
the seminar.

We would also like to thank the Center for Development Studies of the
University of Zacatecas for collaborating in the publication of the case
studies in Spanish as part of its series "Latin America Faces Globalization"

co-edited with publisher Miguel Ángel Porrúa. This English-language edition is largely a translation of the concurrent Spanish volume, *Enfrentando la Globalización: Integración Económica y Resistencia Popular en México* (Mexico City: Miguel Ángel Porrúa: 2003).

From the Mexican Action Network for Free Trade (RMALC), María de la Paz Soriano devoted hours to reviewing drafts. Alejandro Villamar actively participated in developing the project and selecting cases. Eugenia Gutierrez and Ana Grinberg helped with translations, and Ramón Vera was in charge of final revisions, providing his great attention to detail, sharp commentaries, and eloquence. Finally, Maria Atilano, Executive Coordinator of RMALC, deserves special recognition. Her participation in all phases of the project has been essential for both the success and the completion of the project and the book.

Despite the barriers of distance and language, several people at Tufts University's Global Development and Environment Institute have contributed to the project from the beginning. To our colleagues Frank Ackerman, Kevin Gallagher, Eliza Waters, and Regina Flores, we thank you for your support and invaluable commentary. The English edition owes heartfelt thanks to David Palmer, Oliver Brody, and Regina Flores for their translation work. We also appreciate the openness, interest, and contributions of Kumarian Press, especially editor Guy Bentham.

Finally, we would also like to thank the institutions that made this project possible with their financial support and encouragement: Rockefeller Brothers Fund, Charles Stewart Mott Foundation, General Service Foundation, and William and Flora Hewlett Foundation.

Foreword

Jonathan Fox

"The concept of globalization has hit hard. Right in the face. The system no longer hides what's behind it. It openly says 'I'll take your land and exploit you' . . . "
— Ignacio del Valle, leader of the Atenco community
protests against the proposed new Mexico City airport.[1]

The Mexican-U.S. integration process, with its intense flows of capital, commodities, cultures and communities, is a paradigm case for understanding the globalization process. The Mexican experience shows that trade openings are inextricably linked to broader patterns of social, economic, political, and cultural exclusion—both in the popular imagination and at the commanding heights of the ruling political classes. To assess globalization's winners and losers, we need to take into account the breadth and depth of the Mexican experience with international economic integration.

Why Mexico?

Seen from above, the North American Free Trade Agreement led the way for world-wide acceleration of global economic integration between the North and South that followed. The NAFTA experience is directly informing the ongoing negotiations for new trade agreements, both in the hemisphere and specifically with Central America. For example, NAFTA's little-known but powerful Chapter 11, its "investors' bill of rights" that

---

*Quoted in Maria Rivera, "La lucha no se gana con consignas sino con razones, afirma el dirigente Ignacio del Valle." *La Jornada,* 17 July 2002.

trumps national social and environmental laws, is already embedded in early drafts of the proposed Free Trade Area of the Americas.

Seen from below, Mexico's Zapatista rebels fired the proverbial shot heard 'round the world that opened the current cycle of protest against top-down globalization. Their widely-echoed charge that NAFTA spelled a "death sentence" for Mexico's indigenous peoples became a vivid emblem of grassroots struggles against top-down globalization. The rebellion's inclusionary discourse and multimedia-savvy strategy resonated with a wide range of other campaigns for social justice around the world, energizing the emerging concept of globalization from below. Within Mexico, the rebels showed that history still matters and contributed directly to the national democratization process. They revealed that Mexico's neoliberal emperor had no clothes. This is the pattern of Mexican resistance that is best known abroad.

At the same time, *most* Mexicans who challenge top-down globalization follow quite different paths. These grassroots movements often sympathize with the Zapatistas' radical democratic challenge, but they follow strategies that emerge from their own political histories and use tactics that respond to their own specific opportunities and constraints. The chapters that follow show the range of these initiatives, from discreet worker-by-worker organizing for dignity on the shop floor to combined legal, media, and protest campaigns for environmental justice. These cases also help to put cross-border organizing in context, showing that for most grassroots responses to economic integration, transnational coalition-building is just one dimension of political strategies that remain primarily local and national in focus.

Some of these initiatives focus on direct resistance, as in the case of protests against toxic waste dumps. Others try to buffer the process, as in the case of the fight for *maquila* workers' rights. Yet others try to find and expand niches within the globalization process—for example, by building economically viable and sustainable timber cooperatives, or creating new people-to-people "philanthropy from below" in the form of migrant hometown associations. The diverse cases documented here share a common thread, however: they are all stories of people in action, defending themselves, and creating alternatives. Read on to find out more about the multiple meanings of resistance in Mexico today.

Disentangling Winners and Losers

This book differs from most of the literature on Mexican economic integration. The NAFTA debate witnessed a huge battle of the studies. Each side in the debate combined volumes of data with strategic sound bites, thanks in part to the interest groups and private foundations across the spectrum that invested in advocacy research. Some kinds of research counted more than others, though, because the media gave the most credibility to the conventional macroeconomic modeling methods that dominate the U.S. economics profession. These models deployed sophisticated economic techniques, but their results were often determined primarily by their basic starting assumptions, such as how many jobs in Mexican corn production would be displaced by increased imports from the United States—if jobs in corn production were taken into account at all.

Critics fired back with case studies of specific sectors, vivid images of toxic waste and deformed babies at the border, as well as journalistic profiles of individual workers whose jobs had moved to Mexico. The NAFTA opposition certainly had its own contingent of expert specialists, but the dominant frame of the debate was quite lop-sided between expert and local knowledges. Now, after almost a decade of NAFTA in action, both alternative experts and the strategists behind local alternatives are on stronger intellectual ground, based on a sustained track record of practice. Their real world experience gives the new research that follows a powerful comparative advantage—these authors know better than armchair policy analysts what economic integration has meant to specific social actors, in specific sectors, in specific places.

What happened after NAFTA went into effect? Investors kept investing, leading to more but not better *maquila* jobs. Migrants kept migrating, continuing to seek a better life on the border and points north. But what about questions on jobs and the environment that dominated the public and research debates a decade ago? Curiously, the level of research attention to Mexico-U.S. economic integration dropped off significantly once the NAFTA vote was over. Few studies follow up on the many conflicting predictions to see which ones actually held up, though much of the available literature agrees that economic integration has fallen short of its promises.

Causal Stories

When assessing winners and losers from economic integration, the central insight to keep in mind is not to look for answers in terms of countries—whether Mexico, Canada, or the United States benefited. Instead, one must look at specific sectors, regions, social classes, groups of workers, and natural resources as well as visions of alternative futures. Does NAFTA make alternative futures more or less viable? The answers depend on whom one asks. As one of the leaders of the resistance to Mexico City's proposed new airport suggests, globalization unmasks the system, which in turn can embolden and empower resistance by revealing both allies and opponents. At the same time, globalization sometimes poses a challenge by blurring the picture of who is doing what to whom. Local *maquila* managers or crop buyers can blame anonymous international market forces; international financial authorities can blame national policymakers for not following all their prescriptions; environmental regulators can pass the buck while national policymakers can sidestep critics by pointing their finger at supposedly all-powerful international agencies.

How are grassroots actors supposed to figure out where to invest their limited political capital and how to target their campaigns? Activist Mimi Kech's idea of "causal stories" play a key role—accessible narratives that synthesize both the perpetrators and possible pathways to solutions. In the cases that follow here, for example, are several examples of campaigns that embody such causal stories. They include both campaigns to *block* deeper economic integration by the *campesino-ecologista* forest defenders and bioprospecting critics and efforts to *transform* the terms of integration into international markets, like the creative campaigns of Mexico's many indigenous coffee cooperatives. Case studies of grassroots initiatives can play a key role by helping to demystify and explain broader processes, by highlighting the potential power of agency in the face of seemingly all-powerful pressures, and by pinpointing how to most effectively channel anger and advocacy to specific targets or pressure points.

Clearly, there has been increased social polarization within Mexico between those included in and excluded from the dominant economic model. At the same time, significant islands of change and resistance survive. But how large are they? How resilient will they be? Will they be able to grow, spread and form interconnected archipelagos? Will the islands of alternatives be able to join forces and constitute new political counterweights that could affect the national balance of power? Will the two main paths of resistance—protest and proposals for alternatives—manage to reinforce each other?

To sum up, when it comes to grassroots responses to economic integration, we still don't know much about what works and why—just that we should be wary of one-size-fits-all approaches. That is why it is so important to have serious empirical research on the actors themselves, and why this book makes such an important contribution to answering these questions.

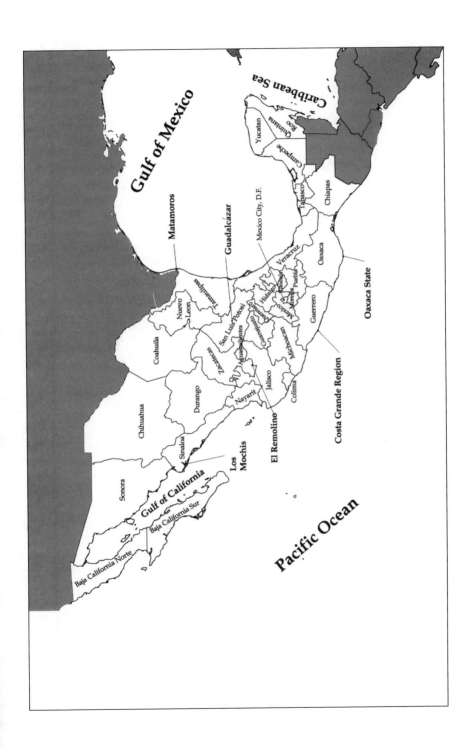

1

Introduction
Globalization and
Popular Resistance in Mexico

Timothy A. Wise, Hilda Salazar, & Laura Carlsen

In 1990, when Presidents George Bush and Carlos Salinas de Gortari opened the first negotiations to widen the Free Trade Agreement between the United States and Canada to include Mexico, civil society organizations began a long process of assessing the agreement's promised benefits for Mexico. The advocates of economic integration promised that with the new North American Free Trade Agreement (NAFTA), Mexico would enter the First World. This would be achieved by using the country's comparative advantages in the international market, attracting foreign investment, and using global competition to stimulate improvements in national production. All this, they argued, would improve the well-being of the vast majority of the Mexican population.

From the beginning, many Mexican organizations doubted such claims. Their skepticism came from nearly a decade of experience with free trade. Opening the Mexican economy began not with NAFTA in 1994, but with the external debt crisis in 1982. It accelerated with Mexico's entry into the General Agreement on Tariffs and Trade (GATT) in 1986, and had already had disastrous consequences in strategic sectors such as agriculture and small and medium-sized industry. For Mexico, international competition with much more powerful U.S. firms seemed to promote a "race to the bottom" in which Mexican society saw its labor, environmental, and agrarian rights eroded. An emerging coalition of social organizations, citizen groups, and researchers feared that NAFTA would only worsen these problems.

These groups were also suspicious of the narrow free-trade perspective shared by U.S. and Mexican leaders, who asserted that the continental trade accord should not deal with environmental protection, labor issues, and equity. In fact, during the formal negotiations (June 12, 1991 until August 12, 1992), these aspects were largely ignored. Meanwhile, networks of environmental groups, *campesino* and women's organizations, labor unions, and academics lobbied to move the "social agenda" into the center of the discussion. They insisted that labor, environment, migration, human rights, and food security—among other issues—should form part of any trade agreement among nations.

For Mexico, NAFTA was, in effect, the icing on the cake of economic integration. Since Mexico's entry into GATT, every Mexican administration has implemented policies to facilitate foreign investment, liberalize trade, and reduce the regulatory intervention of the state, adhering closely to the austerity and adjustment programs dictated by the World Bank and the International Monetary Fund. At present, Mexico has signed more free trade agreements with other nations than any country in the world, and at this writing, it is playing a central role in promoting the Free Trade Area of the Americas (FTAA), a NAFTA for the hemisphere that the United States hopes to negotiate by 2005.

NAFTA formalized the terms of economic integration in Mexico. With its content and scope, NAFTA was more than just a trade opening, transcending the mere reduction of tariffs and customs duties that had begun well before the signing of the agreement. NAFTA established the rules for transnational corporations to locate production and market their goods and services in Mexico, taking advantage of the country's comparative advantages: low salaries, abundant natural resources, weak or unenforced environmental laws, favorable tax structures, and infrastructure. The agreement also guaranteed U.S. companies' technology advantage through its strict intellectual property rules. NAFTA was designed to make Mexico even more attractive for foreign investment.

Economic Integration in Mexico: What Happened to the Promises?

The defenders of NAFTA may still praise Mexico as the most outstanding example of the neoliberal model, but the evidence hardly warrants such glowing assertions. Now, after eight years of NAFTA and more than fifteen years of neoliberal policies, it is possible to go beyond the ideological debates that raged over the agreement's prospective impacts. We can now hold NAFTA's promises—and those of free trade in general—up to the harsh light of economic and social reality. While free-trade advocates still point to a small number of macroeconomic indicators, few can deny that for the vast majority of Mexicans, life has gotten more difficult.[1]

The promise of sustained growth came crashing down the first year NAFTA went into effect, when Mexico was forced to devalue its currency in December 1994, prompting the country's worst economic crisis in decades. The so-called "December mistake" led to an economic contraction of 6.2 percent in 1995.[2] While the country was able to recover slowly from this blow, in the overall period of neoliberal policies, from 1982 until 2000, the Gross Domestic Product (GDP) grew only 0.48 percent per capita annually, in real terms.[3] In 2001, growth again turned negative, falling 0.3 percent, according to Mexican government figures.

Mexico's relative underdevelopment and widespread poverty were barely considered in NAFTA, and few mechanisms were put in place to compensate for them. The economic and social disparities have only become wider since the agreement. After almost two decades of adjustment to the neoliberal model, the toll on Mexico's poor and middle classes has been devastating. Between 1984 and 1996, the percentage of the population living in poverty grew from fifty-nine percent to eighty percent, with almost half living in extreme poverty.[4] In rural Mexico, eighty-two percent of the population currently lives in poverty; fifty-five percent lives in extreme poverty.[5]

While most have gotten poorer, the richest have gotten richer. In Mexico, the richest ten percent of the population receives forty-two percent of total national income, while the poorest forty percent receives just over eleven percent. Since 1984, the richest tenth of the population has increased its share of national income by 4.1 percent.[6] NAFTA has created enormous wealth for the rich; there are Mexican businessmen near the top of *Forbes'* list of the wealthiest individuals on earth.

Falling wages are the main reason poverty rates have increased so sharply. Since 1982, the minimum wage has dropped more than sixty percent in real terms. Since NAFTA went into effect, the minimum wage has lost twenty-three percent of its buying power.[7] Contractual wages have also declined, losing fifty-five percent of their buying power from 1987 to 1999. From their highest point in 1977, contractual wages have lost nearly three-quarters of their value.[8] In the manufacturing sector, workers now earn twelve percent less than in 1994; in the first two years of NAFTA they lost twenty-five percent of their buying power.[9]

The neoliberal model has also failed to generate sufficient employment. Since 1993, 6.2 million jobs were created while the labor force grew by more than ten million, leaving almost four million people without employment. The manufacturing sector, one of the few sectors to show significant growth, has not been a source of job creation. From 1993 to 2000, the sector showed a net loss of 0.3 percent of employment, despite productivity growth of forty-five percent. Of those who are employed, more than sixty percent do not have any of the benefits mandated by law (social security, Christmas bonus, vacation).[10] Some ten million Mexicans currently work in the informal sector, most doing so not by choice but for lack of formal employment.[11] The situation has worsened with the recession in the U.S. economy.

Rural Mexico is in deep crisis, due to rising imports and falling international prices for agricultural products. Corn and coffee, two key products for Mexican agriculture, have lost twenty-seven percent and fifty-eight percent of their value, respectively, since 1994. National policies have failed to promote the recovery and development of the sector, instead abandoning farmers, particularly small-scale farmers, to the global market. The decline in rural production has had strong repercussions for food sovereignty: food dependence grew fifty percent in the last ten years, with a food deficit of 10.4 million tons.[12]

The rural crisis, together with the lack of jobs, has helped create a wave of migration to the urban centers of Mexico and to the United States. In striking contrast to the promises of the neoliberal model, these policies have greatly stimulated the flow of migrants. According to official data, the number of Mexicans leaving for the United States each year grew from 27,000 in the 1960s to 140,000 in the 1970s. In the 1980s the figure rose to 235,000, and by the first half of the 1990s, to 275,000. It is estimated that one-tenth of Mexicans now live in the United States.[13] Ironically, these refugees of economic integration—arguably one of free trade's most dramatic cross-border flows—were not included in the NAFTA negotiations, the United States having rejected from the outset all proposals to discuss the liberalization of the North American labor force.[14]

Many researchers predicted an improvement in environmental conditions in the country as a direct result of economic integration.[15] Three arguments were set forth to support this optimism: 1) economic growth would stimulate investment in ecological improvements; 2) international competition would consolidate economies of scale, thus avoiding the pollution produced by small, "dirty" industries; and 3) NAFTA would raise environmental standards among member nations.

Years later, a few isolated cases of these phenomena can be observed, but only as exceptions that confirm the rule. As the case studies in this book illustrate, the environmental record is poor. There has been pressure to reduce environmental standards and relax enforcement in order to attract investment. Areas of rapid industrialization have experienced severe environmental problems, especially on the northern border. Internal migration has caused uncontrolled urban growth, with insufficient infrastructure and services, generating acute problems of urban and rural pollution. And there are growing threats to biodiversity resulting from regional development projects, biotechnology and the new intellectual property rules, monoculture, and the short-term and unsustainable use of natural resources.

According to official figures, between 1988 and 1999, the cost of environmental degradation and the exhaustion of natural resources reached an average annual rate of ten percent of GDP, far outpacing trade-led economic growth rates. In the NAFTA years, government spending to offset pollution or environmental degradation has fallen by nearly fifty percent.[16] Most environmental problems have been exacerbated with the economic opening. For example, the Institute of Statistics, Geography and Information (INEGI) calculates that since 1988, the annual indices of soil erosion, solid waste generation, and air pollution have increased by a combined average of sixty-three percent.[17]

Despite its rhetorical homage to sustainable development, NAFTA contains terms that contradict and impede the objectives of environmental improvement. It severely limits the state's power to regulate the activity of transnational corporations that operate in national territory. It fosters the exploitation of natural resources and reorients the economy toward dependence on foreign investment, which is free of responsibility for the huge social and environmental costs it imposes. Like the labor side agreement, the environmental side agreement has proven inadequate for the daunting task of addressing the ecological damage from NAFTA.[18]

In sum, the promises of generalized economic growth, employment, infrastructure modernization, efficiency, environmental improvement, and higher salaries have largely evaporated. In contrast, for the great majority of Mexicans, the economic integration of the past fifteen years has left them in more precarious situations, and with little hope for improvement.

These problems are the direct result of the neoliberal model. Many Mexicans now resist the further imposition of neoliberal policies by their government, and they are actively seeking alternatives. It is precisely in this popular resistance that the path to a better future can be found.

Popular Resistance

In the last few years, the international network of social organizations that study, analyze, and take action against corporate-led globalization has matured. In Mexico, the emphasis has shifted from looking exclusively at NAFTA to a wider focus that covers the whole process of economic integration and its impacts. Throughout the country, social organizations are beginning to understand their particular problems in the context of globalization, and they are expanding their networks and alliances accordingly.

This process has led to important changes inside Mexican social movements. The divisions among the traditional sectors—*campesino, labor, barrio*—that defined previous struggles have become blurred in the face of globalization. From one day to the next, a *campesina* becomes a *maquiladora* worker, coffee growers become migrants, and professionals find themselves unemployed. Traditional sectoral demands now intersect with new themes such as environment, gender, human rights, and indigenous issues, serving to revitalize and reshape the movements. The geography of the country is also being transformed. Agricultural areas are converted into industrial corridors, abruptly modifying social relations, cultural identity, and area ecosystems. Entire towns are abandoned, almost from one day to the next, through economically driven emigration as families are broken up and the cultural links to land and territory are lost.

As social movements shift focus, grassroots organizations leave behind obsolete notions that defined common interests in narrow terms. With globalization as the backdrop, today's connections follow a different logic, necessitating new forms of organization capable of confronting the atomizing dynamic of globalization.

As is often the case, the paradigm change closes some doors and opens others. Social movements today are finding new causes and new channels for action that, more than ever, revolve around aspects of globalization. While the negative impacts of globalization are increasingly evident in Mexico, civil society organizations are developing a deeper analysis of the problem, broadening their networks of resistance through new national and international alliances, and gaining valuable experience in constructing alternatives.

This book is both a product and an example of these new international relationships and the attention to globalization in Mexico. In 1999, the Mexican Free Trade Action Network (RMALC) and the Global Development and Environment Institute of Tufts University in Boston began a joint research project to study the experiences of resistance and alternatives to economic integration in Mexico.[19] Together with the social organizations represented in the book, our goal was drawing lessons not only for Mexico and NAFTA but also for other countries and other trade agreements. We were particularly interested in assessing the relevance of Mexico's experience for the proposed Free Trade Area of the Americas, which is being proposed as a NAFTA for the entire hemisphere.

This book documents the responses of Mexican civil and social organizations to economic integration. Some organizations were able to adapt to the new market conditions while developing independent initiatives. Others sought to change government policies that threaten their means of survival. Most use both tactics: as they seek to take advantage of the economic openings created by economic integration, they resist aspects of globalization that threaten their livelihoods, cultures, or environment.

Based on a review of the literature on the subject,[20] we identified three key areas to study: the environment, small-scale agriculture, and the labor sector. It is no coincidence that these are areas of dispute in most trade agreements. The cases were selected according to the following criteria:

- They are paradigmatic, offering important lessons for social organizations, decision-makers, public officials, and politicians involved in negotiating and/or managing economic integration.
- They reveal important aspects of the Mexican dynamic of international economic integration.
- They show experiences in which strategies of collective resistance to the forms of economic integration are developed and concrete alternatives are constructed. They are projects that have achieved a positive impact on local or national policies and demonstrate key characteristics of capacity building: leadership, innovation, internal organization, and negotiation ability.
- They show a wide range of Mexican responses to economic integration in terms of geographic regions, production and commercial sectors, forms of social organization, and strategies of resistance and self-direction. Furthermore, they reflect the distinct ways in which economic integration is expressed in Mexico: the opening of trade, the withdrawal of the state, the role of multilateral organizations, foreign investment, and NAFTA.
- They have the explicit goal of achieving sustainable development, both economically and environmentally.

We selected nine cases, located in distinct regions and sectors of the country, that show a wide range of experience. The actors are diverse, ranging from environmentalist *campesinos* in Guerrero to larger-scale bean producers in the northern state of Sinaloa. They include coffee growers who gain access to international fair-trade markets and *maquiladora* workers who struggle for safe labor conditions. Some of the organizational experiences are regional and relatively small; others are national in scope and include hundreds of regional organizations. Some, as in the bioprospecting case and the case of the Metalclad toxic waste dump, bring together multiple protagonists, united by their opposition to an imposed policy or an economic trend that threatens their cultural or economic survival. The case studies come from various regions of the country: Oaxaca, Guerrero, Los Altos of Chiapas, San Luís Potosí, Sinaloa, Zacatecas, and the northern border of Tamaulipas.

The common thread among them is that they feature forms of resistance to the negative impacts of globalization while also constructing alternatives. The case studies in this book show the human face of economic integration in Mexico, as much for the suffering and the problems it causes as for the resistance that it generates. Together they describe the connections between grassroots experiences and globalization processes as a dynamic process.

The research methodology was also dynamic. Most case studies are written by researcher-activists, as in the bioprospecting and Metalclad cases, as well as the case of the peasant environmentalists from Guerrero. In some, the authors are the principal actors, or are members and advisors of the organizations involved. The Autotrim *maquiladora* struggle and the cases of coffee and basic grain producers fall into this category. Others are written by academics and professionals who conducted extensive fieldwork and are closely linked to the experiences they describe.

Bringing together these diverse experiences was complicated but at the same time immensely rich. The editors convened two workshops involving the case study authors. One brought the researchers together to share their work and develop a common language and methodology. The second, a two-day conference at El Colegio de Mexico, allowed the authors to present their completed studies in greater detail to a small group of highly respected experts in relevant fields. These meetings, with their rich communication and reflection among the participants, allowed us to share experiences and deepen the analyses that link the particular cases to the problems of economic integration.

Organization of the Book

This book presents nine cases in three sections: 1) Integration, Investment, and the Environment; 2) The Crisis in the Countryside: Small Producers Fight Back; and 3) Employment Under Free Trade: Exploitation and Expulsion.

In the first section, the themes of environment, natural resources, and foreign investment are linked in each of the five cases presented. The section opens with the Metalclad case, which has become widely cited in global debates about investment clauses in trade agreements. It tells the story of a toxic waste dump in the state of San Luís Potosí that the transnational corporation Metalclad proposed to build, despite the opposition of local authorities and residents. When the community, through its elected leaders, was finally able to stop the project, Metalclad turned to a NAFTA tribunal under the controversial Chapter 11 on investor-state relations. The tribunal ruled in Metalclad's favor, forcing the Mexican government to pay the company more than $15 million in compensation. The case has become one of the leading examples of the way Chapter 11 undermines local rights, national sovereignty, and governments' ability to regulate the activities of private companies to protect health and the environment.

The next two cases involve the forest sector in the state of Guerrero, but they present contrasting experiences with timber extraction by foreign companies. The Organization of Peasant Ecologists of the Sierra de Petatlán and Coyuca de Catalán was formed in response to the intensive exploitation of area forests by local loggers, politicians, and one of the largest timber companies in the world, Boise-Cascade. The organization's actions were met with fierce repression which in turn provoked an international campaign for the release of two of its jailed leaders, Rodolfo Montiel and Teodoro Cabrera. The case shows the relationship between globalization and human and collective rights, and it underlines the power of international cooperation in the defense of human rights.

Close by, the El Balcón *ejido,* located in Guerrero's Costa Grande, has had a very different experience. It has succeeded in establishing a project for self-management of its natural resources that appears viable within the global context. The success of this project is due in part to El Balcón's efforts to build a strong and respectful relationship with a U.S. buyer for the wood.

The last two cases in this section introduce the complex and important subject of the commercial exploitation of genetic and biological resources.

In the north of the country, agricultural producers from the state of Sinaloa have seen their markets for the export of yellow beans to the United States closed due to a registered patent in that country. The patent gives exclusive rights of commercialization to a bean dealer in the United States, who claims he "invented" the Sinaloan mayocoba bean. The case study highlights the ways in which the intellectual property regime favors U.S. corporate interests, even to the point of restricting trade.

The bioprospecting case relates four experiences with bioprospecting contracts in Mexico. Despite their differences, all four examples have generated local and national resistance, which is based on the threat of losing rights to the country's genetic resources through patenting. The public debate about the subject, and the national campaign for a moratorium on these contracts, form part of a larger process to democratize policies concerning the use of natural resources.

The second section considers the crisis in rural Mexico, provoked in great part by the policies of liberalization. The first case recounts the story of ANEC, an organization of small- and medium-scale farmers who produce basic grains, a strategic sector for Mexican food security and a significant source of employment. Despite having negotiated long periods (ten to fifteen years) for the elimination of tariffs under NAFTA—with the goal of controlling the opening while the sector prepared itself to enter into international competition against the world leader in the production of grains—the Mexican government decided unilaterally to permit the massive importation of basic grains above the established quotas. Flooded by U.S. imports, ANEC farmers have undertaken efforts to improve efficiency, market directly and collectively, and modernize their operations. In the face of the sudden trade opening, ANEC is helping to construct a viable alternative for thousands of small farmers while pressing for policies that protect this vital sector.

The case of coffee producers in the state of Oaxaca recounts the experience of the Coordinadora Estatal de Productores de Café de Oaxaca, or CEPCO, a grassroots organization of almost 30,000 small, indigenous producers. CEPCO is a pioneer in the direct and collective marketing of its "fair trade" coffee, which is produced and sold in accordance with principles of social justice and equity. The organization has generated an impressive array of independent initiatives that range from the establishment of its own credit union to community women's projects. Its experience in producer-led efforts to market products on a newly opened international market highlights the possibilities and limitations for such peasant-led initiatives.

The cases presented in the third section illustrate the related impacts of economic integration in Mexico's labor sector: intensive exploitation and growing expulsion from existing sources of livelihood. The first case relates the struggle of workers in the Autotrim factory in Matamoros, Tamaulipas. Combining contextual data about the *maquiladora* industry with direct testimonies from workers, the case illustrates the deterioration in working conditions and the possibilities and limitations of international solidarity in the defense of labor rights. It portrays a struggle of small advances, significant setbacks, high risks, and large obstacles.

While the Autotrim case depicts the struggle of Mexican workers on the Mexican border, the chapter on migrants from the state of Zacatecas deals with the problems of the thousands of migrants who work in the United States and their creative efforts to pool their wage remittances to generate economic development in their communities of origin. The chapter studies migrants from El Remolino, whose commitment to their hometown community is translating into concrete development projects. The case examines the emergence of this "collective migrant" and explores the development potential of pooled remittances.

Despite the explicit criticisms of the current situation, neither of the two cases argues for the abolition of the *maquila* sector or international migration. Both have become escape valves for the pressures that accumulate in the interior of the country due to the absence of genuine national development. As Armando Bartra says well: "Without a doubt, it is necessary to denounce the criminalized migration and the prison-like regime in the factories, but it also necessary to work to humanize these situations, which for many are unavoidable."[21] This is precisely the approach of the Zacatecan migrants and Tamaulipan workers presented here.

The last chapter of the book presents our efforts to draw general lessons from these diverse cases. We distilled from the cases some of the key factors in both resisting neoliberalism and creating alternatives, including: grassroots democratic organization; community management of natural resources; social mobilization to influence public policy; strengthening internal and regional markets; and the demand for jobs with security and dignity. The chapter goes on to discuss the important role of the state, which has been greatly undermined by neoliberalism, and ends with a discussion of the implications of these cases for negotiating other trade agreements, in particular the FTAA.

We see these cases as a source of inspiration. In spite of many obstacles, these organizations have developed the capacity to make inroads in the international market in a collective and organized way and have opened alternative markets for their products. They have made their cultural differences into a force for promoting social justice, in a homogenizing environment that grows increasingly hostile. Together with these accomplishments, the cases also demonstrate the limits of local and national resistance in a context dominated by the global market and multinational corporations. One of the most important lessons is that the barriers imposed by the neoliberal model can only be overcome through broad international alliances.

Mexico is the birthplace of the movement that has become a symbol of the resistance to the current model of economic integration. NAFTA became effective the same day the Zapatista Army for National Liberation burst on the scene in San Cristóbal de las Casas and in other cities in Chiapas. In an enormous blow to business and government interests, the celebration of the beginning of NAFTA was challenged by a group of poor and poorly-armed indigenous people who refused to believe that NAFTA was their salvation. That first day of January 1994 has since acquired profound symbolic significance, as the differences between these two mutually exclusive visions for Mexico grow more stark with each passing day.

We are constantly told that economic integration is inevitable, that the "backward" sectors of society must change and adapt to the new reality. However, in every corner of Mexico, community organizations, farmers, and workers have refused to sacrifice their cultures, their identities, and their ways of life at the altar of globalization. This book shows the rich processes of learning, organization, and consciousness-raising that have led to these creative organizational responses to economic integration.

Faced with the challenge of the FTAA a new hemispheric movement, the Hemispheric Social Alliance, has emerged which does not reject the realities of economic integration but instead struggles for a model of integration that benefits the majority.[22] We hope this book makes a small contribution to this movement for economic, ethical, and social alternatives, both in Mexico and globally.

Notes

1. For recent positive analyses of NAFTA and economic integration in Mexico, see, for example: Rudiger Dornbusch and Alejandro Werner, "Mexico: Stabilization, Reform, and No Growth," *Brookings Papers on Economic Activity*, volume 1, 253–315; Nora Lustig, *Mexico: The Remaking of an Economy* (Washington, D.C.: Brookings Institute, 1998).

2. Alberto Arroyo P., et al., *Resultados del Tratado de Libre Comercio de América del Norte en México: Lecciones para la negociación del Acuerdo de Libre*

Comercio de las Américas (Mexico City: Red Mexicana de Acción Frente al Libre Comercio, 2002), 20.

3. Arroyo, et al., *Resultados,* 16.

4. Arturo Alcalde, Graciela Bensusán, Enrique de la Garza, Enrique Hernández Laos, Teresa Rendón, Carlos Salas, *Trabajo y Trabajadores en el México Contemporáneo* (Mexico City: Miguel Angel Porrúa, 2000). The authors analyze methodologies for measuring poverty and use the methodology developed by Enrique Hernández Loas, *Prospectiva demográfica y económica de México y sus efectos sobre la pobreza* (Mexico City: Universidad Autónoma Metropolitana (mimeo), which incorporates minimum costs for transportation, housing, services, and recreation as part of the minimum necessary for a dignified life. These figures are only slightly higher than official Mexican government calculations, which show a seventy-three percent poverty rate for 1996, up 9.6 percent since 1984. INEGI, *Encuesta Nacional de Ingresos y Gastos de los Hogares 1996* (Mexico City: INEGI, 1998).

5. Information provided by Julio Boltvinik in an interview with Ricardo Rocha, *Detrás de la Noticia,* supplement to *El Universal,* January 20, 2001.

6. Alcalde, et al., *Trabajo y Trabajadores,* 103.

7. Arroyo, et al., *Resultados,* 70.

8. Alcalde, et al., *Trabajo y Trabajadores,* 79.

9. Boltvinik, *Detrás de la Noticia.*

10. Arroyo, *Resultados,* 68–72.

11. Cited in Victor Ballinas, "80% de la microempresa mexicana surgió como opción de sobrevivencia." *La Jornada,* December 18, 2000.

12. Data from a study carried out by the University of Chapingo and the Centro de Estudios Estratégicos Nacionales, cited in *El Universal,* May 19, 2001. See also Blanca Rubio, "El modelo económico neoliberal y el problema alimentario," in *El neoliberalismo en el sector agropecuario en México* (Mexico City: Facultad de Economía de la UNAM, 2001).

13. Juan Manuel Sandoval, "Migración Laboral," in Arroyo, et al., *Resultados,* 115.

14. Sandoval, in Arroyo, et al., *Resultados,* 111.

15. For a discussion of the positive hypotheses and their critics, see Bruce Campbell, *Moving in the Wrong Direction: Globalization, The North American Free Trade Agreement and Sustainable Development* (Ottawa, Canada: Canadian Center for Political Alternatives, 1993), 11.

16. Institute of Statistics, Geography and Information (INEGI), *Sistema de Cuentas Económicas y Ecológicas de Mexico* (Mexico City: INEGI, 2000).

17. Institute of Statistics, Geography and Information (INEGI), *Sistema de Cuentas Económicas y Ecológicas de Mexico* (Mexico City: INEGI, 2000).

18. For an analysis of the limitations of the North American Agreement on Environmental Cooperation, see Hilda Salazar and Laura Carlsen, "Limits to Cooperation: A Mexican Perspective on NAFTA's Side Agreement and Environmental Institutions," in *Greening the Americas: NAFTA's Lessons on Hemispheric Trade* (Boston, Mass.: MIT Press, 2002).

19. The project was based on prior work carried out by RMALC, the Sierra Club, and the Mott Foundation.

20. See Timothy A. Wise and Elisa Waters, "Community Control in a Global Economy: Lessons from Mexico's Economic Integration Process," *G-DAE Working Paper 01-03*, February 2001, available at http://ase.tufts.edu/gdae.

21. Armando Bartra et al., *Mesoamérica: Los Rios Profundos* (Mexico City: Instituto Maya, 2001), 48.

22. For a detailed presentation of the Hemispheric Social Alliance's alternative framework for the FTAA, *Alternatives for the Americas,* see: http://www.web.net/comfront/alts4americas/eng/eng.html.

PART 1

INTEGRATION, INVESTMENT, AND THE ENVIRONMENT

2

Investment, Sovereignty, and the Environment: The Metalclad Case and NAFTA's Chapter 11

Fernando Bejarano González

THIS IS THE STORY OF CITIZENS' STRUGGLES TO PREVENT THE REOPENING OF A toxic waste site managed by a U.S. company, Metalclad, and to demand the cleanup of more than 20,000 tons of toxic residue still buried on land known as La Pedrera in Guadalcázar in the state of San Luís Potosí.[1] The Metalclad investment, initially touted as a shining example of NAFTA's promise to modernize hazardous waste management in Mexico, became the first lawsuit by a foreign company against the Mexican government under the agreement's controversial investor-protection rules, known as Chapter 11. NAFTA's tribunal ruled in favor of Metalclad's claim that the decision by local authorities to prevent the company from reopening the waste site was unfair, and the Mexican government ended up paying more than $16 million in compensation to the company.

The case has grave repercussions for the future of democracy and municipal and state sovereignty, not only in Mexico but in the United States, Canada, and all of Latin America. And its implications go deeper, because a similar investment clause has been proposed for the Free Trade Area of the Americas (FTAA), which is currently being promoted by U.S. President George W. Bush. If a foreign corporation can override the efforts of elected governments to protect the health of its citizens and the integrity of its environment, democracy itself is undermined. The Metalclad case highlights the urgency of rethinking such provisions in future trade agreements.

A History of Deception

At the beginning of the 1990s, a local Mexican company, Confinamiento Técnico de Residuos Industriales SA (Coterin), owed by the Aldrett de León brothers, began drilling what it said were wells in La Pedrera, in the municipality of Guadalcázar. Guadalcázar is situated on San Luís Potosí's central plateau. Even though today it is quite poor, it flourished in colonial times due to its rich deposits of gold and silver. The municipality is now rural, with a population of 26,974 dispersed in 110 villages; only six have a population of more than 1,000. Like many other poor communities, its population lives primarily from seasonal, rain-fed cultivation of corn, beans, sorghum, and feed crops for small herds of cattle and goats. Because of their low incomes, some residents migrate temporarily to urban centers in Mexico, or to the United States.[2]

The company Coterin maintained that it was drilling to distribute potable water to neighboring settlements and that the surplus would be used to irrigate tomato fields in an agricultural cooperative. To the surprise and anger of neighbors, however, it left thousands of barrels of hazardous waste out in the open around the La Pedrera drilling site, without even fencing the area. The Aldrett de León brothers had a history with toxic waste. In 1989, state environmental officials (from the agency Sedue) had closed one of their toxic waste sites in Mexquitic de Carmona after residents protested the unsafe burial of more than 70,000 tons of toxic waste from the brothers' mercury recycling plant.[3]

From the beginning, Coterin's hazardous waste dumping in La Pedrera was illegal. Although it is not known exactly when the company began bringing waste onto the site, the official registry shows that from November 1990 through May 1991 the company deposited about 55,000 barrels containing 20,500 tons of hazardous waste. Most of this waste can be traced to sixty-one companies, primarily in the chemical, auto, metal mechanics, and agrochemical industries. Some 170 tons consisted of expired medication from the Mexican Social Security Institute (IMSS).[4]

A below-ground hazardous waste site, which depends on the indirect detection of leaching to prevent groundwater contamination, presents grave risks to health and the environment. The leaching process can be slowed, but not eliminated, through good site selection and strict monitoring of site construction and operation. In the United States, such sites must meet strict technical requirements and generally include funds for closing the site and monitoring subsequent contamination. Still, many experts contend that such underground hazardous waste storage is inherently dangerous.

They call for above-ground sites, that allow for more efficient inspection and monitoring, thus reducing risks of environmental contamination.[5]

The Coterin waste dump lacked even the most minimal safety features. The 814 hectares at La Pedrera are situated in a narrow valley tucked in the mountains. A river, dry for most of the year, cuts through the area. In 1991, a torrential rainstorm swept away several barrels of hazardous waste, contaminating the reservoir for the community of El Huizache, which borders the toxic waste site. The population, angered by what they felt were the company's lies and frustrated that state authorities had not acted on their petitions to address the issue, decided to mobilize. On the night of September 24, 1991, more than 200 people with machetes in hand stopped the unloading of twenty hazardous waste trucks and held them for three days, forcing environmental authorities to carry out inspections. The authorities finally closed and sealed the site on October 3, 1991.

The irregularities in waste handling and in the process of obtaining permits in the Coterin operation were serious enough to eventually lead to a ruling by the National Human Rights Commission. Federal authorities from Sedue gave Coterin a temporary permit on October 31, 1990, to operate a transfer station for toxic waste after the drilling work had already been carried out. They failed to demand an environmental impact study, as required by Mexico's General Law for Ecological Equilibrium and Environmental Protection (LGEEPA). This favored Coterin, which was seeking an alternative disposal site following the closure of the Mexquitic dump.[6] In Mexican environmental law, the term transfer station has no standing, a fact that would later provide the basis for a legal challenge to Sedue's authorization of the site.

When the so-called transfer station was closed, contaminated with 20,000 tons of hazardous waste, federal authorities still did not force Coterin to clean up the site. Instead, officials in January and August 1993, authorized the company to operate a toxic waste confinement site in La Pedrera.[7] Also questionable was Coterin's success in obtaining the required land-use permit from Sedue, which it got on May 11, 1993, with the help of San Luís Potosí Governor Teófilo Torres Corzo, of the Institutional Revolutionary Party (PRI), shortly before the end of his term.[8] With the federal permit to operate the site and the state land-use permit, Coterin had two of the three legal permits needed to operate a toxic waste dump. All that was missing was the municipal building license, a requirement that was left to a new actor in the conflict, the transnational Metalclad Corporation.

The Entry of Metalclad

NAFTA created favorable conditions for Metalclad, which before the agreement was a small, publicly-traded company headquartered in Newport Beach, California, specializing in the removal of industrial insulation and asbestos. Even though it had no prior experience in the area, Metalclad's goal became dominating the market for the treatment or final deposit of hazardous waste in Mexico. It sought to achieve this through acquisitions and alliances with Mexican companies as well as through a public relations campaign to win over creditors and investors in the United States and Europe.

The timing with the NAFTA negotiations was impeccable. In July 1991, Grant Kesler, a large stockholder in Metalclad, entered as a partner into Environ Technologies, Inc. (ETI). ETI had joined with four Mexican investors to establish a company called Eco-Administración. In November 1991, Kesler arranged the acquisition of ETI by Metalclad, thereby consolidating his influence in Eco-Administración. Eco-Administración was trying to develop several investment projects, among them a hazardous waste incinerator in Santa María del Río, in San Luís Potosí. The same group acquired the stock of two other waste disposal companies in 1992: Descontaminadora Industrial de Veracruz and Eliminación de Contaminantes Industriales in Tamaulipas.[9]

Even though none of these projects prospered, Metalclad was able to promote itself—and even increase the value of its stock—by advertising its plans to invest in Mexico. In one press conference, Kesler announced that the incinerator project in Santa María del Río would generate approximately $150 million annually. Later he announced that they had received a proposal from Chase Manhattan Bank for a $250 million loan.[10]

Metalclad's campaign dovetailed with the NAFTA negotiations, where the relationship between trade, foreign investment, and the environment was generating heated debate in the U.S. Congress and among NAFTA opponents. Mexico and the United States were already discussing cooperation on environmental affairs. In this context, Kesler presented Metalclad as the solution to Mexico's hazardous waste problems.

In mid-1992, Metalclad was still trying to get the incinerator project in Santa María del Río off the ground. Plans for two other projects in Veracruz and Tamaulipas had already been abandoned. Despite growing difficulties in obtaining financing,[11] the company embarked upon yet another project: the construction of a hazardous waste dump in the state of San Luís Potosí.

In June 1993, Metalclad approached the newly elected governor of San Luís Potosí, Horacio Sánchez Unzueta, with the offer to supply cutting-edge technology to develop infrastructure for hazardous waste treatment. The proposal was well received because the governor wanted to promote industrial growth in the state and was seeking such investments. State environmental officials in San Luís Potosí warned Metalclad not to invest in La Pedrera, because studies by the Autonomous University of San Luís Potosí had revealed that the site was not geo-hydrologically sound, and that the site had a number of legal, political, and economic problems created by Coterin. They offered their support in the search for an alternative site.[12]

Metalclad, however, did not heed these warnings. In October 1993, the company acquired ninety-four percent of Coterin's capital with the goal of reopening and expanding La Pedrera to receive 30,000 tons of toxic waste annually over twenty-five years. Metalclad informed its stockholders that it expected profits of $12.5 million in the first year alone. At the end of 1993, the state government called unsuccessfully for a review of the 1993 permit granted by Sedue.

Metalclad wanted to buy Coterin, despite its enormous environmental liabilities in La Pedrera, because the property was close to important highways connecting it with border cities and the center of the country. Above all, it was attractive because Coterin had obtained two of the three authorizations needed to operate a hazardous waste dump. Metalclad was apparently aware of the risks the purchase implied when it bought Coterin and apparently knew the construction permit was still missing, though later, during the Chapter 11 hearing, the company claimed it was not adequately informed about this requirement. Metalclad's contract to buy Coterin's stock options contained the agreement that Metalclad would pay three-quarters of the purchase price under two conditions: that the governor of San Luís Potosí authorized construction to proceed, and that the municipal construction permit would be granted, or in case of legal action, that a final judgment would permit the company to proceed legally with construction.[13]

A key figure in the contract between Metalclad and the governor and with the Aldrett de León brothers, owners of Coterin, was Humberto Rodarte Ramón, the former state-level Sedue official who had closed the La Pedrera site in 1991, and who first orchestrated the meetings between Metalclad and the Aldrett de León brothers. This same official was special advisor to the National Institute for Ecology (INE) and served as a Coterin real estate agent in the sale of La Pedrera. He received a $100,000 commission for arranging the sale. His wife—who went by the name Ratner—received

money from Metalclad in exchange for stock she held as a founding partner of Eco-Administración, bought by Metalclad in 1991. According to the
Mexican government, "The payments in Metalclad stock and cash to Mrs.
Ratner were designed, among other things, to expedite the federal permits."[14] The federal official was later named general director of Metalclad's consulting company, Consultora Ambiental Total.

The evidence of this official's corruption and the violation of Mexico's
Federal Law of Public Service Responsibilities were the basis for a 1999
criminal lawsuit, which was brought by Semarnap, Mexico's environment
ministry (which later became Semarnat). As the Mexican government
pointed out in the suit, Metalclad acquired Coterin believing that, with the
federal official helping it obtain the permits, it could force the opening of
the site.[15]

Metalclad formed a holding company and offered its stock to investors
in Europe and the United States, promising fast profits and high rates of
return. To promote its acceptance in these markets, it associated with First
Analysis Corporation, a Chicago-based financial company that specialized
in the environmental market and in investment fund management, and with
Oakes Fitzwilliams, a New York firm with a franchise in London.

The Metalclad holding company was called Ecosistemas Internacionales, SA (Econsa). In 1995 it included four businesses: 1) Ecosistemas de Potosí, SA (Ecopsa), which would operate the site in La Pedrera,
thanks to the acquisition of Coterin; 2) Química Omega, a Mexican company acquired in 1994 that recycled oils and other hazardous waste to sell
as alternative fuel for cement kilns; 3) Consultora Ambiental Total, SA
(Catsa), which offered environmental consulting and auditing to mining
companies and foundries, and which was left in charge of obtaining the
permits for four additional dump sites in Mexico for Metalclad; and 4)
the hazardous waste incinerator in Santa María del Río, San Luís Potosí,
the old Eco-Administración project that never happened.[16]

Metalclad made its clean-up of La Pedrera conditional on the reopening and expansion of the hazardous waste site. In response, federal environmental authorities, both at INE and the Federal Attorney for the
Protection of the Environment (Profepa), agreed to consider reopening the
site. An environmental audit paid for by Metalclad and supervised by Profepa was carried out from late 1994 through March 1995. Even during the
audit, Metalclad carried out construction at La Pedrera without obtaining a
municipal construction license. The fieldwork for the audit was completed
in only one month.[17] Despite the fact that it found eighteen violations of

environmental rules and demanded a plan to correct them, the audit concluded that the site was suitable for reopening the toxic waste dump.

In 1994, the 20,000-plus tons of toxic waste in La Pedrera lay buried in three cells at a depth of five meters, with a plastic membrane at the bottom and ventilation tubes designed to prevent the accumulation of toxic gases. This work, however, was poorly done—according to the environmental audit, in two of the three cells the risk of explosion was extremely high. In the words of local residents, the place was a "time bomb."

Local Resistance and National Alliances

The problems caused by the Coterin toxic waste site generated protests from several municipal administrations in Guadalcázar. They sent letters to state and federal authorities—and to Mexico's president—demanding the cleanup of the site and stating their opposition to the reopening of the dump. The protests increased following the birth of several children with birth defects. Many of these defects were never recorded on death certificates.[18] Suspicions grew after it became known that the former Sedue official who had closed the site was now a promoter of the project for Metalclad. The municipal council named a special *regidor* (administrator) for ecology in 1993 to address the problem, leading to better organization by opponents of the project and a search for new allies. Opponents asked for the support of the environmental groups Pro San Luís Ecológico and Greenpeace-Mexico.

Meanwhile, Metalclad was under pressure to show progress to its shareholders. With the favorable results of the environmental audit in hand, it announced the formal reopening of the site for March 10, 1995, and promised that the governor, federal environmental officials, members of President Zedillo's cabinet, and U.S. embassy officials would be present at the event.[19] The company made this announcement even though it still lacked a municipal construction permit and had not reached full agreement with federal or state authorities on the project. Even the Mexican Embassy in Washington sent a communiqué to Kesler cautioning that it was premature to give a public announcement of the reopening.[20] The company became more tentative in its statements, but it went ahead with its "grand opening," inviting the press and arranging for three busloads of invited guests.[21]

When local residents found out about the event, they mobilized, blocking access to food and beverages at the event. Metalclad's publicity stunt, and the popular response, ended up making relations between Metalclad and municipal and state authorities even more tense. One national newspaper erroneously reported that the toxic waste site had been opened.[22]

The Role of Environmental Organizations

Thanks to additional protests in the capital of San Luís Potosí, a meeting with federal Profepa authorities was arranged. Greenpeace and Pro San Luís Ecológico had access to the information from the environmental audit. Greenpeace formed a Citizens' Technical Committee, with the participation of geologists and civil engineers from the Regional School for Earth Sciences of the Autonomous University of Guerrero, and members of Pro San Luís Ecológico, who analyzed the audit, carried out assemblies and interviews with residents, and visited La Pedrera and the toxic waste site. In June 1995, the Citizens' Technical Committee issued a report detailing the history of violations of Mexican environmental legislation and documenting the company's failure to comply with existing environmental rules about the site-selection process.

The committee's report stated that the environmental audit was inconclusive, and that the studies were partial and preliminary, hiding the magnitude of present and future contamination, which included the risk of surface and groundwater contamination. The report also pointed out the lack of a cleanup plan and other irregularities.[23] After meetings and discussions with federal authorities and the companies that participated in the environmental audit, the Committee recommended further studies and evaluations. Metalclad and Profepa resisted these recommendations.

The opposition movement grew, gaining support from *ejidos* and communal land authorities in the municipality and from other groups in San Luís Potosí. Greenpeace generated national publicity for the demand that the La Pedrera installations remain closed, that the previously given permits should be revoked, and that the site should be cleaned up. The peaceful protests included a letter to the head of Semarnap, signed by more than fifty important environmental and social organizations in Mexico, and demonstrations at Profepa offices in Mexico City. The conflict even gained international publicity, with solidarity protests by members of the group Mothers of East L.A. at Metalclad's offices in California and press conferences in Chicago in August 1995.

With federal authorities refusing to carry out more field studies, and armed with information about the political pressure put on authorities to authorize reopening the site, Greenpeace and Pro San Luís Ecológico brought criminal charges against state and federal officials from both INE and Profepa. The complaint for "ecological crimes" was presented to the attorney general's office on September 14, 1995.[24]

The municipal opposition to Coterin and Metalclad, and the statewide resistance to federal authorities, must be understood in the historical context of San Luís Potosí's vibrant civic movements. The so-called *navista* movement—named for Dr. Salvador Nava, municipal president of San Luís Potosí in 1958, and candidate for governor in 1997—mobilized strong opposition to the state's *caciques* (political bosses) and to the ruling PRI's electoral fraud.[25] Like the *navista* movement, the municipal opposition to Coterin and Metalclad was not led by any political party. Rather, men and women from Mexico's three largest parties—the PRI, President Fox's National Action party (PAN), and the center-left Party of the Democratic Revolution (PRD)—and people without political affiliation mobilized to pressure municipal presidents to clean up the waste site and prevent it from reopening. Particularly important was the activism by women from Pro San Luís Ecológico, including Dr. Angelina Nuñez and Guadalcázar teachers, homemakers, and peasants, who became active when they learned about children with birth defects, miscarriages, and other reproductive health problems.

Metalclad's Search for Influence

Metalclad resorted to both legal and illegal means to promote its investment project. It intervened in municipal politics to promote a candidate for the municipal presidency who favored its interests.[26] It carried out a propaganda campaign in San Luís Potosí newspapers. As would later be revealed in the Chapter 11 hearings, Metalclad tried to bribe the municipal environmental official from Guadalcázar—one of the leaders of the opposition—and then-governor of San Luís Potosí, Horacio Sánchez Unzueta, with one million dollars.[27]

Metalclad also used its influence in the United States to further the project, using its stockholders' influence with U.S. senators and the U.S. Ambassador to Mexico. Senator Paul Simon (D-Ill.) and Barbara Boxer (D-Calif.) took actions to support Metalclad's effort to open the site.[28] In August 1995 Brian Hand, representative of the First Analysis Corporation in Chicago and a member of the Metalclad board of directors, wrote a letter to then-president of Mexico Ernesto Zedillo, asking him to intervene to avoid a delay in the reopening of the waste site.[29] James Jones, the U.S. ambassador to Mexico, directly pressured the Mexican Secretary of

Commerce and told the governor of San Luís Potosí that he would place the state on a blacklist to slow U.S. investments if the governor did not allow the waste site to reopen, something the governor now says he considered a blackmail attempt.[30]

Under such political pressures, federal authorities refused to continue field research to clarify the existing technical uncertainties, as demanded by the citizens' committee. They also sought quick approval for the project from other institutions—the college of Civil Engineers, the Geological Institute of the National Autonomous University of Mexico (UNAM), and the National Water Commission—which confirmed the suitability of the site without deep analysis or even acknowledgment that there were serious problems.[31]

On November 24, 1995, Profepa signed an agreement with Coterin-Metalclad, with the support of INE and the head of the Semarnap. The agreement committed Coterin to clean up the site in three years provided the company be allowed to operate the waste dump, subject to an inspection by Profepa after five years. Coterin agreed to pay the municipality two pesos for each ton of waste that entered the municipality, to employ local workers, to offer free health consultations once a week to residents, and to give a ten-percent discount for its services to companies located in San Luís Potosí. Profepa agreed to set up a technical committee to oversee the clean-up of the three existing cells and agreed to accept citizen oversight.[33]

The Opposition Builds

Because the agreement was signed behind the backs of state and municipal authorities, they rejected it publicly. The governor of the state published a manifesto in various national and state newspapers, affirming that he did not know of nor agree to the terms of the agreement, calling for full respect for the will of the people, and urging the authorities of the municipality of Guadalcázar to resolve the issue. He stated he would not accept any commitments that were against the will of the people and called for negotiations to find a solution.[33]

Days later, the municipal council of Guadalcázar, meeting in open session with the participation of more than 500 individuals and *ejido* representatives, reiterated its opposition to the toxic waste site. The people rejected the federal agreement and the company offers, because, in their words, "the health of the people is not for sale." In this same session the council called for the formation of a common front, made up of the seventeen municipalities in the San Luís Potosí plateau, to keep the site from opening and to ensure respect for the sovereignty and autonomy of the municipalities, as guaranteed in Article 115 of the Mexican Constitution.[34]

In January 1996, Guadalcázar municipal authorities, with legal support from the state government, filed a lawsuit to have the agreement between federal environmental authorities and Coterin-Metalclad declared invalid. The lawsuit took more than four years to resolve. The court ultimately ruled against the municipal authorities, finding that in their roles as public agencies they could not base their lawsuit on individual rights. The suit kept the site from opening, however, since the judge had provisionally suspended its operation while the case was being litigated.[35]

Greenpeace, for its part, filed three lawsuits when it learned of the agreement: one against the Federal Comptroller for administrative irregularities related to the actions of public officials; one before the National Human Rights Commission; and one that broadened the criminal suit previously filed with the attorney general's office.[36]

In January 1997, Metalclad, beset by falling stock prices and fearing charges of fraud from its stockholders, filed its claim under Chapter 11, demanding $130 million in compensation from the Mexican government for its unfair treatment. Before the suit could be heard, though, and with municipal litigation against the federal agreement still pending, state officials took one further action: on September 27, 1997, they declared the area of Real de Guadalcázar a Protected Natural Area with "biosphere characteristics."

The Protected Natural Area

The state decree justified the creation of a Protected Natural Area based on the contention that the region is the center of the most important concentration of cacti species in the Great Chihuahua Desert, which extends from the southern United States to central Mexico. This makes the region of general ecological importance.[37] In it there are eighteen endangered cacti species, five of which are endemic to the region. The area also serves as a transitional habitat for a variety of animal species of ecological and economic importance, including the black bear, puma, white-tailed deer, and wild boar, among others. It also contains more than 200 archaeological sites.[38]

Representatives of local *ejidos* and agrarian communities had asked that Guadalcázar be declared a Protected Natural Area because of the diversity of cacti for two years. Greenpeace, along with thirty-five Mexican environmental and social organizations and some U.S. environmental organizations (including the National Wildlife Federation), had proposed the designation in an open letter to Semarnap.[39] The proposal was based on an extensive study of cacti in the area by the Biological Institute of UNAM.[40]

Metalclad's Chapter 11 Lawsuit

Metalclad alleged in its lawsuit that the Mexican government, by permitting the actions of the municipal authority of Guadalcázar and the government of San Luís Potosí, violated Article 1105 of NAFTA, because it did not give the company fair and equal treatment. The company also charged that Mexico violated Article 1110 when the municipal authority denied Metalclad a construction permit, which resulted in a *de facto* "expropriation" of its investment. When the state of San Luís Potosí later decreed Real de Guadalcázar a protected natural area, Metalclad argued that this measure also constituted an indirect expropriation of its investment.

NAFTA's Chapter 11 establishes a series of obligations for host governments in order to give protection and security to foreign investment. Article 1105 obligates the governments to treat foreign enterprises in accordance with international law, including fair and equitable treatment and full protection and security. Article 1110 states, "No Party may directly or indirectly nationalize or expropriate an investment of an investor of another Party in its territory or take a measure tantamount to nationalization or expropriation of such an investment ('expropriation'), except: (a) for a public purpose; (b) on a nondiscriminatory basis; (c) in accordance with due process of law and Article 1105(1); and (d) on payment of compensation in accordance with paragraphs 2 through 6."

The difficult question raised by Chapter 11 is how to interpret the concepts of "fair treatment," "indirect expropriation," and "tantamount to nationalization or expropriation." Governments have traditionally recognized foreign companies' rights to compensation when their land or installations are expropriated for public use. Under Chapter 11, the meaning of expropriation has been extended to the commercial value of company property, including the value of a company's stocks and its future utilities. According to Chapter 11, a government may be liable for any action that harms the investments of a foreign company, including laws, rules, proceedings, requirements, administrative practices, or measures to protect the environment or public health.

The Metalclad case calls into question the sovereignty of the municipality and the state government, making an exaggerated claim for compensation.

The claim for $130 million is based on the company's overestimate of the value of its investment in La Pedrera ($20 to $25 million, according to the company), $90 million for lost future earnings because it could not operate, and another $20 to $25 million for the drop of stock prices in related Metalclad-owned companies affected by the conflict.[41]

The Dispute Resolution Process

Disputes under Chapter 11 are resolved undemocratically, through an arbitration tribunal under the International Centre for the Settlement of Investment Disputes (ICSID), an institution linked to the World Bank and based in Washington, D.C.[42] For the Metalclad case, the ICSID arbitration panel was set up on May 19, 1997, with three people designated to hear the case; the arbitration was set for Vancouver, British Columbia, Canada, by the agreement of the parties.[43]

More than two years later, the tribunal held a hearing in Washington from August 30 through September 9, 1999, in which both parties presented their witnesses. Among them were Julia Carabias, head of Semarnap; Horacio Sánchez Unzueta, former governor of San Luís Potosí; Pedro Medellín Milán, former general coordinator for Ecology and Environmental Management for the state government of San Luís Potosí; Leonel Ramos, former municipal president of Guadalcázar; and José Mario de la Garza, formerly Metalclad's lawyer in San Luís Potosí, who, according to his testimony, resigned when Metalclad's Kesler proposed that he bribe Sánchez Unzueta, among others.[44]

On August 30, 2000, after a long exchange of letters, extensions, contestations, and replies, the tribunal decided in favor of Metalclad, judging that the municipality, by denying the local construction permit, "acted outside its authority," which constituted a measure equivalent to unfair treatment and indirect expropriation of the investment. It criticized Mexico for permitting or tolerating this conduct. Furthermore, it ruled that the state decree creating a protected natural area "could, in and of itself, constitute an act equivalent to expropriation." For these reasons, the Mexican government was ordered to pay Metalclad $16,685,000, and a cumulative six percent annual interest beginning forty-five days after the date of publication of the decision.[45]

The tribunal's decision validated most of Metalclad's complaints, but it failed to explain why it did not accept the Mexican government's evidence. The tribunal also exceeded its authority when it disqualified the constitutional competence of the municipality of Guadalcázar to deny the

construction permit to Metalclad, in effect passing judgment on the juridical structure of one of the countries that is party to NAFTA.

Mexico Appeals

The Mexican government appealed the tribunal's decision. According to
the agreement, appeals are heard in the courts where the tribunal deliber-
ates, so Mexico's case went to the Supreme Court of the Province of
British Columbia in Vancouver. This was the first Chapter 11 case to be
appealed, and the trial created a lot of interest in Canada. Since the case
dealt directly with NAFTA's ability to override local government decisions, the provincial government of Quebec took an interest, and the City
Council of Vancouver even petitioned to be part of the process, though the
request was denied. Many civil society organizations got involved as well,
including the Canadian Union for Public Employees (CUPE).

The Canadian court held public hearings in February and March 2001,
where the Mexican government presented its defense. On May 2, 2001,
Judge David E. Tysoe, of the Supreme Court of British Columbia, issued
his decision. He threw out the tribunal's finding that Mexico had violated
Article 1105 on discriminatory treatment, and he overruled two of the
three Article 1110 findings related to expropriation, the issue that most
concerned the Mexican government. But on the basis of the remaining
charge—the ruling that the creation of the protected natural area was "tantamount to expropriation"—he let stand the decision to compensate Metalclad, reducing the amount slightly to approximately $15.5 million.[46]

It was a complicated finding. According to Chapter 11 rules, the Canadian judge could review the rulings of the ICSID panel, but only insofar as
they overstepped their authority, and, in such cases, he could only annul or
accept the finding or any of its parts.[47] Judge Tysoe recognized that the tribunal had exceeded its authority in finding that the denial of the local construction permit was equivalent to expropriation simply because it
determined such decisions not to be the province of local government, in
effect questioning a governmental structure based in Mexico's constitution
and laws. Thus he threw out most of the tribunal's decision. Still, he
accepted the finding that the creation of the protected natural area was a
measure of indirect expropriation, overruling Mexico's arguments that the
decree did not in a strict sense impede the waste site's operation, and in
any case was not retroactive and therefore would not imply the expropriation of the site under Mexican law.[48]

Judge Tysoe's decision was controversial, because on the one hand he recognized that "the panel used an extremely wide definition of expropriation with respect to Article 1110."[49] Still, he concluded that he did not have the authority to revise the panel's decision regarding the protected natural area. The decision created an ominous precedent for Canadian courts in Chapter 11 arbitration appeals. According to a legal expert who advises Canadian public employee unions and environmental organizations, the decision's most problematic aspect is that, in this conflict between a private foreign company and governments, it used the same limited criteria applied in a conflict between persons in a commercial contract. Chapter 11 gives investors the right to sue foreign governments for actions that reduce their profits, under certain conditions, a right not granted to U.S. companies within the United States. Obviously, this conflict is not merely a private affair, as it profoundly affects the environment and health of communities.

Critics of the decision also argued that the judge gave too little weight to the evidence of corruption presented by the Mexican government. Even though the Canadian judge recognized that Metalclad paid large amounts—in stock and cash—to the wife of a federal environmental official, he ruled that this did not constitute conclusive evidence of corruption carried out in the name of Metalclad, and he did not question the credibility of the federal official.[50]

Metalclad's Reaction

Grant Kesler, president of Metalclad, criticized the decision, declaring that future trade agreements should incorporate stricter measures to protect investors. He complained that the judge denied him the interest he should have received—approximately $1 million—and declared that the award did not compensate him for the $90 million in profit he had expected to earn if the waste site had opened. Kesler threatened to initiate a second lawsuit in Mexican courts because of local opposition to another waste dump he had considered developing in the state of Aguascalientes, even though he had already sold most of his properties in Mexico. Ultimately, Kesler declared he would not return to the country.[51]

The U.S. International Business Council also decried the decision, demanding stricter measures to protect investors in free trade agreements negotiated by the White House. The group also called for a better appeals process for the FTAA.[52]

Initially, the Mexican government appealed the Canadian judge's decision, which could have been taken to the Canadian Supreme Court, prolonging the case for years. In the end Mexico decided to negotiate a settlement with Metalclad. On October 23, 2001, the Mexican government paid Metalclad $16,002,433 as compensation. In addition, the settlement establishes the conditions for the turnover of the land to the federal government and stipulates that the Treasury Department will provide the resources to Semarnat to clean up the site, still contaminated by the 20,000 tons of hazardous waste buried by Coterin.

Metalclad may not have gotten all it wanted, but it made out well. The company got paid and was absolved of any responsibility for the cleanup. Thanks to NAFTA, the polluter did not pay; rather, it was paid—and by the taxpayers of the country suffering the effects of the contamination. A more just solution would have been to establish a fund to clean up the site, with money from the parties that generated the problem: Coterin and the companies that illegally deposited 20,000 tons of hazardous waste, as well as the federal and state authorities who gave out the initial permits.

Mexican taxpayers will also have to foot the cleanup bill, which Semarnat estimates could cost as much as $8 million.[53] The cleanup must include full restoration of the contaminated soil, as well as a study of possible contamination of the aquifer. One has to question the Semarnat official who told a San Luís Potosí newspaper that the La Pedrera dump does not represent a risk because it is in an isolated area and people cannot enter.[54] The more time it takes to start the clean-up, the worse the environmental and health problems may get, problems that will be passed on to future administrations and generations.

Several important issues are still pending. Guadalcázar needs to establish a system of epidemiological monitoring in the communities exposed to the hazardous waste when it was unsafely stored, first in the open and later in the three cells that lacked adequate monitoring of gas emissions and leaching. Those who were exposed should be offered medical attention. And the government of San Luís Potosí, together with area citizens and experts, needs to develop a management plan for the new protected natural area, hopefully one that can create employment opportunities for residents.

Conclusion: A Flawed Model

The Metalclad decision illustrates the ways in which NAFTA's Chapter 11 elevates the rights of corporations above the rights of citizens—especially poor citizens—and above the protection of the environment. In so doing, it creates uncertainty for state and municipal governments that consider imposing environmental regulations that may affect corporate interests.

Chapter 11's investor-protection language is serving as a model for other multilateral trade agreements.[55] According to various experts, the rights Chapter 11 gives to foreign investors go further than anything previously negotiated by the United States or Canada, further, in fact, than any other bilateral investment agreement.[56] Previously, corporations could only pursue claims of unfair treatment through their own governments; this agreement gives corporations the status of international actor with the right to sue a foreign government.[57]

Chapter 11 does not assign any responsibility to foreign investors: they only have to consider their self-interest. The principal process to resolve problems—through the investor-state dispute mechanism—can only be initiated by foreign investors against the host government, not vice versa. In examining the Chapter 11 cases heard to date, many analysts have concluded that the arbitration tribunals have interpreted states' obligations toward foreign enterprises in a sweeping way. Since Chapter 11 makes no specific reference to its objectives, the panels have commonly given a narrow interpretation to NAFTA's stated objectives, emphasizing the agreement's goal of promoting investment opportunities. The have given less weight to the goals of protecting public welfare or preserving the environment.[58]

Chapter 11 has, in effect, converted trade provisions traditionally designed to defend corporations from unfair acts by a foreign government into an offensive weapon, an instrument that allows corporations to threaten government entities at the expense of environmental protection, public health, democracy, and state and municipal sovereignty.[59]

The Metalclad case also confirms the undemocratic character of the trade arbitration process, which is modeled on private arbitration procedures and therefore excludes public participation in order to protect confidentiality. Many critics have observed that Chapter 11 proceedings are closed-door.[60] Access to written documents in the cases is limited and discretional; some documents are made public only when the arbitration process is complete, and there is no public access to the hearings themselves unless all parties agree to open hearings, something that has not happened at this writing. Community, municipal, and state government cannot participate in the arbitration process or have access to the files, even if they are directly interested or affected. They must rely on their national government to present the case.

There are other shortcomings as well. The decision of the NAFTA tribunal is final, with no internal process of appeal. The only recourse the losing party (such as Mexico in the Metalclad case) has is to ask for the decision to be reviewed in the courts where the tribunal took place. Unlike a real appeals process, this review cannot take up the case itself, only questions related to the tribunal's jurisdiction and competency. There also are no requirements to ensure that the arbiters are qualified for the case, not only as experts in international trade issues but also in other relevant areas, such as environmental law and public health in the Metalclad case.[61] Chapter 11 fails to provide a level of transparency comparable to national judicial processes.

Even institutions and analysts who are not opposed in principle to the idea of free trade as a way to achieve sustainable development have recognized the illegitimacy of the Chapter 11 process. As one excellent analysis of the issue states, "In short, the investor-state process as currently designed and implemented is shockingly unsuited to the task of balancing private rights against public goods in a legitimate and constructive manner."[62]

"What this is about is to have a mechanism that gives a basic line of comfort to foreign investors," declared Ko-Yung Tung, vice president and general consul of the World Bank and Secretary of the ICSID, to the *New York Times*. He added, "If increasing direct investment is the primary objective, then making the proceedings public could be of lesser importance" than protecting investors.[63]

ICSID has heard most of the Chapter 11 cases in dispute, in addition to Metalclad. By the end of 2000, another sixteen corporations from the United States and Canada had demanded millions in compensation from the governments of the United States, Canada, and Mexico. Ten of these cases are environmental, based on alleged discriminatory treatment, measures tantamount to expropriation, and reduced future profits related to government actions to protect the environment. Among the government measures being challenged are the prohibition of toxic additives in gasoline, the prohibition on exporting toxics contaminated by PCB, the prohibition of pesticides, a moratorium on exporting water in order to conserve the scarce resource, and the revocation of concessions to manage hazardous or municipal waste.[64] These include two cases against the Mexican government, cases which have since been thrown out by the NAFTA arbitration panel.[65]

Even though the majority of these cases are still pending, a number of companies have benefited from the arbitration process and the negotiations, receiving substantial compensations at taxpayers' expense. The mere notification that a corporation intends to sue a government, and the acceptance of a case by the arbitration tribunal, have been sufficient to intimidate government officials. The most illustrative case is that of the U.S. company Ethyl, which, in April 1997 filed a $201 million claim for compensation for the Canadian Parliament's ban on the importation of or trade in the gasoline additive MMT, a proven neurotoxin. Once the arbitration panel decided to hear the case, the Canadian government gave in, negotiating a $13 million settlement with Ethyl, retracting the MMT ban, and, notwithstanding claims by scientists and environmental groups, giving Ethyl a letter stating that there was no scientific evidence for health risks from MMT.[66]

The payment of millions in compensation to Metalclad, thanks to Chapter 11, creates a precedent that will be invoked by foreign companies to pressure federal, state, and municipal authorities not to interfere with their investments and not to undertake measures to protect citizens' health or environment. The Mexican government should call for the renegotiation of NAFTA Chapter 11. It should also submit the investor-protection provisions of the proposed Free Trade Area of the Americas to broad public debate and rethink its bilateral investment agreements that contain similar provisions.[67]

Mexico needs national and foreign investment to expand and improve the country's infrastructure to treat hazardous waste, as it currently has only one site in the whole country, in Mina, Nuevo León. Still, such sites should not be imposed on poor communities against their wills and without adequate environmental and health safeguards. It is an act of environmental injustice to impose environmental and health risks on poor communities, while absolving the polluters of any responsibility to reduce their waste through cleaner production methods. NAFTA's Chapter 11 should not allow foreign corporations to override citizens' rights to a healthy environment. This is a threat that can only be stopped through organized resistance and public debate, which becomes particularly important if Chapter 11 serves as a model for the Free Trade Area of the Americas promoted by the Bush administration.

Notes

The author was the coordinator of the Greenpeace-Mexico Toxics Campaign from 1993 to the end of 1996, and was directly involved in this case. He was invited by the Canadian Union of Public Employees and Greenpeace Canada to be an observer in the public hearings on the appeal of the Metalclad case before the Supreme Court of British Columbia in February 2001.

1. A good summary of the conflict through 1996, can be found in Greenpeace articles in the supplement, *La Jornada del Campo* of the Mexico City newspaper *La Jornada*, May 30, 1995, and August 28, 1996.

2. Data from the 1995 census, cited in Vicente Ugalde Saldaña, *La gestión ambiental en el ámbito municipal: dos estudios de caso.* Master's Thesis in Urban Studies, Centro de Estudios Demográficos y de Desarrollo Urbano (CEDDU), El Colegio de México, June 2000.

3. The company Manejo y Disposición de Desechos Químicos, SA operated this site. The reason for its closure was citizen pressure not because "it had gotten to the end of its useful life," as Profepa affirmed. These and other erroneous affirmations can be found in Procuraduría Federal de Protección al Medio Ambiente (Profepa), Semarnap, *De La Pedrera a Metalclad. El conflicto en torno al confinamiento de residuos peligrosos en Guadalcázar, San Luís Potosí* (México, 2000), 13. To date, there has been no evaluation of the environmental or public health implications of the 70,000 tons of waste still buried in Mexquitic de Carmona. According to Dr. Angelina Nuñez, of the environmental group Pro San Luís Ecológico, the mercury recycling company still operates in Mexquitic.

4. Ugalde Saldaña, *La gestión ambiental,* states that it is imposible to determine the exact date when waste deliveries to La Pedrera began, but others say the first shipments were in 1989. (See López Farfán, "El municipio frente a la problemática ambiental. El caso de La Pedrera en Guadalcázar," *Gerencia pública municipal. Conceptos básicos y estudios de caso* (México City: Miguel Ángel Porrúa, 1999).

5. See Fred G. Lee and Anne Jones-Lee, *Recommended Design, Operation, Closure and Post Closure Approaches for Municipal Solid Waste and Hazardous Waste Landfills* (El Macero, Calif., August 1995); James V. Walters, Tola B. Muffet, Jerry D. Sellers, and W. Adrian Lovel, "Elevated Concrete Buildings for Long Term Management of Hazardous Wastes," in *Environmental Progress* 7, no. 4 (November 1988); K.W. Brown and David C. Anderson, "Section 10.7 Aboveground disposal" in *Standard Handbook of Hazardous Waste Treatment and Disposal,* ed. Harry M. Freeman (Washington, D.C.: U.S. Environmental Protection Agency/McGraw Hill, 1984); Peter Montague, "The Limitations of Landfilling," in *Beyond Dumping: New Strategies for Controlling Toxic Contamination,* ed. Bruce Piasecki (Westport, Conn.: Quorum Books, 1984).

6. Strangely enough, the Profepa report acknowledges this, stating that the temporary permit for the transfer station "had as its objective to permit C. Aldrett to comply with its previous obligations before the imminent suspension of the Mexquitic site." Profepa, Semarnap, *De La Pedrera a Metalclad,* p. 14.

7. The permits were granted by René Altamirano of INE. The official version of this procedure is found in Profepa, Semarnap, *De La Pedrera a Metalclad.* A description of the irregularities is found in the Declaration of Facts prepared by Greenpeace-Mexico and Pro San Luís Ecológico for the Attorney General of the Republic in September 1995: Exp: AP-7821-FEDEC-95 Mesa cuarta.

8. Generally, the land-use permit is issued by the municipality. According to the Urban and Ecological Code of San Luís Potosí, the permit could be given by the state executive branch through the Secretariat for Urban and Ecological Development. But the code states that the local government gives out the building license. The municipality generally has more authority in these matters.

9. Hugo Perezcano Díaz, et al. (Consultor Jurídico de Negociaciones. Secretaría de Comercio y Fomento Industrial, Estados Unidos Mexicanos), *Escrito de Dúplica del Gobierno Mexicano ante el honorable tribunal arbitral establecido al amparo del capítulo XI del Tratado de Libre Comercio de América del Norte (TLCAN)*. The lawyer Perezcano coordinated the case assisted by the law firms Thomas & Davis and Pittman, Potts & Trowbridge. This document was presented by the Mexican government in the arbitration panel, prior to the British Columbia Supreme Court hearings in Vancouver in February 2001. It constitutes the Mexican government's public record of the initial Metalclad hearings.

10. Perezcano, et al. *Escrito de Dúplica*, 47.

11. On June 30, 1992, Metalclad reported working capital of only $880,000, down from $1,925,000 the year before; by September 1992, it had dropped to $678,000. Perezcano, et al., *Escrito de Dúplica*, 53–54.

12. Interview with Pedro Medellín and Horacio Sánchez Unzueta in San Luís Potosí, February 11, 2001. The Universidad Autónoma de San Luís Potosí (UASLP) had carried out two evaluations of the site. One was a geologic study by engineer Sergio Alemán, researcher in the engineering department, who concluded the site was unsuitable. The second evaluation was by Dr. Fernando Díaz Barriga of the department of toxicology of the medical school, who found aberrations in the chromosomes and an elevated level of arsenic in the hair and urine of transfer station workers who were given inadequate safety equipment.

13. Perezcano, et al., *Escrito de Dúplica*, 80.

14. Perezcano, et al., *Escrito de Dúplica*, 12.

15. Perezcano, et al., *Escrito de Dúplica*, 87–88. Interview with Hugo Pérez Cano, Secofi (now Secretariat of the Economy), General Director for Juridical Consultancy in Negotiations, February 18, 2001.

16. Oakes Fitzwilliams, *Metalclad Corporation. Cleaning Up the Mexican Waste Market*. Howard Tisshaw, London-New York, March 1995 (mimeo).

17. Profepa, Semarnap, *De La Pedrera a Metalclad*.

18. Dr. Angelina Nuñez, interview, February 12, 2000. She documented thirty cases with family name, date, and place where they received medical attention. The majority of these cases did not have death certificates.

19. Grant S. Kesler, Metalclad Corporation, Letter to Shareholders, March 6, 1995.

20. Raúl Urteaga, letter to Grant Kesler, March 8, 1995, cited in Profepa, Semarnap, *De La Pedrera a Metalclad*, 19.

21. According to Profepa, the event on March 10 was only a simple site visit, though it recognizes the opposition, devaluing it as "the opposition of at least a part of the local community." Profepa, Semarnap, *De La Pedrera a Metalclad*, 19.

22. Adriana Bermeo, "Abren primer cementerio de toxicos," in *Reforma* newspaper, March 11, 1996.

23. Escuela Regional de Ciencias de la Tierra, Universidad Autónoma de Guerrero, Greenpeace-México, and Pro San Luís Ecológico, AC, *Dictamen ciudadano a la auditoría ambiental de la estación de transferencia de residuos peligrosos, ubicada en el sitio La Pedrera. Guadalcázar, San Luís Potosí. Informe de Auditoría 1*. México, June 28, 1995.

24. Greenpeace, press release, September 14, 1995. Denuncia de Hechos ante la PGR EXP AP 7821-FEDEC 95 Mesa Cuarta.

25. Arturo Borja Tamayo, *The New Federalism, Internationalization and Political Change in Mexico: a Theoretical Analysis of the Metalclad Case* (Mexico: División de Estudios Internacionales, CIDE, 2001).
26. Hermilio López, former ecology official, interview, February 10, 2001. On May 13, 1994, the inhabitants of Guadalcázar sent a letter to the governor of San Luís Potosí in which they complained of Metalclad's support for candidates for the municipal presidency.
27. The attempt to bribe the ecology official was alleged in the February 10, 2001 interview. The attempt to bribe the governor was alleged in an interview with the governor on February 11, 2001, and in the statement by the Mexican government: "The then-judicial advisor to Metalclad in San Luís Potosí, De la Garza, testifies that after the failed opening at the end of April 1995, Grant Kesler communicated the idea of offering a bribe of one million dollars to the governor in exchange for his support in opening the site. De la Garza refused, and later resigned from representing Metalclad." Perezcano, et al., *Escrito de Dúplica,* 11.
28. Letter from Senator Paul Simon to Silva Herzog, the Mexican ambassador in Washington, June 16, 1995, and letter to President Zedillo, August 11, 1995. The senator describes Metalclad as a company with significant investment in Illinois (remember that First Analysis Corporation was the primary stockholder) and warned that the situation would dampen similar investment by U.S. companies. In the opinion of governor Horacio Sánchez Unzueta, the support of Senator Barbara Boxer was also important in the White House. Interview, February 11, 2001.
29. Letter from Brian Hand, First Analysis Corporation, to President Ernesto Zedillo, August 31, 1995.
30. Horacio Sánchez Unzueta, Interview, Ferburary 11, 2001.
31. The institution with the best technical capabilities, the Geological Institute of UNAM, recognized that the information presented by the consulting firm GIMAS was disorganized, without all the necessary geological and hydrological information, and recommended a regional flow analysis where the position of the aquifers, the depth of the wells, and other evidence about subsurface water could allow them to better analyze the relationships among the different aquifers in the region. Still, it somehow deemed the site apt for the waste depository. It is also contradictory that the College of Civil Engineers recognized that there was inadequate integration of the design and engineering for the site and little coordination among the specialists involved in the project. Profepa, Semarnap, *De La Pedrera a Metalclad,* 85–96.
32. Semarnap, Profepa, Subprocuraduría de Auditoría Ambiental, *Convenio de concertación de acciones resultantes de la auditoría ambiental.* Empresa, Confinamiento de Técnico de Residuos Industriales, SA de CV, November 24, 1995.
33. "A los Potosinos," *El Financiero,* México, November 26, 1995.
34. *La Jornada,* December 6, 1995; also a videotape made by participants in the meeting.
35. The details can be read in Profepa, Semarnap, *De La Pedrera a Metalclad.*
36. Press Release, Greenpeace, February 2, 1996.
37. The Great Chihuahua Desert extends from the south of the United States in the states of Arizona, New Mexico, and Texas to the center of Mexico, including parts of the states of Chihuahua, Coahuila, Durango, Nuevo Leon, Zacatecas, San Luís Potosí, Tamaulipas, Aguascalientes, and Guanajuato.

38. Official Paper of the Government of San Luís Potosí, September 27, 1997.

39. Since October 21, 1995, the majority of the representatives from *ejidos* and communities have favored declaring the protected area because of the importance of the cacti, based on the research by the Biological Institute of UNAM. Press Release, Greenpeace, November 3, 1995, with attached letter to Julia Carabias, head of Semarnap.

40. On September 19, 1995, in a letter directed to Julia Carabias, the director of the Biological Institute of the UNAM, Hector Hernandez Macías, had pointed out the importance of the diversity of cacti, of the idea of converting it into a protected area, and his worries about the reopening of the toxic waste site. This letter was never answered by Semarnap. Part of the research was published in *Conservation Biology* 9, no. 5 (October 1995), and Vol. 10, no. 4 (August 1996).

41. CIADI (ICSID), *Certificado Metalclad Corporation vs Estados Unidos Mexicanos* (Caso CIADI, núm. ARB AF/97/1) Washington, D.C., August 30, 2000, 40.

42. Article 1120 of NAFTA establishes that the claims of an investor against a NAFTA government are to be examined by an international trade tribunal, which will act according to: a) the ICSID Convention, provided that both the disputing Party and the Party of the investor are parties to the Convention; or b) the Additional Facility Rules of ICSID, provided that either the disputing Party or the Party of the investor, but not both, is a party to the ICSID Convention; or c) the UNCITRAL Arbitration Rules approved by the General Assembly of the United Nations on December 15, 1976. The tribunal has to be integrated by three arbiters, one chosen by each of the parties and the third with the agreement of both. (Article 1123)

43. The tribunal included Sir Eliu Lauterpacht, CBE, QC (president), Benjamín R. Civiletti, and José Luis Siqueiros.

44. Perezcano, et al., *Escrito de Dúplica,* 114–16. De la Garza's testimony is cited in the document as "Contestación a la demanda, primera declaración de José Mario de la Garza, páginas 9 a 12."

45. CIADI (ICSID), *Certificado Metalclad Corporation vs Estados Unidos Mexicanos* (Caso CIADI, núm. ARB AF/97/1) Washington, D.C. 30 de agosto del 2000. The compensation was less than Metalclad had originally demanded, because the tribunal argued that the waste site never functioned and it would be speculative to establish compensation based on future earnings. The tribunal also excluded compensation for the effect on other commercial operations, arguing that other factors influenced drops in the price of Metalclad's stock. It also refused to compensate for expenses incurred by Coterin, before Metalclad acquired the company. The Mexican government estimated the investment in La Pedrera at only $3 to $4 million, not the $20 million claimed by the company.

46. Supreme Court, British Columbia, "The United Mexican States vs. Metalclad. Reasons for Judgment of the Honorable Mr. Justice Tysoe," May 2, 2001. *Boletín de prensa de la Secretaría de Economía,* May 3, 2001.

47. In a case of a total annulment, the case would return to the NAFTA tribunal for additional consideration. It is not an appeal in the strict sense that it would permit the Canadian court to change the tribunal's findings. Such findings are not subject to appeal.

48. Interview with Hugo Pérez Cano, June 13, 2001. The Mexican government gave proof to this respect. Of the same opinion was Pedro Medellín Milán,

former coordinator for Ecology and Environmental Management of the government of San Luís Potosí, interviewed on February 11, 2001.

49. Comments by lawyers Steven Shrybman and Sack Goldblatt Mitchell of the firm Sack Goldblatt Mitchell Barristers & Solicitors, Toronto, Canada, May, 6, 2001.

50. A summary of the judge's ruling can be found in "Reasons for Judgment of the Honourable Mr. Justice Tysoe. The United Mexican States v Metalclad Corporation," Supreme Court of British Columbia. May 2, 2001, Vancouver, Canada. pages 38–39. See also Steven Shrybman, of Stack Goldbatt Mitchell Barristers & Solicitors, "Mexico vs Metalclad. Reasons for Judgment," Ottawa, Ontario, May 6, 2001.

51. Tali Nauman, "Metalclad, Mexico Feels Little Solace in Ruling," *Eco-americas* (Santa Monica, Calif.: Fourth Street Press Inc., September 2000).

52. Steven Shrybman, "Canada Court Ruling Prompts Calls for Stronger Investor Rule," *Inside US Trade*. May 11, 2001.

53. Declaration by Víctor Lichtinger, Head of Semarnat, in an article by Óscar Alejandro Martínez, *Pulso*, San Luís Potosí, August 17, 2001.

54. Declaration by Víctor Lichtinger, August 17, 2001.

55. For a detailed description and analysis of Chapter 11, see International Institute for Sustainable Development and World Wildlife Fund, *Private Rights, Public Problems: A guide to NAFTA's controversial chapter on investor rights* (Washington, D.C.: IISD and WWF, 2001).

56. Howard Mann, Konrad von Moltke and collaborators, *NAFTA's Chapter 11 and the Environment: Addressing the Impacts of the Investor-State Process on the Environment* (Winnipeg, Canada: IISD, 1999), 3.

57. Juli A. Abouchar and Richard J. King, "Environmental Laws as Expropriation under NAFTA," *RECIEL* 8, no. 2 (1999): 209–14.

58. See IISD and WWF, *Private Rights*.

59. Mann, et al., *NAFTA's Chapter 11 and the Environment,* 17–24.

60. Only appeals hearing documents have been published.

61. Among many good critiques, a few stand out: Public Citizen, Friends of the Earth, *NAFTA Chapter 11 Investor-to-State Cases: Bankrupting Democracy. Lessons for Fast Track and the Free Trade Area of the Americas* (Washington, D.C.: September 2001); Center for International Environmental Law, Third World Institute, Preamble Center, *Investment Agreement of the Americas: Economic, Environmental and Social Perspectives* (Washington, D.C.: 1999); Mann, et al., *NAFTA's Chapter 11 and the Environment* (Winnipeg: 1999).

62. IISD and WWF, *Private Rights,* 46.

63. Anthony DePalma, "NAFTA's Powerful Little Secret; Obscure Tribunals Settle Disputes, but Go Too Far, Critics Say," *New York Times,* March 11, 2001.

64. For a list and a description of the different cases of companies that have resorted to Chapter 11, see Public Citizen, Friends of the Earth, *NAFTA Chapter 11 Investor-to-State Cases,* and IISD and WWF, *Private Rights.*

65. One case involves the U.S. company Waste Management, whose claim for $60 million was not accepted initially by the NAFTA court because other proceedings had already been initiated in a Mexican court. The case is still open. The second case involves Robert Zinin, majority stockholder of Desona, who demanded $19 million for the revocation of a contract to manage solid waste in the

municipality of Naucalpan. The case was thrown out by the NAFTA tribunal when the irregularities of the contract, the inexperience of the company, and the failure to comply with certain clauses were proven. See Public Citizen, Friends of the Earth, *NAFTA Chapter 11 Investor-to-State Cases.*

66. Abouchar and King, "Environmental Laws," 209–12.

67. See "An analysis of the draft investment chapter of the FTAA," Hemispheric Social Alliance, available at http://www.asc-hsa.org.

3

Human Rights, Ecology, and Economic Integration: The Peasant Ecologists of Guerrero

Enrique Cienfuegos and Laura Carlsen

In memory of Digna Ochoa

On May 2, 1999, members of the 40th Infantry Battalion entered the community of Pizotla, Guerrero, firing their weapons. They killed Salomé Sánchez Ortíz[1] and arrested two environmentalist leaders, Rodolfo Montiel Flores and Teodoro Cabrera García. The army took Montiel and Cabrera to a nearby checkpoint, where they were held for two days, interrogated, and tortured. Later they were transferred to the battalion's base in Ciudad Altamirano, where they were again tortured and interrogated. The two leaders were held incommunicado for three days and finally forced to sign confessions of federal crimes under torture and threats.[2] Montiel and Cabrera were charged with possession of firearms for exclusive use of the army, possession of firearms without a license, and growing marijuana.

Rodolfo Montiel, a traveling clothes salesman with little formal education, learned the basics of ecology in Uruapán, Michoacán, where he had worked for a university professor. When he returned to his community, he founded the Organization of Peasant Ecologists of the Sierra de Petatlán and Coyuca de Catalán (known by its Spanish acronym, OCESP). The organization, made up of regional peasant farmers and workers, began to protest the rapid deforestation of the surrounding mountains and called attention to the ecological impact of the uncontrolled logging being carried out in the area. They petitioned the state and federal governments for support to stop clandestine logging and establish community and environmental recovery programs.

This activism had made targets of Montiel and his fellow peasant ecologist. After remaining in prison over a year, the two were sentenced on August 28, 2000, Montiel to six years, eight months, and Cabrera to ten years. The sentence was imposed even though the only evidence against them were confessions signed under torture, and despite a recommendation from Mexico's official National Human Rights Commission, just months before sentencing, that a full review of the case be conducted due to the many legal and human rights violations.[3] The peasant ecologists spent another year in prison before they were finally released on November 8, 2001, "for humanitarian reasons." Their release was the product of an intense international campaign and outrage at the assassination of Digna Ochoa, one of their defense lawyers.

The repression against Rodolfo Montiel and Teodoro Cabrera, and the Organization of Peasant Ecologists' fight to save their forests, gained international attention. For many environmental groups, the pair became a symbol of local resistance to environmentally destructive forces unleashed under the terms of trade liberalization. To really understand the peasants ecologists' struggle in the southern state of Guerrero, it is necessary to step back and analyze the history of a region coveted for its abundant natural resources, exploited by extractive industries, and plagued by social instability.

Forestry and Agriculture in Guerrero

The history of ecocide and resistance in the mountains of Guerrero did not begin with Montiel and Cabrera, nor is it likely to end there. Armando Bartra, one of the foremost experts on the region, points out that Montiel and Cabrera continue a long legacy of resistance in the mountain communities and form part of a third generation of struggle for the forests of Guerrero.[4] Commercial relations in the region have always been based on the power of intermediaries. More important than actually owning the land or producing goods, the key to getting rich lay in the control over regional marketing. Whoever had the means to warehouse, process, and market agricultural and forestry products controlled profits and, in a vicious cycle, also controlled the peasants who produced them.

In the early part of the twentieth century, three Spanish marketing companies dominated commercial and production activity in Guerrero's Costa

Grande. These companies controlled the roads and means of transportation, the maritime sea routes and ships, the land and its products, the markets and merchandise, and the civil and military authorities. Other important interests also held sway: U.S. businessman Roberto Silberber Sucesores owned nearly 40,000 hectares of forest near Atoyac; local landowners held some 31,722 hectares; and 150,000 hectares were under concession to a company called the Guerrero Land and Timber Co., which operated in Tecpan, Atoyac, and Coyuca de Benitez.[5] The looting of natural resources and exploitation of the local workforce led to scores of local uprisings, which eventually found expression in the "radical wing" of the Mexican Revolution led by Emiliano Zapata.[6]

In the mid-1950s many Costa Grande peasant organizations initiated their own grassroots development projects as an alternative to privatization of the region and its resources. Most self-help initiatives never took off in forestry. Although eighty percent of Guerrero's forests are *ejidos* or communal lands—part of Mexico's unique social property sector—community groups did not have access to financial resources, roads, or transportation to get their timber down to the sawmills. When the communities were unable to develop their own projects, privatization moved ahead, despite vehement but isolated local opposition.[7] In this period, a firm called Maderas Papanoa, property of the lumber magnate Melchor Ortega, began clear-cutting in the area. In 1955, Maderas Papanoa opened a road into the mountains and set to work felling trees on the *ejidos* of San Vicente de Jesús, El Naranjal, Mezcaltepec, Agua Fría, and El Camerón. By the 1960s, four-fifths of the state's forested area was controlled by a handful of companies.[8] Uprisings against these companies converged with the guerrilla insurrections led by Lucio Cabañas Barrientos and Génaro Vázquez Rojas and brought about a virtual suspension of logging.

To pacify local discontent over poverty, oppression, and environmental degradation, the government of President Luís Echeverría designed a strategy to address the crisis in agriculture and livestock production and win back the allegiance of local peasants, who formed the social base of the guerrilla movements. Promoted as an alliance between the government and peasant farmers, the Echeverría model increased government investment in rural economic activities, taking a direct role in financing, processing, and marketing agricultural, livestock, and forestry goods. The government created a number of extension agencies and state-owned enterprises. Conceived in part as a necessary counterinsurgency measure, the Echeverría model also built major public works and infrastructure in the area. The plan did not, however, diminish the fierce power of traditional rural strongmen, or *caciques*.[9]

⋅ As part of the plan, in 1972, the government established the Vicente Guerrero Forestry Agency. The purpose of the decentralized agency, which was given exclusive concession for logging in the region, was to absorb the private lumber companies that operated in the zone. Relations between the Vicente Guerrero Forestry Agency and local communities were less conflicted than with the private companies. The state-owned enterprise, for example, hired local workers, in contrast to the private companies' custom of employing outsiders for logging and extraction. With the conversion to state-owned logging operations, the battle against company abuses, non-compliance with contracts, and depredation of the forests had a new actor—the government.

Many peasant organizations, some independent and others allied with powerful interests, were founded and grew during this period, often tangibly improving standards of living for mountain communities. Government control of marketing activity, at least at that time, was preferable to the brutal, despoiling control exercised by local *caciques*. But when José Francisco Ruíz Massieu became governor of Guerrero in 1987, the limited advances of the Echeverría model were quickly wiped out. Ruíz Massieu was a prominent member of the group of politicians led by his former brother-in-law, Carlos Salinas de Gortari, who came to power in the late 1980s. As governor, Ruíz Massieu imposed an economic model adapted from the ambitious designs of President Salinas. The Guerrero version of the model was laid out in the state's Six-Year Plan, presented in 1988, which emphasized development of the economy's service sector—especially tourism, which supplied seven of every ten pesos of the state budget. The plan placed a high priority on the development of offshore assembly plants and set in motion four megaprojects: the Punta Diamante/Marina Ixtapa tourism complexes, the Sun Highway to connect Acapulco to Mexico City, the Filo Mayor highway, and the reconstruction of irrigation systems in the Tierra Caliente. These projects were conceived as doors to the global market and formed the foundation for projected economic growth based on foreign investment.

The Six-Year Plan also implemented the decision to cut back government spending, as it proposed dismantling government programs for rural extension, agricultural subsidies, and regulation. The primary sector, employer of seven out of every ten Guerrerans, was practically abandoned under the plan. The government was betting that open markets would automatically make agriculture competitive; but without a well-planned and supported strategy the situation in the countryside hit crisis proportions almost overnight.

NAFTA and Boise Corporation

The North American Free Trade Agreement (NAFTA) caused major adjustments in the use of forestry resources in Guerrero.[10] The forestry section of the agreement stipulated that tariffs on wood and wood products be phased out by 2003. Although the member countries already had zero tariffs or, in Mexico's case, relatively low tariffs (between zero and fifteen percent), after NAFTA international trade in wood and wood products in Mexico increased significantly.[11] This increase stemmed from two factors: the entry of transnational timber companies and intensified logging activities by national companies seeking to maintain their domestic market share.

In 1995, a year after NAFTA took effect, a U.S.-based wood-products company, the Boise Corporation (formerly known as Boise Cascade Forest Products), signed an agreement with then-governor of Guerrero, Rubén Figueróa Alcocer, granting it purchase and logging rights on *ejidos* of the Costa Grande of Guerrero. It was an opportune moment for the transnational because the 1995 peso devaluation that had plunged Mexico into crisis had also lowered labor costs in Mexico, and U.S. markets for wood products were growing. Although the Boise Corporation has denied having signed an exclusive contract to log the region, investigations by Greenpeace concluded that such a contract existed, and local and national press reports also refer to such a contract.[12] According to reports and interviews in the region, the contract was for five years (1995–2000) and involved twenty to thirty million board-feet a year.[13]

Based in Idaho, Boise Corp. had annual sales of $7.4 billion in 2001, and ranked 246 on the Fortune 500 list.[14] It logs 2.3 million acres of forest in the United States. In the past years, the company has closed U.S. sawmills to open up activities in foreign countries, claiming a lack of accessible forest in the United States due to "extreme environmentalism" that restricts logging in areas designated for conservation or as habitat for endangered species.[15] A group of researchers from Idaho, however, cited evidence that the main motive for moving operations abroad was not so much a lack of raw materials but to lower operating costs and avoid criticism from U.S. environmental groups.[16] The study concluded that Boise Corp. directed its operations to countries—among them Mexico, Chile, and

Brazil—where environmental laws were more lax and where conditions of poverty allowed it to reduce labor costs and forest management costs.

It is worth looking closely at Boise Corp. activities in the Costa Grande of Guerrero. In 1995, Boise associated with NDG, Inc., a Mexico-incorporated office run by a joint venture lawyer from Puebla and later bought out by Boise, to carry out logging and sawmill operations in the forests of Guerrero. It formed a wholly-owned subsidiary called Costa Grande Forest Products, which operated a sawmill in Papanoa[17] and bought production from another sawmill in Tecpan.[18] The company contracted the Union of *Ejidos* Rubén Figueróa to log the forests. Representatives of the Boise head office directly supervised operations, making frequent trips to the region.[19]

Boise Corp. began by paying significantly higher prices than local buyers,[20] and the Papanoa sawmill received lumber twenty-four hours a day.[21] However, few of the benefits of the wood sales reached local workers, who were paid twenty to thirty pesos per cubic meter. José Laderos Ortíz, a peasant farmer from the *ejido* El Mameyal, states: "I worked a year as a trimmer, but we were paid thirty pesos a day. The loggers were below us and above us were the *caciques*. They were the ones who paid us."[22] The profits generated by the huge quantities of wood sold to Costa Grande Forest Products apparently remained in the hands of the leaders of the Union of *Ejidos* Rubén Figueróa and the transnational.

The Costa Grande Forest Products sawmill got most of its logs from the Sierra de Petatlán and Coyuca de Catalán. Although precise data is scarce, a comparison of satellite shots taken in 1992, and 2000, by Greenpeace experts reveals massive deforestation in the area. During that time, which includes the 1995–1998 period of intense logging by Boise Corp., the Sierra lost 86,000 hectares of forest—nearly forty percent of the region's 226,203 hectares of forest in just eight years.[23] The report stated that excessive logging and destruction of vegetation in the zone meant that bare soil increased 130,595 hectares between 1992 and 2000. Greenpeace concluded, "If illegal logging in Guerrero continues at this rate, in ten years there will be no forest in Sierra de Petatlán and Coyuca de Catalán, just as Montiel and Cabrera have warned."[24]

The scars of the forestry practices of Boise Corp. are evident in the region. Employing methods of clear cutting and old growth harvesting that are severely limited in the United States and other countries, the transnational set out to log as much as possible, in as little time as possible and at minimum cost. According to the Miguel Agustín Pro Center for Human Rights and local inhabitants, Boise did not reforest in the zone.[25] The peasants of the region observed that the rivers were drying up, some species were growing scarce, soil erosion had increased considerably, and the rainy season had gotten shorter.[26] The region's rapid environmental deterioration severely impacted the peasant agricultural economy.[27] According to a peasant from the Sierra de Petatlán: "We used to harvest over three tons per hectare without fertilizer, now we don't get half of that using fertilizers. Now we don't even harvest enough for the family."[28]

According to interviews of OCESP members, the difference between the activity of Boise Corp. and previous logging activities had to do with the quantity of trees felled and the intensity of the operations, as well as the top-down relationships later imposed on the *ejidos*. On the second point, a leader of the movement explains: "The industrialists only want to take out the wood and make off with it, whatever the cost to us. The difference between locals and Boise is that before at least they didn't deceive the people so blatantly, because the timber interests would go and sign contracts with the assembly of this or that *ejido* and only the *ejido* in which they were working was involved. But now, first they stir up the people, promising things, they take them to Chilpancingo [the state capital] to meetings and start to get the people involved in a political dynamic that in the end they can't stop."[29]

Although little is known about the alliances between state officials and the transnational, Boise Corp. chose a local partner with one of worst reputations in the state for environmental and social abuses. The Union of *Ejidos* Rubén Figueróa managed a signed contract with the Costa Grande Forest Products sawmill, the Boise-owned subsidiary, in which the twenty-four *ejido* members of the union were committed to deliver their product. The union is under the control of Bernardino Bautista, a local *cacique* and staunch supporter of former governor Rubén Figueróa. Bautista has been accused of setting forest fires and planning assassinations in the area, and is well known for clear cutting in the *ejidos* under his control.[30] Through a network of political relations and armed assistants, he maintains iron law in the region.[31] It was predictable that Bautista would employ similar methods to assure delivery of the millions of board-feet promised under the contract with Boise Corporation.

Boise Corp. has repeatedly denied having anything to do with the case of the peasant ecologists. However, when Boise intensified logging in the area, it contributed significantly to the problems associated with deforestation and also increased the stakes for local bosses. This raised the temperature of the conflict in an already unstable zone. According to the interpretation of local residents and organizations including Amnesty

International and Sierra Club who took up the cause of Montiel and Cabrera, the two grassroots leaders were arrested when local *caciques* and politicians decided to come down on the peasant ecology movement in order to reestablish control and avoid future losses.[32]

The repression of local environmentalists is a global phenomenon. In a report on environmental campaigns around the world, Sierra Club and Amnesty International conclude that globalization has in general increased human rights violations against local defenders of natural resources:

> *From emerging economies in the South to economic superpowers in the North, governments are lowering environmental standards to increase global trade and are allowing their foreign policies to be driven and directed by corporate, instead of democratic, values. In many parts of the world, corporations and governments are colluding to violate the rights of environmental activists in the name of profit and economic development. Millions of dollars are on the line and environmental activists who protest are being persecuted and punished.[33]*

A Powder Keg in the Costa Grande

The region Boise Corporation chose to log features an explosive, three-part mix: extreme poverty, environmental degradation, and endemic violence. One of the poorest parts of the state located at the foot of the mountains, its main economic activity is cattle ranching, followed by agriculture. Landless peasants work for ranchers or logging outfits; others work on leased lands or help with the harvest. Annual crops of corn, beans, sesame seeds, watermelon, chile, and tomato characterize agriculture in the Costa Grande of Guerrero. Some areas are planted in coffee, coconuts, bananas, mangos, papayas, and lemons. In the higher regions, loggers report that the only viable option is to sell pine, the only marketable species in the zone since other species such as mahogany and cedar have been logged out.

Over eighty-five percent of land in Petatlán is *ejido* land. Local production combines commercial crops—such as honey, coffee, coconut, and wood—with products for family consumption, including corn, fruit, and small livestock. Most peasants grow corn for subsistence; those who venture into papaya and other tropical crops have had serious problems since they are forced to accept the prices offered by intermediaries, and prices for coffee and coconut have plummeted on the international market.

Environmental destruction in the region has been a steady process, resulting from the uncontrolled exploitation of natural resources. Inhabitants of Petatlán communities have converted many hectares of forest into crops or pasture, since without governmental support or technical assistance to create alternative projects they were left with no other options. The expansion of cattle ranching, often with the aid of government programs, has contributed heavily to deforestation.

Local residents report that the contract with Boise Corp. did not improve their living conditions. One ecology movement leader explained that while the U.S. company operated, much money circulated but it rarely filtered down to the communities. In numerous interviews local residents say the company dedicated itself only to logging the forests, and public works were limited to repairing necessary access roads.[34]

Finally, area violence has many roots. During the 1970s, army forces occupied the mountains of Guerrero, as part of the "dirty war" against the guerrilla groups of Genaro Vázquez and Lucio Cabañas. After exterminating rebel groups, the army continued to occupy positions, justifying its presence by claiming the need to fight drug trafficking in the area. The drug trade is indeed a real problem, but residents claim that army occupation is not the answer. In fact, several army officials charged with combating drugs in the state are now behind bars for corruption and drug trafficking. Municipal and state authorities, as well as the army, have served the interests of local *caciques,* consolidating the oligarchic control of the state in the hands of a few families. The oligarchy maintains power through the violation of individual liberties, persecution, kidnapping, cooptation, and the murder of grassroots leaders.

Between April and June 1999, members of the Mexican Army occupied eleven communities in the mountains of the Costa Grande of Guerrero, while they searched for suspected guerrillas, something that had not happened since the counterinsurgency war of the 1970s. The consequences of the army operation have not been adequately documented, but there were at least two deaths, and daily life was punctuated by regular patrols of foot soldiers, armed vehicles, and helicopters. Human rights organizations have documented many illegal detentions, and entire communities were forced to flee higher into the mountains.[35]

The presence of the army and private paramilitary groups has been a key factor in the breakdown of the region's normal community life. Far from bringing peace, the army has served to protect the interests of the *caciques* and commit abuses against the communities. The Miguel Agustín Pro Center for Human Rights reported that in 1995, 113 human rights violations were reported, sixty-six of which had to do with repression of groups opposed to the government.[36] The most notorious of these came in June 1995, when police killed seventeen unarmed peasants, members of the Peasant Organization of the Southern Sierra (OCSS) who were meeting near the village of Aguas Blancas to protest the entry of foreign companies and demand government support. The Aguas Blancas massacre eventually cost Rubén Figueróa Alcocer the governorship, when a police film of the incident documented his involvement.

The Peasant Ecologists

In February 1998, in response to the environmental destruction by Boise Corp. and local groups, peasants and vendors from the region formally registered their civil association under the name Organization of Peasant Ecologists of the Sierra of Petatlán and Coyuca de Catalán (OCESP). The group had already been organized and active for several years, but their activities intensified in 1998. OCESP began by writing letters to government officials, explaining the situation of environmental deterioration and requesting government intervention to stop logging in the zone.[37] In March 1998, they filed a complaint with the Federal Office of Environmental Protection (Profepa), charging "exploitation of pine-wood, without respecting the norms established in the Law of Ecological Balance." In other letters they requested support for regional development programs and volunteer reforestation programs.

The OCESP also launched an awareness campaign among the communities, which included reaching out to the truck drivers and chainsaw operators employed by the logging companies. The campaign focused on issues of reforestation and used grassroots organizing to request the intervention of government officials charged with local and state environmental protection. The organization implemented what members called "wood stoppages" by blocking trucks as they drove cut logs from the mountains, trying in the process to open up a dialogue with the drivers. Alongside these activities, the organization members developed a publicity campaign in the local and national media on OCESP's fight to preserve the forests. They also invited national and international nongovernmental organizations to support their movement and help communicate their cause to a broader audience.

In April 1998, three years after coming to Mexico, Boise closed down operations, citing "difficult business conditions."[38] Members of the OCESP considered the withdrawal of the transnational a major victory.

But the departure of Boise Corp. opened a new and dangerous chapter in the life of the OCESP. On the one hand, the deforestation of the region has not been deterred. According to interviews, new groups of loggers backed by paramilitary forces came in to cut down the forests where Boise left off. In part as punishment for OCESP's wood stoppages and for breaking the Boise contract, repression and violence increased against the peasant ecologists' organization, with threats; arrest orders for its members; and assassinations, torture, and physical abuse in several communities.[39]

In summer 1998, *cacique* Bernardino Bautista requested the intervention of the Mexican Army, alleging that he had been attacked by armed groups. At that moment, a new stage of sustained militarization and harassment began, which has only gotten worse. It was in these volatile conditions that Montiel and Cabrera were arrested and Salomé Sanchez was killed on May 2, 1999.

The OCESP has had to combine the fight to free its leaders and members[40] with campaigns for environmental protection and efforts to build alternatives in the region. In various events, the organization has presented state authorities with an alternative regional development plan that includes building new roads, paving highways, installing electricity in the communities, building irrigation systems (to which Rodolfo Montiel contributed the entire sum of his Goldman Prize—see below), and setting up quality health and education services. The organization has worked to develop productive projects, emphasizing sustainable development alternatives that do not deplete forestry resources. It has also advocated more serious regulation of logging activities.[41]

One difficulty the OCESP has faced since its inception is its political isolation. In spite of its international strength, it has not been able to build strong relations with the many grassroots organizations in the region. Organizations such as the Union of *Ejidos* Hermenegildo Galeana (see chapter 4) that manage self-run forestry projects have maintained a certain distance from the ecologists, criticizing their work as "ultra-conservationist." Lately these groups have come closer, recognizing that conservation and community-run projects are two facets of the same struggle to defend the forests through sustainable regional activities. With the murder of Digna Ochoa and the freeing of Montiel and Cabrera, OCESP has received broader national support. The organization continues to stress the need to maintain national and international attention on the region to protect the lives of Montiel and Cabrera and prevent more acts of repression against the movement.

The Campaign for Montiel and Cabrera

The OCESP case is perhaps most noteworthy for its impressive use of cross-border alliances and Internet-based campaigns. Mass communication networks—undeniably a part of globalization—now make it possible to exchange information and rapidly mobilize groups and individuals, even in geographically isolated communities. The new communications technology has become an essential tool for building the support necessary to bring a local struggle to international attention, as OCESP found in its campaign to win the release of Montiel and Cabrera.

The international coalition built quickly. It began on July 30, 1998, when residents of the community of El Mameyal, in the municipality of Petatlán, reported being harassed by members of the Mexican Army to a regional human rights group, the Human Rights Committee "The Voice of the Voiceless" in Coyuca de Benitez. This catalyzed the participation of nongovernmental organizations and human rights groups in the regional conflict.

The Miguel Agustín Pro Center for Human Rights became involved in August 1999, when OCESP presented Montiel and Cabrera's case. After reviewing the facts, the group considered it "a paradigmatic case, very representative of what is happening in Mexico to people who work for ecology."[42] The group agreed to take on the defense of Montiel and Cabrera. Greenpeace-Mexico also began to work on the case, providing data on regional deforestation and environmental effects. The Mexican Network for Action on Free Trade (RMALC) helped publicize the case, as part of its work on issues of foreign commercial activity and free trade following NAFTA. RMALC and Greenpeace have actively denounced, in Mexico and abroad, the environmental and social consequences of Boise Corp. activities in Guerrero. Various national and international NGOs (Greenpeace, Sierra Club, Amnesty International, Rainforest Action Network) also took up the cause of the peasant ecologists of Guerrero, perceiving the case as particularly important for illustrating environmental issues in the era of globalization. They saw the need to combat the violation of the human rights of individuals recognized as stewards of their lands and defenders of their environment. They wanted to highlight the lack of a clear legal definition in NAFTA that assures real defense of the environment. They sought to highlight the destruction of the social and natural environment as a consequence of the economic interests of foreign capital. And they wanted to draw attention to the absence of laws to regulate the behavior of transnationals.

Through the efforts of the OCESP and these groups, Montiel and Cabrera's case quickly gained international momentum. The front page of the *New York Times* featured their plight and the paper also dedicated an editorial to the case.[43] When the Goldman Foundation awarded its prestigious

Goldman Environmental Prize to Rodolfo Montiel on April 6, 2000, it marked a watershed in the international campaign to free the ecologists. Recognized as the equivalent of the Nobel Prize in environmental activism, the Goldman prize is delivered each year to six "environmental heroes" from each of the six continents of the world. This places Montiel in the company of environmental activists such as Chico Mendes of Brazil, Ken Saro Wiwa of Nigeria, Wangari Maathai from Kenya, Medha Patkar from India, and Russian Aleksandr Nikitin.

The campaign accelerated. On May 31, 2000, Amnesty International declared Montiel and Cabrera "prisoners of conscience."[44] Months later, in president-elect Vicente Fox Quesada's first visit to the United States, the president of Amnesty International, Pierre Sané, demanded in person that as proof of the new government's commitment to respect human rights Fox should free the ecologists within the first hundred days of his administration.

On February 7, 2001, Rodolfo Montiel also received the Chico Mendes Prize, awarded by the Sierra Club, one of the oldest and most respected environmental organizations in the world, in recognition of his struggle to defend the forests of Petatlán. The prize was delivered to Montiel behind bars in the federal penitentiary of Iguala, by human rights activist Ethel Kennedy, widow of Robert F. Kennedy.

The global solidarity campaign for Montiel and Cabrera and the public questioning of Boise's actions in Guerrero were not well received by the transnational. In response, the company unleashed a campaign against those who criticized its practices in Mexico. When the Rainforest Action Network (RAN) publicized the case of Montiel and Cabrera on its web site, the legal department of Boise Corp. wrote a letter accusing RAN of publishing false declarations and fabricating evidence.[45]

The company's belligerent response clearly reflected the power of the peasant ecologists' international campaign. The widespread support of nongovernmental organizations all over the world has been crucial, and the publicity in the mass media and international networks gave OCESP the leverage to finally win Montiel and Cabrera's release—but not before the tragic death of one of their foremost defenders.

The Death of Digna Ochoa

On October 19, 2000, two lawyers found their partner—the former nun, lawyer, and human rights activist Digna Ochoa— dead in her office with a bullet hole in the head. Through early 2000, Digna Ochoa had directed the defense of Montiel and Cabrera for the Pro Center for Human Rights.[46]

Ten days before her death she had visited several communities in the area, under the heavy vigilance of the Mexican Army. Ochoa had already received death threats, and on October 28, 1999, she had been kidnapped, beaten, and left tied to an open gas tank.

Ochoa's apparent murder shook the population and put President Vicente Fox in an uncomfortable position. Nationally the crime provoked a hail of criticisms accusing the new government of failing to protect the life of the human rights activist and taking few steps to improve the human rights situation in the country. The president's lack of response, along with the many protest messages from around the world, increased pressure not only to clear up the crime but to show a real commitment to human rights.[47]

Bernardo Batiz, Attorney General of the Federal District where the crime occurred, was assigned responsibility for investigating Ochoa's death, and he confirmed the Guerrero case as one of the main lines of investigation. His declaration points out the role of Boise Corporation, noting that the state of Guerrero has "a history of violence, *cacicazgos*, with a new ingredient: the concession for the exploitation of wood to an important company, where these peasants in some way interfered in large investments and considerable resources."[48]

With the death of their lawyer, Montiel and Cabrera's case returned to the front pages of the national newspapers and mobilized human rights activists around demands to resolve the assassination and attain justice for the jailed ecologists. On November 8, Rodolfo Montiel and Teodoro Cabrera were released from prison. In an unsatisfying evasion of justice, the official explanation for their liberation was "humanitarian reasons" owing to their precarious state of health, which gave them their freedom but did not recognize their innocence or acknowledge the many abuses committed in the case. Organizations and individuals that had supported the peasant ecologists' cause wondered aloud why the government had waited so long if it had always known of the many irregularities in the case against the ecologists. Neither the Zedillo administration before it nor the Fox administration could claim ignorance of the facts involved; the publicity campaign in Mexico and the rest of the world had made awareness of the case nearly unavoidable. At the beginning of his administration, Vicente Fox Quesada announced that the case of the jailed ecologists would be reviewed and responded to Pierre Sané of Amnesty International saying: "We want them out." René Juarez Cisneros, governor of Guerrero, and the new Secretary of the Environment, Victor Lichtinger, visited the ecologists in jail in largely symbolic acts. Despite the federal government's stated interest, the government reviewed the case and offered legal advice from the Ministry of the Interior, and the court still ratified Montiel and Cabrera's sentences.

Montiel and Cabrera spent 900 days behind bars, and Digna Ochoa had to die, before the peasant ecologists were finally released.

Human Rights: An Expression of All Rights

On August 15, 1999, the Pro Center for Human Rights assumed legal defense of the pair. In a paper analyzing the Montiel-Cabrera case, the Pro Center notes several lessons that make the case important. First, the case shows how corrupt Mexico's judicial system is. In testimony gathered from the accused and military officials involved, military members confessed to having held the ecologists incommunicado and torturing them. Subsequent investigations provided evidence of additional suffering. Nonetheless, the Fifth District Court refused to receive evidence of improper procedure in the case; only as a result of an appeal on December 7, 1999, was the evidence finally admitted. Even then, in July 2000, their sentences were ratified. Meanwhile, the Public Ministry turned over the file on torture to the Military Justice Office,[49] and Military Justice sent the case to the Military Public Ministry of the 40th Infantry Battalion—the same unit responsible for the alleged torture. Besides assigning the accused to judge themselves, this procedure violates the Mexican Constitution.[50]

Second, the case shows how this corruption serves the political interests of those who benefit from economic globalization. Perhaps most important, it shows the need for a definition of human rights that integrates political and civil rights with economic, social, and cultural rights. The case presents clear violations of both kinds of rights. On the one hand, the government violated individual guarantees of free association in defense of their local environment, as well as the personal security and due process for Montiel and Cabrera. On the other hand, the government failed in its obligation to guarantee the rights of the communities of the Costa Grande to a healthy environment, adequate food, and a decent standard of living, free from violence. An overall absence of the rule of law and respect for basic rights forms the backdrop for the case in particular and for the region's problems in general.

The analysis by the Pro Center emphasizes how applying an integral definition of human rights serves to strengthen the work of those who defend these various rights. An integral defense of Montiel and Cabrera, and of the cause of the ecologists in the region, helped activate human rights organizations, ecologists, and groups opposed to free trade. The Pro Center concludes that human rights can be a mobilizing discourse to unite forces in the struggle against globalization in its current form. "Seen integrally, civil, political, economic, social and cultural rights of women, of migrants, of ethnic and racial minorities, of children, of ecologists, etc. make up a political platform that covers the wide range of demands postulated by grassroots movements that oppose top-down economic integration. . . . The sum of our wills (in the case of Montiel and Cabrera) shows that although we have different agendas, our interests and objectives converge in a world where transnational capital places itself above nature and human life."[51]

Outstanding Issues

OCESP must still travel a long, difficult road to attain the economic and political power it needs to actively participate in the management of natural resources. Up to now, peasant ecologists have faced a government unwilling to deal with their complaints on the ecological impact of deforestation, repression of their leaders, and the militarization of their communities by army, police, and paramilitary forces. Despite continued repression in the Sierra de Petatlán and Coyuca de Catalán, the local ecology and forest defense movement has been able to mobilize large numbers of inhabitants in the mountains of Guerrero. Environmental consciousness —encouraged by the strong link of the peasants with the land, the sad evidence of environmental destruction in the region, and the help of environmental organizations— is incipient but growing. Even children in the region are aware that their parents' struggle is for them and that someday they too will take it up.

Without a clear legal framework and honest application of the law, the achievements of OCESP could be ephemeral. On April 6, 2001, Profepa lifted the suspension on logging activities that had been decreed for the *ejidos* of San Antonio de las Tejas, El Carrizal, Zihuaquio, San José de los Olivos, and La Botella, and the private lands of El Chivo and Chaneque located in the Sierra de Petatlán and Coyuca de Catalán. According to press reports, by lifting the sanction won by the organization, the government has authorized the harvest of 50,000 cubic meters of round wood.[52] Roads opened by Boise Corp. to remove timber from the forests are currently being used by clandestine logging operations.[53] Illegal logging in the state accounted for 800,000 cubic meters in 2000—half of all trees felled. Moreover, despite the experience with Boise, the region is once again open to foreign investment without having resolved the environmental and social problems exacerbated by the previous contract. A new logging concession was recently granted to a Spanish company, Tableros y Chapas of Guerrero.[54]

Boise Corp. has argued that Mexican environmental laws are comparable to those of the United Sates. Without embarking on a comparative study, the problem in Mexico is not only the laws but also their application. According to a study by Mexico's National Institute of Statistics and Geography, since the signing of NAFTA the budget for environmental protection has fallen forty-five percent and the number of inspections has similarly dropped.[55] Rodolfo Lazy Tamayo of the Environmental Ministry states that environmental inspectors refuse to go into some parts of Guerrero due to the violence that prevails, or that they have to be accompanied by the judicial police or army to do their work.[56] Given the purported complicity of the police and army with local loggers, and the distrust that exists between them and local residents, the possibility of carrying out effective monitoring and punishment of illegal loggers is severely limited.

The result is that in many regions of the country illegal logging continues with total impunity. The Environmental Ministry reports that half the 23,000 hectares of forested area lost in Guerrero every year is lost to uncontrolled logging. And this situation is not limited to the Costa Grande. Recently, the Commission on Environmental Cooperation, an institution established by the environmental side agreement of NAFTA, asked the government to respond to a citizen petition in the Sierra Tarahumara of Chihuahua for failure to apply its environmental legislation to the processing of citizen complaints, the persecution of environmental crimes, the consultation with indigenous peoples regarding timber exploitation, and access to environmental information.[57]

One OCESP leader notes that for his organization, economic integration—particularly NAFTA—has been a way of "legitimizing the looting of our natural resources. . . . With this situation of backwardness, in education and technology and everything, we think that we're never going to compete with the United States. What we see is that the government legitimizes commerce in order to sell what it wants to the United States and loot the country like they've been doing and then say that legally what they're doing is 'business.' . . . But how does it help us that foreigners come and invest here when the money the businesses make they just take right back to the U.S?"[58]

The liberation of Rodolfo Montiel Flores and Teodoro Cabrera Garcia, though significant, does not close their case. Their communities still live in poverty and are marginalized, with the added factor of a growing climate of violence. The Union of *Ejidos* Rubén Figueróa continues to deforest the zone. Military forces, which have intensified their presence in the area under the Fox administration, continue to harass local residents. The presence of "white guards" and paramilitary groups has become a constant in the daily life of the people.[59] Badly needed roads, schools, and hospitals have not been built, and proposals for productive alternatives have received no support. The government instead has offered a new forestry plan based on privatization of the nation's forests.[60]

In the protection of human rights, the only gain has been the construction of a more effective and active grassroots citizens' movement. In legislation, there have been few advances: Mexican law continues to consider confessions signed under torture valid. Still, Montiel and Cabrera are free, and dozens of human rights and environmental groups all over the world have championed the demands of the peasant ecologists. Their lawyers say they will take their case to the Interamerican Commission on Human Rights to denounce the torture of the defenders of the forest. The Organization of Peasant Ecologists of Guerrero has asked the Secretary of the Environment to evaluate the environmental impact caused by Boise Corporation's logging.

The case of Montiel and Cabrera remains open. OCESP, for its part, has before it the double challenge of confronting local *caciques* to stop the deforestation of its hillsides and designing and applying programs of sustainable forestry. Resolving the region's serious social problems will depend in part on the force of the innovative network of peasant groups, human rights centers, environmentalists, and organizations for global justice that was woven during the long battle to free Montiel and Cabrera.

Notes

1. To date, no one has been apprehended in the assassination of Salomé Sánchez.

2. The torture of Montiel and Cabrera was certified by a commission of doctors from the organization Doctors for Human Rights from Denmark, who met with them July 28–31, 2000. See Jimena Camacho, "Montiel y Cabrera: Los campesinos ecologistas presos y torturados," Greenpeace-México, 2000.

3. Comisión Nacional de Derechos Humanos, June 14, 2000. Recommendation 8/2000 of the CNDH was directed to General Enrique Cervantes Aguirre, then Secretary of National Defense.

4. Armando Bartra, "En defensa del bosque," *Ojarasca, La Jornada,* March 2001. Some OCESP members have been environmental activists for more than

thirty years. Felipe Arriaga and others participated in the first protests against logging during the governorship of Rubén Figueróa Figueróa in the 1970s.

5. Armando Bartra, *Guerrero Bronco: Campesinos, Ciudadanos y Guerrilleros en la Costa Grande* (México City: Ediciones Sinfiltro, 1996), 32.

6. Bartra, *Guerrero Bronco*, 40–49. However, the same source indicates that the Costa Grande was the exception to the state's support of Zapata.

7. Bartra, *Guerrero Bronco.*

8. Chapas y Triplay, SA, administered since 1967 by Nacional Financiera; Celulosa del Pacífico, SA, affiliate of Industria Forestal del Poniente, S. de R.L.; and Silvícola Industrial, SA., associated with Fábrica de Papel San Rafael and Loreto y Peña Pobre. See Bartra, *Guerrero Bronco*, 107.

9. According to Bartra, *Guerra Bronco,* the government's investment in Guerrero during the years of the guerrilla activity under Lucio Cabañas resulted in over 200 roads, 200 km of paved highway from Chilpancingo to Atoyac, ninety water projects with an investment of 400 million pesos, and 180 million pesos in rural loans to small and medium producers, quite a contrast with the prevailing custom of financing only large interests. In 1975, after the death of Lucio Cabañas, investment dropped dramatically, and such credit dried up. Only recently, with new signs of guerrilla activity, it has picked back up.

10. The 1992 reforms to Article 27 of the Constitution prepared the ground for forestry concessions. The new Forestry Law, enabling legislation to Article 27, was designed to attract foreign investment to the sector and move toward privatization of forestry resources. The government programs that followed, including President Fox's most recent program, have favored the private sector even though eighty percent of forestry resources are in the social sector. See http://info.juridicas.unam.mx.

11. See Mary Kelly and Cyrus Reed, "The Forestry Industry in the State of Chihuahua: Economic, Ecological and Social Impacts Post-NAFTA," Texas Center for Policy Studies, 2001. http://www.texascenter.org.

12. John Ross, "Treasure of the Costa Grande: NAFTA opens Mexico to U.S. timber giants," *Sierra,* July/August 1996, reports: "The front page of El Sol de Acapulco features a full-color photo of Rubén Figueróa, then-governor of the Mexican state of Guerrero, with a brace of timber barons from Boise Cascade. All are smiling broadly as they sign a five-year agreement in the spring of 1995 to bring the timber giant to the Costa Grande. . . ." See also Camacho, "Montiel y Cabrera," 4, and Centro de Derechos Humanos Miguel Agustín Pro, "Por la libertad de Rodolfo Montiel Flores y Teodoro Cabrera García, campesinos ecologistas presos en Guerrero," press release, 2000.

13. Interview with Chris Cooper of Westwood Forest Products in Bray and Merino, Chapter 4 of this book on the *ejido* El Balcón. Ross (*Sierra* July/August 1996) reports twenty million board-feet a year.

14. Boise Cascade Corporation, Annual Report 2001, www.boisecascade.com.

15. See Dave VanDeGraff, manager of Boise Corp., "Extreme Environmentalism Often Occludes Path to Good Forest Science," in *The Idaho Statesman,* June 23, 1997.

16. William Wines, Mark Buchanan, and Donald J. Smith, "The Critical Need for Law Reform to Regulate the Abusive Practices of Transnational Corporations: The Illustrative Case of Boise Cascade Corporation in Mexico's Costa Grande and Elsewhere," originally published by the *Denver Journal of International Law and*

Policy, School of International Law, University of Denver, Vol. 26, Number 3, Spring 1998, and retracted in the Journal's Summer 1999 edition after the company had contacted the publishers. When the University of Denver refused to republish the article, the authors filed a lawsuit against the University for defamation damages and breach of contract. In mediation, the authors and university reached a settlement on May 30, 2001 in which the University agreed to pay the authors legal and additional costs and the authors regained rights to the article. For a discussion of the suppression of the article see Peter Monaghan, "A Journal Article Is Expunged and Its Authors Cry Foul: They say a university caved in to the corporation they criticized," in *The Chronicle of Higher Education,* December 8, 2000; and Kent Paterson, "Mexico logging wars spark legal battle over academic freedom at U.S. university" September 28, 2000, Pacific News Service. See also, George Draffan, "Global Timber Titan: Profiles of Four Wood Products Corporations Driving the Globalization of the Industry," June 1999. Report commissioned by the Committee on Corporations of the International Forum on Globalization, copyright Public Information Network.

17. Property of the government and abandoned at the time.

18. George Draffan, "Global Timber Titan," and the Mexican monthly magazine *Ojarasca,* March 2001.

19. John Ross, *Sierra* (July/August 1996).

20. Bray and Merino, chapter 4 this volume, report fifty percent more initially. Ross cites sources that suggest the price may have been three times prevailing levels.

21. According to information from members of the *Ejido* Union Hermenegildo Galeana, in 1996 Boise Cascade unilaterally lowered its prices to prevailing national levels. This was a factor in breaking the contract with the transnational. See chapter 4 of this book.

22. Interview with Enrique Cienfuegos, January 29, 2001 in the *Ejido* El Mameyal of the Sierra de Petatlán.

23. Camacho, "Montiel and Cabrera," 9–10.

24. Press bulletin, Sept. 4, 2000. Declarations of Alejandro Calvillo, director of Greenpeace-México.

25. Centro de Derechos Humanos Miguel Agustín Pro, "Por la libertad de Rodolfo Montiel Flores y Teodoro Cabrera García, campesinos ecologistas presos en Guerrero"; *Ojarasca,* October 2000. See also Angelica Enciso, "Boise Cascade harmed forests in Guerrero" (translation by authors) *La Jornada,* March 28, 2001. In this article, Rodolfo Lazy Tamayo, Coordinator of Advisors of the Secretary of the Environment, states that forty percent of the wooded zones of the state have been deforested and cites the Union of *Ejidos* Rubén Figueróa and Boise Cascade as major culprits.

26. Testimonies of local residents abound and have been reprinted in various sources: see Rocha, www.rocha-detrasdelanoticia.com, Camacho, "Montiel and Cabrera," *Ojarasca,* March 2001.

27. Montiel described the relation between deforestation and the peasant economy: "When there are trees in rows, the clouds crash and the rains fall, but if there are no trees in a row the clouds pass over and only a few drops fall so the crops are lost, it hurts the peasants and the professionals who eat the peasants' harvest."

28. Amnesty International USA and Sierra Club, "Environmentalists Under Fire: 10 Urgent Cases of Human Rights Abuses. Defending Those Who Give the Earth a Voice," January 2000. Available at www.sierraclub.org/human-rights/amnesty/report.pdf.

29. Interview by Enrique Cienfuegos with Maximino Pineda Barrientos, January 28, 2001.

30. Greenpeace-Mexico documents three major cases of nonsustainable clear-cutting and burns carried out by the UERF. Camacho, "Montiel and Cabrera," 11. Rocha, www.rocha-detrasdelanoticia.com and Ross (1996) also document abuses by Bautista and the UERF.

31. See, for example, the report by Maribel Gutierrez, published in *El Sur,* September 8, 1998.

32. Amnesty International and Sierra Club, op. cit. and Goldman Prize Recipient Profile: Rodolfo Montiel. Available at www.goldmanprize.org/recipients/recipientProfile.cfm?recipientID=104.

33. Amnesty International and Sierra Club, "Environmentalists Under Fire," Sierra Club, *Planet Newsletter, January–February 2001;* Centro de Derechos Humanos Miguel Agustín Pro, "Por la libertad de Rodolfo Montiel Flores y Teodoro Cabrera García, campesinos ecologistas presos en Guerrero," press release, 2000.

34. "The arrival of Boise Cascade was a 'flash in the pan.' They went for the business, they pay for the cubic meter you sell them and though they supported some requests for a footbridge or something, it's not like they dedicated themselves to social work because then, what would happen to their profits?" Interview with Maximino Pineda Barrientos by Enrique Cienfuegos, January 30, 2001.

35. The inhabitants of the mountains describe a situation of war. For more information on these months see the Mexican newspaper *El Sur,* especially reports by Maribel Gutiérrez from April to June 1999.

36. Miguel Agustín Pro Center for Human Rights, "Guerrero 95: Represión y Muerte." 1996. Report available at www.sjsocial.org.

37. Camacho, "Montiel and Cabrera," 7.

38. Boise Corporation, FAQs: "When did operations of Costa Grande end? Due to difficult business conditions, we decided in late 1997 to permanently terminate our Costa Grande operations in 1998, which was done by the end of April of that year. Eligible employees were provided with severance pay. Since closure, employees were provided with severance pay. Since closure, that subsidiary has been dissolved." (Costa Grande is the name of the Mexican subsidiary.)

39. Among the members of the organization killed: May 31, 1998, Aniceto Martínez; July 2, Elena Barajas; July 10, Romualdo Gómez García. See Ricardo Rocha, "Vergüenza nacional," November 6, 2000, *Detrás de la Noticia,* http://www.rocha-detrasdelanoticia.com; and Camacho, "Montiel and Cabrera," 15–16. November 1, 2001, in El Venado unidentified persons fired at a truck and three people died, among them a six-month-old baby, while the mother and her two brothers were wounded. Members of OCESP think the shots were meant for them, since it was known they would pass by the spot on the way to Mexico City. *La Jornada,* November 8, 2001, 13.

40. Still in prison at this writing: Pilar Martínez Pérez, Francisco Bautista Valle, and Gerardo Cabrera González. Arrest orders are pending for: Jesús and Servando Bautista Fuerte, Rodolfo and Eutiquio Cabrera González, Palemón Cabrera González, Rogelio Carrillo Mendoza, and Roberto Cabrera Torres.

41. The plan to rescue the Sierra was presented October 28, 2000, in the First Meeting for the Defense of the Forests of Guerrero and for the Liberty of Rodolfo Montiel and Teodoro Cabrera, *ejido* Banco Nuevo, Sierra de Petatlán, Guerrero.

42. Interview by Enrique Cienfuegos with lawyer Aurora de la Riva Copete, member of the legal defense team for Montiel and Cabrera, November 2000.

43. *New York Times,* April 1, 2000.

44. Amnesty International considers a political prisoner anyone jailed for: opposing grave violations of the right of all people to maintain and freely express their convictions and not be discriminated against; oppose grave violations of the right of all people to physical and mental integrity; and in particular, oppose by all appropriate means, independently of political character the imprisonment, reclusion or imposition of other physical restrictions on any person by virtue of his or her political, religious or other conviction arising from motives of conscience, or based on ethnic origin, sex, other circumstances, when that person has not resorted to violence or espoused its use in the future.

45. Letter from Boise Corp. to Rainforest Action Network, mimeo.

46. After Digna Ochoa, Mario Patrón Sánchez and Aurora de la Riva took over the legal defense in the Pro Center under the direction of Edgar Cortéz.

47. President Fox remained silent on the case for several days, then declared that the investigation was "commonplace" and under the jurisdiction of the Federal District, and just another of the many crimes committed in that city. The comment, considered insensitive, caused protests from human rights activists.

48. Gabriela Romero, "A la fecha 39 personas han declarado . . . " *La Jornada,* November 14, 2001.

49. Then under the direction of General Rafael Macedo de la Concha, now Attorney General of the Republic, a post legally reserved for civilians.

50. Pro Center, "Guerrero 95," 20.

51. Ariadna Estévez López, "Comentarios a la ponencia sobre derechos humanos y ecología" presented at the "Social and Environmental Impacts of NAFTA: Grassroots Responses to Economic Integration Seminar," El Colegio de México, August 17–18, 2001.

52. Matilde Pérez, "Levantan la suspensión de aprovechamiento forestal a ejidos de Petatlán y Coyuca de Catalán" en *La Jornada,* April 6, 2001, 33.

53. Rosa Rojas, "Cárcel, persecución y muerte," *La Jornada,* October 23, 2001.

54. Rocha, "Vergüenza nacional." "It unleashed widespread deforestation by gangs of loggers, backed up by paramilitary groups like Los Santoyos who, according to documented testimony, are trained and armed by the army. . . ."

55. Kevin Gallagher, "Fast Track: Fix It or Nix It," in *Foreign Policy in Focus,* January 25, 2002. www.fpif.org.

56. Angélica Enciso, *La Jornada,* March 28, 2001.

57. Info CEC bulletin, November 7, 2001. www.cec.org.

58. Interview by Enrique Cienfuegos with Maximino Pineda Barrientos, member of the OCESP leadership, Sierra de Petatlán, January 30, 2001.

59. According to Montiel: "[the government] has armed people of Bernardino Bautista, Heladio Peñalosa, Lucas Sánchez and the Santoyo [. . .] armed and trained to combat the peasant ecologists." Rocha, "Verguenza Nacional."

60. Rosa Rojas, "Critican grupos sociales plan forestal del gobierno foxista," *La Jornada,* July 25, 2001.

4

El Balcón, Guerrero
A Case Study of Globalization:
Benefiting a Forest Community

David Barton Bray and Leticia Merino

IT HAS OFTEN BEEN NOTED THAT GLOBALIZATION HAS BOTH WINNERS AND LOSERS. It is less frequently noted that the winners and losers can sometimes be found within the same sectors and levels of society. Although clearly the poorest and most marginalized people in less-developed countries are most commonly losers, some organizations and communities have been able to position themselves to take advantage of the opportunities presented by globalization. The forest *ejido* of El Balcón, because of its forestry assets and specific organizational history, provides an example of a community that has benefited from economic globalization by establishing a relationship with a mid-sized forest products corporation from the Northwest United States.

History and Context

El Balcón is located in the Costa Grande region of Guerrero, on the Pacific coast north of Acapulco, up the mountain from the coastal city of Tecpan. Situated in the segment of the Sierra Madre Sur known as the Cordillera Costera del Sur, it has an average elevation of 7,200 feet, with a very rugged topography that leaves parts of the area isolated during the rainy season, when some fifty-five inches of rain falls. The *ejido* was constituted in January 1966, with an endowment of 2,400 hectares. In October 1974, it received an additional 19,150 hectares, including most of its current

65

forest lands, for a total land area today of 25,565 hectares. Its current land area and perimeter were legally established in the resolution of a boundary dispute with the neighboring *ejido* of Cuatro Cruces in 1986, when it ceded 3,085 hectares of forest in exchange for 7,100 hectares of dry scrub forest. El Balcón has a main village, Pocitos, and two outlying population centers or *agencias,* La Lajita and Mesa Verde, with 136 *ejidatarios* in all three villages and a total population of around 600.

The population was formed from small groups of *mestizo* families who lived off corn farming and goat herding. Its local history is marked by severe violent interfamily and intercommunity clashes over land, which have characterized the history of the state of Guerrero in general. In the early 1960s, this region of the Sierra was described as "enmeshed in terror and killing,"[1] and El Balcón also found itself embroiled in land conflicts. Community members from El Balcón sought the intercession of the Mexican government in 1961, initiating the application for *ejido* status to fix their land boundaries. Although the claim was recognized in 1966, they did not receive the final title until 1972.

In the late 1960s and early 1970s, armed guerrilla movements further roiled the Costa Grande, accompanied by frequent military confrontations, and many local communities were once again forced to relocate. Some community members from El Balcón fled to a community to the north called La Laguna, which had been operating its own sawmill and logging operation since the late 1950s. When they returned to resettle El Balcón in the early 1970s, they carried with them the realization that their forests were a potential economic resource—the seeds of a demonstration effect had been planted. Community members began lobbying for a new land grant, which was given in 1974. Thus, their most important natural asset— the forest—was awarded to them by the Mexican government, albeit in the context of violent social conflict in which the action was part of the government's effort to pacify the region.

Under President Luis Echeverría (1970–1976), the early 1970s initiated a major new wave of government activism in the rural sector. El Balcón's land grant was part of a process of trying to deliver new benefits to a region unsettled by the rise of a guerrilla movement and consequent repression in an area just south of El Balcón. Their land grant, like many at the time, formed part of a government program of rural pacification, which combined economic and social programs with strong military repression. In addition, the grant responded to the need to create a new source of supply for a state-owned timber company. It is nonetheless extraordinary in comparative global terms that the Mexican mechanism for achieving both rural pacification and a new source of timber was to grant local communities major forest areas, with the potential for the growth of autonomous local management.

The high levels of regional and local violence that characterized its past make the current relative peace of the zone all the more remarkable. Today, most El Balcón residents combine their forestry work with small-scale livestock raising, and about sixty percent of the *ejidatarios* still plant corn, especially in the warmer lands on the lower slopes toward the *tierra caliente* of Guerrero.

The Community Enterprise:
Vertical Integration, Asset Building, and Human Capital

As noted earlier, El Balcón's most significant productive asset, its forest land, was granted to the community by the Mexican government as a part of overall agrarian policies in 1974. From the beginning, the *ejido* leadership's vision was building a community enterprise such as they had seen in La Laguna. When El Balcón first began selling logs in 1980, it sold directly to the Guerrero state-owned Forestal Vicente Guerrero (FOVI-GRO), with about twenty community members working as laborers. Thus El Balcón never passed through a classic *rentista* stage where timber buyers come in and take complete charge of extraction, paying only a stumpage fee (*derecho de monte*) to the community.

As has been the case with other successful communities, El Balcón was able to use the significant profits from the first round-wood (felled log) sales to begin to expand its capital assets. In 1982–83, it acquired five logging trucks and two winches and was thus able to deliver round-wood directly to the sawmill, capturing more of the value chain. In 1986, *ejido* members traveled to San Juan Nuevo, Michoacan, to study its model of community forest development. In 1986, El Balcón acquired a new community asset, the sawmill, in a joint investment with a state development-financing agency, the National Trust Fund for Ejido Development (FIFONAFE). FIFONAFE dissolved ten months later, with El Balcón assuming full ownership of the mill. Thus, in six years, El Balcón went from its first logging, essentially as employees of the state-owned enterprise, to full control of its own logging business from the forest to the mill.

However, El Balcón quickly confronted its serious human capital deficiencies in training and experience in managing a complex industrial enterprise. They encountered problems in meshing the hierarchical discipline required of an enterprise with *ejido* notions of equality. Accounting was absent, managerial skills were weak to nonexistent, and the enterprise quickly tumbled into disorganization and debt. Similar scenarios have led to years of social problems in many forest communities.

The Introduction of Professional Management

In 1988, *ejido* leaders were able to convince members to hand over the enterprise to a professional manager, John Vala, a former employee of FOVIGRO. The process that ensued can only be described as entrepreneurial shock treatment. The manager renegotiated debts, hired a professional managerial and technical team, and made substantial investments in infrastructure. In both the sawmill and the forest logging operation, community members were almost entirely excluded, since the manager felt they were not disciplined workers. As a counterbalance to this new managerial dominance, the Council of Principals was formed in 1989. The manager had to submit his investment plans to the Council, which reportedly approved most proposals, but often directed more money toward community investments.

The combination of professional management with community involvement and decision-making power began to shore up the enterprises productive assets. It also created financial flows that were directed toward economic and cultural assets such as houses, investments in cattle and pig breeding, as well as some dividend sharing. The reinvestment in capital assets was particularly impressive: from 1992–1995 the *ejido* invested some $1.6 million in improvements to the sawmill and the acquisition of dryers. As a result of the dramatic turnaround in the fortunes of the community, El Balcón won two National Merit Forest and Wildlife Prizes, one in 1993, in the category "Cultivation and Logging" and again in 1994, in the category "Transformation–Forest Industry." In the early 1990s, the enterprise slowly began to hire *ejidatarios* again, and today more than seventy percent of the labor force is made up of locals, some of whom hold skilled jobs.

El Balcón's professional management has also introduced important efficiency gains, such as using logging trucks with double trailers, which significantly lowered transportation costs. All this has led to what is reported to be a relatively healthy financial profile. The enterprise reports a twenty to thirty-five percent profit margin in recent years, and an average of $1 million annually in net profits. Fixed capital assets are reported to be $4.2 million. Their current debts are three million pesos (about $330,000) with commercial banks, in addition to short-term loans for operating capital from Westwood Forest Products, its main buyer.

The previous sawmill burned down in 1997, but it was entirely rebuilt with insurance money and commercial credit. The two drying ovens and the sawmill represent an investment of $2.3 million. The dryers, purchased in Portugal and Italy, are operated using sawdust, introducing significant environmental efficiencies, and they are equipped with pollution-reducing chimneys. Among other assets, El Balcón also has a sharpening shed and a chip mill, as well as two front-end loaders, seven winches, and six tractors.

Community Organization: The Foundation for Success

El Balcón's success is particularly striking because it started out with limited organizational experience or social cohesion, what is often referred to as a very low social capital endowment. The community does not have the communal institutions of many indigenous communities or a decade-long history as a self-governing *ejido*. It was formed out of violently quarrelling families with extremely low levels of trust who did not begin learning how to govern themselves under *ejido* structures and practices until the late 1960s. This makes the relatively rapid accumulation of social capital particularly noteworthy.

Sources of social capital accumulation can be traced to the participation of several communities in the Tecpan region in a national small farmer federation, the Central Independiente de Obreros Agricolas y Campesinos (CIOAC). In the 1970s, local CIOAC leaders negotiated social peace between the neighboring communities, although the final agrarian solution did not occur until 1986, with the land exchange previously mentioned. Nonetheless, the social peace pacted in the late 1970s enabled El Balcón to begin commercial logging in 1980. The *ejido* president at the time was a "visionary leader who saw community organizing and regional peace as necessary precursors to the establishment of a community forestry enterprise."[2]

As El Balcón struggled to form its forest community enterprise, in 1986 several *ejido* members traveled to San Juan Nuevo Parangaricutiro in Michoacán. This Purépecha Indian community was at the time already establishing itself as a national model in community forestry. One of the most important lessons the visitors from El Balcón took away was the need to create new organizational structures that would permit timber business management to be separated from *ejido* politics. In 1989, the *ejido* made a dramatic decision to turn forest enterprise management over to an outsider. To ensure channels of community participation within the scheme of professionalizing its forestry business, El Balcón created its own Council of Principals, modeled after San Juan Nuevo's Communal Council. The Council of

Principals functions as a sort of community oversight committee for the professional manager, approving general investment and policy guidelines, but leaving day-to-day management to him. It represents a further accumulation of social capital, both as an organizational innovation and as a new space to build accountability, mechanisms for forest monitoring, and experience in conflict resolution.

The Council of Principals reports to the *ejido* General Assembly and is said to represent each family in the community. It is made up of young people, seniors, men, and women, with current numbers reported to be between 26–32. Its relationship to other community administrative organs and authorities is shown in Figure 4.1.

The function of the Council of Principals is to monitor all activities of the enterprise, under the management of a professional. The Council itself does not make decisions. Rather, it discusses and analyzes enterprise issues and then recommends new rules or policies to the General Assembly. However, members report that the Council's recommendations are invariably accepted by the General Assembly. Since El Balcón has almost no families without agrarian rights (*avecindados*), community cohesion is aided by the fact that nearly everyone participates in the larger decisions on local resource use.

The professional manager is responsible for drawing up an annual enterprise work plan to present to the Council. The Council can modify the plan, although it only tends to do so in requesting more employment positions. For example, the manager may indicate that sixty *ejidatarios* are needed for a given level of production, but the Council may propose hiring

Figure 4.1 El Balcón's Organizational Structure

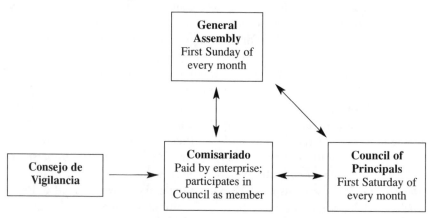

additional people and giving the manager the power to decide where they work. The work plan and modifications are then presented to the General Assembly. All daily production and management decisions are in the hands of the professional manager. The Forest Technical Director may give monthly reports to the Council, with the professional manager giving reports annually.

El Balcón belongs to the regional Unión de Ejidos Hermengildo Galeana. The nature of the relationship has varied, depending on the level of interest of El Balcón's elected authorities. Unlike other *ejido* unions, where the most powerful member typically withdraws from the organization having achieved a high degree of economic self-sufficiency, El Balcón has always remained in the union, although it hired its own Forest Technical Director early on. Authorities recognize the value-added of regional organization, another expression of social capital. Through the *ejido* union, El Balcón has gained access to regional development projects by government agencies such as Sedesol and Semarnat, which prefer to work with *ejido* unions rather than individual *ejidos*.

In recent years, tension has existed between the logging *ejidos* and national environmental organizations. In Tecpan, there has been resentment of environmentalists who oppose all logging without recognizing the efforts of logging *ejidos* to generate income for communities and sustainably manage the forests. While residents in the Tecpan region acknowledge that organizations like the Organization of Peasant Ecologists of the Sierra de Petatlán, led by Rodolfo Montiel, are motivated by genuine ecological concerns, they assert that they—the community forest sector—are "the real ecologists." According to some accounts, the recent conflicts between illegal loggers and environmentalists have brought conservationists and community forestry workers closer together within the *ejido* union.[3]

Although El Balcón has two smaller communities, the *ejido* has apparently been effective in balancing micropolitical interests, and there have been no reports of friction between the communities. Power-sharing appears to be part of the formula, since the current *Comisariado* is from the smaller community of La Lajita. Unlike some other forest communities in Mexico, emigration is reported to be low in El Balcón with reportedly only two young people moving to the United States.

Ecosystems and Forest Management

The community enterprise has implemented a sustainable forestry plan that should allow the community to benefit from its forestry resources while preserving the forest as a long-term natural resource. The current uses of El Balcón's forest lands are shown in Table 4.1.

The forest lands of El Balcón are dominated by conifer stands mixed with firs, particularly oyamel (*Abies Religiosa*), oak, and other broad-leafed species. Until recently, El Balcón practiced the Mexican Method of Forest Management (Método Mexicano de Ordenación de Bosques). As of 2001, in a new ten-year management plan, it adopted the System of Conservation and Silvicultural Development (SICODESI-*Sistema de Conservación y Desarrollo Silvícola*), a variant of the Silvicultural Development Method.[4]

SICODESI is a software program, developed under the Mexico-Finland Agreement in the early 1990s. The program takes into account ecological protection, socioeconomic and legal variables, and also permits the generation of management alternatives with predictive models. It includes a suite of silvicultural treatments, including liberation and pre-clearing cuts, regeneration cuts, small clear cuts, and selection cuts. In ideal conditions, the silvicultural sequence would begin with a liberation cut, followed by regeneration cuts, clearing cuts, and selection cuts. Priorities can be established based on volumes and increments in a particular stand.

SICODESI includes two planning levels: strategic planning and operative planning. Strategic planning has a thirty-year time horizon that looks at the interactions between the forest, its owners, and other economic activities while operative planning divides the thirty years into six five-year periods. In the five-year periods the focus is on the precise location of extraction and quantities of wood to be removed and with which silvicultural techniques. The forest inventory is based on a ten percent sample established on permanent sampling plots, forming a network of monitoring and control. The *ejido* currently contains 650 strategic sampling sites and 8,500 operational inventory sites. The most recent inventory was carried out from January–April 2000, with a ten percent sampling intensity. The largest volume of trees in the commercial forest area is in the sixty-to-seventy year age range, and the cutting strategy involves a slow removal of these

Table 4.1 El Balcón's Forest Land Use

Forest Production	10,968 ha.
Conservation Areas	4,059 ha.
Other Uses	874 ha.
Restoration Area	163 plantations

Source: El Balcón, Program de manejo para el aprovechamiento forestal maderable persistent (Tomo I), 2000.

older trees. El Balcón applies a silvicultural management of regeneration by selection, individually and in groups, and seeks to maintain the present structure of the forest.

The *ejido* reports some 500 hectares of former cultivated lands are being converted to forest plantations of native species. They are planting in fenced areas with seeds of pine species obtained from their own forest. It is expected that the plantations will generate an additional 1,000 cubic meters of production yearly by 2035.

A forest brigade, composed of twenty people, chops up the ten percent of the volume that is left in the forest, to reduce the risk of forest fire and hasten decomposition. The brigade also has cut twenty-eight miles of firebreaks. Since 1993, the *ejido* maintains a nursery in the forested area that has an annual production capacity of 100,000 plants, and is used for reforestation activities. The nursery contains pseudostrobus, ayacahuite, chiapensis, and patula, among others.

El Balcón places 4,058 hectares of the forested area under protection where no logging is permitted. These include permanent and seasonal watercourses (twenty-meter and ten-meter strips, respectively), fringes along roads, forested areas around the population centers, and a forest area with low production potential held as a wildlife reserve. Table 4.2 shows the distribution of these protected areas. Some twenty-seven percent of the forested area is currently under protection.

The forested land on the El Balcón *ejido* contains specimens of *pinus chiapensis,* a species protected under Mexican law. The *ejido* gives special protection to this species, marking all individual trees as they are found to prevent their being logged and seeks to expand its presence in the forest through reforestation. Other conservation measures include leaving trees with nests in them (or large dead trees suitable for nesting), closing logging roads that are not needed in the short term, leaving piles of branches as wildlife refuges, and segregating important habitat areas from logging areas.

Table 4.2 Protected Areas in El Balcón (hectares)

Permanent Watercourses	80
Seasonal Watercourses	315
Principal Roads	230
Secondary Roads	357
Special Areas (population centers, springs, waterfall)	243
Wildlife Reserve	2,835
Total	4,059

Source: El Balcón, Program de manejo para el aprovechamiento forestal maderable persistent (Tomo I), 2000.

A list of the fauna found in the *ejido* is contained in the management plan. Although jaguar is not listed in the management plan, sources in the *ejido* report that three jaguars have been seen attacking livestock. White-tailed deer (*odocoileus virginuanus*) are considered abundant in the *ejido* and in former years were extensively hunted for subsistence. A few years ago, the *ejido* imposed a conservation measure, prohibiting hunting of any kind. This regulation is enforced by the forest brigades who patrol for fires, illegal logging, and hunting. Interestingly, community members often are too busy with paid *ejido* employment to hunt, a collateral benefit to biodiversity conservation of the forest enterprise's success.

Entering the Global Market

The ability to enter the international market independently and finance its own operations has been critical to the success of the community enterprise, particularly in the context of tight to nonexistent credit in rural Mexico. El Balcón has established a successful commercial relationship with a Washington-based timber marketing company called Westwood Forest Products. A Westwood representative first visited El Balcón in 1995 and came away extremely impressed by the sawmill. He was also impressed by El Balcón's management plan, which he thought would assure a steady supply of logs, and by the high quality of its product.[5]

Westwood proposed a business partnership while at the same time noting the need for some changes in El Balcón's operations. First, Westwood representatives pointed out the need to increase efficiency in the use of forest resources. ("They were still throwing away a lot of the log," one representative observed.) Later the company began to integrate more of the processing on site, in an effort to increase efficiency but also to benefit the *ejido*. One company representative stated, "We used to bring up all lumber, but then we wanted to get more added value—the more money I can bring here the better."[6]

Westwood invested considerable time and effort in building the relationship and providing technical assistance and financing. Its representative spent one week a month at the Guerrero site for a couple of years. Westwood is currently importing both sawn wood and moldings to the United States from El Balcón, shipping to its warehouse in El Paso, Texas. El Balcón also sells sawn wood in national markets. For top-quality pine sawn wood, in 2001, it receives 10.7 pesos a board foot in the export market, and nine pesos in the national market, including transportation costs.

The lower quality wood was sold only on the national market. El Balcón also sells wood chips in Mexico City, Tuxtepec, Oaxaca, and Jalisco. Small pieces of wood are sold for broom handles.

From 1996–2001, El Balcón exported forty to forty-five percent of its production, which represented sixty-five percent of total sales, with all first-class timber exported through Westwood. From late 1995 to late 2001, El Balcón exported approximately $19 million of timber to Westwood. Westwood has also been crucial in financing both capital assets and operating costs over the last several years. Westwood loaned El Balcón $200,000 to put in dry kilns, in addition to helping arrange for a six percent loan from the manufacturer. In 1999, and 2000, Westwood loaned El Balcón $400,000–$500,000 in start-up operating capital, all of which was repaid within months. In 2001, only $100,000 was loaned because El Balcón had sufficient operating capital.

El Balcón and Boise Cascade in the Costa Grande Region

El Balcón's experience with Westwood Forest Products contrasts markedly with the controversial incursion of Boise Cascade in the Costa Grande (see Chapter 3). El Balcón and the Unión de Ejidos Hermenegildo Galeana were briefly suppliers for Boise Cascade. Shortly after the North American Free Trade Agreement went into effect in 1994, Boise Cascade began exploring logging options in the Costa Grande of Guerrero. In the words of one official from the Unión de Ejidos Hermenegildo Galeana, "The market came to look for us."[7] Sources in the region report that Boise Cascade first entered the region through a contracted agent charged with setting up the operation in the Costa Grande. The company's interest was based on the supposition that it could find large supplies of high-quality raw material, which it needed to replace dwindling supplies following the closure of some forests in the Northwest United States.

The agents first made contact through the Unión de Ejidos Hermenegildo Galeana and El Balcón, but then expanded to communities all the way to Chilpancingo. They soon had contracts with some thirty communities for an annual volume of 100,000 cubic meters. Even though 1995 was a year of economic crisis in Mexico, markets were booming in the United States, and a devalued peso meant that Mexican labor was especially cheap.

In 1995, Boise Cascade paid 450 pesos (about $60) per cubic meter for logwood, when the national price was 300 pesos. Most *ejidos* felt that the contracts were transparent and that Boise Cascade treated them fairly; in commercial terms there was never any problem, and payment was made promptly upon delivery. The communities also expressed an interest in other benefits, such as clinics and schools, and Boise Cascade reportedly agreed to the possibility, but apparently none was ever built. Fellowships to study at the University of the Americas were also mentioned, but it is not known if any were actually given.

Interviews with officials of the Unión de Ejidos Hermenegildo Galeana suggest that Boise Cascade "did not want to know what was going on in the forest,"[8] and no support was given for reforestation or forest management. In 1995, El Balcón sold most of its timber to Boise Cascade, under what is known in Mexican law as an "asociación en participación" (participating association), selling the remainder to Westwood. Also in 1995, El Balcón was approached by Boise Cascade about selling its sawmill. El Balcón had decided to sell it and use the money to build another one, but Boise Cascade backed out.

But in 1996, problems began to surface and El Balcón stopped selling to Boise Cascade, which finally left the region in 1997. Interviews indicate various reasons behind the rapid entry and exit of the transnational in the Costa Grande region. In 1995, Boise Cascade purchased relatively little logwood, since the mill at Papanoa was not finished for most of the harvest season. They mostly bought sawn wood from El Balcón and the few other community sawmills in the region. In 1996, with the mill completed, they were interested only in buying logwood, not sawn wood, so El Balcón stopped selling to them and began exporting much more through Westwood. Also in 1996, according to local reports, Boise Cascade lowered the price to prevailing national levels, giving no price stimulus for selling to them. The original contracts were for five years, but Boise Cascade modified them to be annual contracts. Also, the contracts were originally for logwood delivered to the mill (*puesto en planta*). When prices were high in 1995, communities could afford to rent extraction equipment and trucks to do this, but when the price went down, it became impossible for them to absorb the transportation costs. Boise Cascade no longer offered a higher price than local buyers, so the communities were no longer interested in selling to them. These factors, added to the protests against deforestation, prompted Boise Cascade's early exit. A Westwood representative noted, "Boise Cascade came down here to get as much timber as they could. They needed thirty million board-feet a year from this area. That's a lot of timber; it was too high an expectation."[9] One year later, facing the difficulty of supplying the industry it had acquired, and foreseeing growing losses, Boise Cascade left the region and the country.

New Challenges

El Balcón currently faces some difficult changes in its production strategies. First, in 2001 El Balcón had to lower its annual cutting volume substantially. The *ejido* had been working on a fifteen-year management plan
devised in 1987, that authorized harvest of 400,000 cubic meters over the
entire period. But because of managerial problems in the early years,
the annual cuts for these years were far below the authorized volume. Thus
the forest managers decided to log at much higher volumes in recent years
to achieve the full 400,000 cubic meter volume over the period.

As El Balcón launches its new management plan, this means that the
logging volume is now reduced by approximately half, from 40,000 cubic
meters annually to around 20,000, which would lead to an underuse of the
sawmill. El Balcón's strategy for dealing with this decline has apparently
not been fully developed. The management is considering making up the
rest of the volume by buying round wood from other communities, but
they have never done this before.

A second challenge lies in timber certification, to be able to compete
on the global market. El Balcón is not currently certified as producing sustainable lumber, but it has requested the visit of a certification team from
the Mexican Civil Council for Sustainable Silviculture (CCMSS). Westwood has strongly encouraged them to seek certification, noting that
"[Forestry Stewardship Council]–certified wood is the future."[10] Westwood already has "chain of custody certification"—which assures that certified wood is accounted for in every step of the marketing chain—from
Smartwood, a program of the U.S. environmental group, Rainforest Alliance. Since getting the license in late 2000, Westwood has purchased certified pine from Brazil.

Although certification has not yet led to substantial sales increases for
those Mexican forest communities that have obtained it, the Westwood connection gives El Balcón a marketing link most communities lack. Westwood
does significant business with the huge supplier Anderson Window, which
sells to Home Depot. Anderson is moving toward sustainable timber but
claims this is difficult given their large number of suppliers. Nonetheless,
Anderson has promised special treatment to those who have certified wood.

Westwood also sells to high-end producers in California. These companies currently pay a ten percent premium for certified timber from
Brazil, and Westwood notes that while some customers still look for the
lowest prices, others increasingly inquire about harvesting methods.[11]

The species of pine that grows in Guerrero is a more resinous, five-
needle pine and is not as well accepted as pine from the states of Oaxaca

(*Pinus patula,* similar to Ponderosa) and Chihuahua. The Guerrero pine is closely related to sugar pine and is about twenty percent heavier than Ponderosa; only specific customers will use it. For example, Anderson Window does not use the Guerrero pine because it lacks a uniform light color. But Westwood has found a market for the cut stock from El Balcón with a small window manufacturer in Ste. Genevieve, Missouri.

El Balcón still faces enormous challenges in human capital development. Current managers note that many *ejido* members and forest managers learned basic logging skills under the state-owned FOVIGRO.[12] El Balcón does not currently have a systematic training program, but some members have received on-the-job training in some of the more sophisticated mill operations. For example, the young operator of the highly sophisticated automated saw is from El Balcón. Jesús García, the current professional manager, while not from El Balcón, learned management from the previous professional manager while he was Forest Technical Director.

Finally, El Balcón faces a dilemma common to community-run enterprises regarding the distribution of benefits between employment, enterprise investment, community investment, and profit-sharing. The entire forest enterprise employs 140–145 people, but only twenty-six are employed for the entire year. For most other employees, the enterprise generates about eight months of work a year. Almost all sawmill employees are from Tecpan, although some of the more skilled technical positions are filled by *ejidatarios.* In forest extraction and transportation, about eighty percent of the employees are from El Balcón, with seventy percent of all *ejido* members now employed in the enterprise, particularly during the peak months from November to July. All workers receive benefits, social security, retirement payments, and a Christmas bonus. In addition, the *ejido* administrative positions of Commissary, Secretary, and Treasurer are all paid positions, and the Commissary receives 126,000 pesos (about $14,000) annually in expenses. The Oversight Committee is also paid, although at a lower rate.

The first social benefits paid out from the enterprise were widows' pensions, a much-needed benefit after years of violent conflicts. The pensions currently support some twenty widows at 1,500 pesos a month. The forestry business also provides fifteen retirement pensions at 2,000 pesos a month each, and offers complete medical coverage for both *ejidatarios* and non-*ejidatarios,* through a voucher program with a doctor in Tecpan.

From 1986 to 1989, the *ejido* implemented direct profit-sharing. However, the distribution included a loan for working capital, which subsequently contributed to the financial collapse that led to the decision to hire a professional manager. In all, there have been only four profit-sharing distributions in the last fifteen years, since almost all profits are reinvested either in the business or in collective community development projects.

The professional manager estimates that from 1988–1998, the *ejido* invested about sixty percent of profits in the business and forty percent in community infrastructure and social services. In the most recent period, 1998–2001, about ninety percent has been invested in the community, because the business has not required further investments. It is estimated that some $1 million has been spent on roads alone, particularly the road from the community to the *tierra caliente*. Other community investments include potable water, solar energy, and housing. To date, the *ejido* has built thirty-two houses and is currently experimenting with a lower cost home that requires a contribution from the homeowner. The *ejido* has also invested in productive projects such as pig-raising and organic agriculture.

Finally, El Balcón has invested in human resources, with a heavy emphasis on providing educational opportunities for its children. The *ejido* provides full fellowships for high school and college study and has turned out eight or nine college graduates, and two or three forest technicians, most of whom have returned to the community. The cost of the fellowships exceeds many of the salaries, and there has been some discussion that with the reduction in logging, this is a benefit that would have to be looked at more closely.

The case study of El Balcón suggests that strong community organization combined with professional management, forestry assets of substantial value, and the market link with Westwood Forest Products have positioned this community to be one of the relatively few winners in the globalization processes that are sweeping rural Mexico.

Notes

The authors would like to give special thanks to the authorities in El Balcón and to manager Jesús García González for their willingness to participate in this research. In addition to the particular interviews cited in the text, this report is based on interviews with: Bernardino Ramírez, former president of the Consejo de Vigilancia for the Union de Ejidos Hermenegildo Galeana (UEHG); Alejandro Albarán, UEHG Forest Technical Director; Mario Cedillo, El Balcón Forest Technical Director; Leónidas Chávez, president of the UEHG Administrative Council; Fidel López, *ejidatario* from the *ejido* Bajos de Balsemar; Jorge Villa, Forest Technical Director and *ejidatario* in El Balcón; and Jesús López, Comisariado Ejidal, El Balcón.

1. Matthew B. Wexler, "Learning the Forest Again: Building Organizational Capacity for the Management of Common Property Resources in Guerrero, Mexico," Ph.D. Dissertation, Department of Anthropology, Boston University, 1995. Other good sources on El Balcón are: Tomás Bustamante Álvarez, "Los Recursos Forestales de Guerrero, su Aprovechamiento Social y la Apertura Comercial. El Caso de Ejido El Balcón," in *La Sociedad Rural Mexicana Frente al Nuevo Milenio, Vol. III: El Acceso a los Recursos Naturales y el Desarrollo Sustentable,* ed. Horacio Mackinlay and Eckhard Boege (Mexico City: Plaza y Valdez, 1996); and El Balcón's forest management plan, Ejido El Balcón, *Programa de manejo para el aprovechamiento forestal maderable persistente (Tomo I),* Tecpan de Galeana, Guerrero, 2000.

2. Wexler, "Learning the Forest Again." This President was assassinated in 1986, so the forest enterprise has also been able to survive the loss of a charismatic leader.

3. See Armando Bartra, "En Defensa del Bosque," *Ojarasca,* March 2001.

4. The Mexican Method of Forest Management calls for selective logging, with the other two management plans carry out more intensive cutting. Still, the former system has greater environmental impacts as it changes the composition of species in the forest. The other two methods make it possible to take advantage of the forest's natural productivity while encouraging the efficient regeneration of trees.

5. Chris Cooper, Westwood Forest Products, personal communication. Cooper noted that the quality was actually much higher than needed at the time.

6. Cooper, personal communication.

7. Author interview with Fidel López, March 2001.

8. Interview, Fidel López.

9. Chris Cooper, personal communication.

10. Chris Cooper, personal communication.

11. Chris Cooper, personal communication.

12. "FOVIGRO was the school for a lot of people in felling and extraction." (Mario Cedillo, personal communication.)

5

Biopiracy on the Border: The Battle for the Yellow Bean

Laura Carlsen

"Intellectual property is the oil of the 21st century. Look at the richest men a hundred years ago; they all made their money extracting natural resources or moving them around. All today's richest men have made their money out of intellectual property."
—Mark Getty, grandson of oil magnate, J. Paul Getty[1]

The term "biopiracy" was coined in 1992, and has since gained wide usage in the battle against scientists and businesses that simply take biological material from developing countries and patent it back home. According to a growing body of research on the subject, a biopirate—unlike the high-seas variety—launches attacks from behind a desk, financed by coffers of venture capital and U.S. government grants, and backed by armies of scientists and lawyers. Considered an arch villain of the global justice movement, these modern-day corsairs are portrayed as faceless Gene Giants (huge biotech transnationals such as Monsanto or Novartis) that plunder tropical rainforests and mine the lore of native *curanderos* for plants that can cure baldness or dissolve obesity.

With his red beard and swashbuckling manner, Colorado bean broker Larry Proctor fits the stereotype of the old-fashioned pirate much more closely than that of the biopirate. Yet his battle has spurred a cross-border turf war in the long fight against biopiracy. The little yellow bean he claims to have invented has become emblematic of the inequities between the North and the South in an age that measures riches not in buried treasure

81

but in the multidigit patents that form what the biotech industry likes to call its "intellectual property estate."

Proctor's unapologetic use of patent laws to take over an emerging U.S. market for Mexican yellow beans highlights both the inequities and the injustices in the current intellectual property regime. In this case the victims are not poor farmers but a well-organized group of modern producers seeking to take commercial advantage of NAFTA's opening of cross-border trade.

The Battle for the Yellow Bean

In 1994, Larry Proctor bought a bag of bean seed in Sonora, Mexico, and took them home to sow. He began to breed a yellow bean, and in 1996 he applied for a patent from the U.S. Patent and Trademark Office. Patent number 5894079, issued on April 13, 1999, gives his company, Pod-ners, L.L.C., exclusive monopoly rights to market what he calls the "Enola" bean—after his wife's middle name.

Meanwhile in the northwestern state of Sinaloa, Mexico, the farmers who have been producing the yellow bean for generations learned that it was no longer theirs. Proctor's patent bars them from what had become a lucrative market for their beans in southern California. But the powerful Rio Fuerte Growers Association (RFGA) of Los Mochis, Sinaloa, has vowed to fight back. As one member put it, "What Mr. Proctor has done is plagiarism of the product of years of research in Mexican experimental fields."[2]

Housed in a hexagonal white building that dominates the nondescript urban landscape of Los Mochis, the 1,000-member RFGA is proud of its collective achievements. Founded in 1932, Rio Fuerte is one of the largest and most successful growers associations in the country. Made up of small- to medium-scale farmers who work between thirty and one hundred hectares of irrigated land, the RFGA has developed collective services to the producer, including more than 90,000 tons of grain storage capacity; distribution of fertilizers, seed and fuel; accounting services, and a "parafinancing agency" that provides credit in-kind to members. In 1994, following passage of NAFTA, the RFGA began a major effort to export its yellow beans to the United States. Although Mexican growers had exported yellow beans before, particularly in the Los Angeles area, in 1996, the RFGA teamed with Tutuli Produce, a Tucson, Arizona, importer and began to chisel out a market in California. By 1999, they were exporting 4,000 tons, a healthy complement to domestic sales. The bean obtained a fifteen to twenty-five percent price advantage on the U.S. market, so the growers decided to expand their export business, investing several million dollars in machinery to provide the quality required for the U.S. market.[3]

The yellow bean exported by Sinaloa farmers developed out of a long process of collaboration between scientists and farmers throughout Latin America. When the Sinaloa growers set out to improve the quality of their traditional yellow beans in the 1970s, the Colombia-based International Center for Tropical Agriculture sent bean samples for breeding and selection. By 1978, the Mexican Institute for Forestry, Agriculture and Livestock Research and the growers had produced what they dubbed the *mayocoba* and were ready to market it. The bean rapidly became a favorite in Northern Mexico.

When NAFTA opened up new export opportunities, the RFGA, unlike most agricultural producers in the country, was well positioned to take advantage. A consolidated organization of farmers, favored with fertile lands and adequate water supplies, the RFGA began to look toward the export market. With the help of Tutuli Produce they first built a market among nostalgic Mexican-Americans, later branching out to new consumers. Tutuli actively promoted the bean among retailers and taught consumers how to cook the pale beans. After a while exportation of yellow beans, albeit on a small scale, began to look like one of Mexico's very few agricultural success stories under NAFTA.

Then in 1999 the bean export business came to a grinding halt. Armed with a U.S. patent and a plant variety protection certificate, Larry Proctor went to court to enforce his patent against the Mexican growers. He sued Tutuli Produce for patent infringement and royalties. Tutuli promptly countersued, challenging the validity of the Enola patent. The Rio Fuerte Growers Association and the Mexican Agricultural Ministry joined forces with Tutuli to revert the patent.

As the ink flows and the accusations fly, policymakers and dealmakers view the yellow bean patent as a precedent-setting case within the murky realm of international biotech protection. Across borders, lawyers, scientists, farmers, activists, trade officials, and now even the United Nations have all taken up arms in the *battle of the bean*.

A Bean by Any Other Name . . .

The legal case hinges on the physical characteristics of this unpretentious legume. In the fifteen patent claims, Pod-ners—formed in 1999 to handle the budding yellow-bean business—maintains that Proctor complied with patenting requirements by creating a "new, useful and nonobvious" product. The claim describes a field bean variety with a yellow seed coat that falls within defined points of a color card similar to that used by interior decorators. Proctor says he worked "about twenty-four hours a day" to develop a bean with uniform color and leaf size, a defined hilar ring, and stable pod characteristics. His patent prohibits unauthorized commercialization, importation, or use of the bean for commercial or research purposes.

From the mundane properties of the bean, the case expands into the no-man's land that lies between agricultural practices and intellectual property law covering plants. Plant patenting began in 1931, in the United States, with a patent granted for a trailing rose.[4] Since then, three landmark court decisions have opened the door to patenting nearly anything that walks, squiggles, or grows on the face of this earth:

- The 1980 U.S. Supreme Court decision to allow a patent for a genetically engineered microorganism. This decision referred to plasmids allegedly useful in cleaning up oil spills. It remains the legal basis for decisions to broaden the scope and power of biological patents.
- The 1985 U.S. Patent and Trademark Office decision to include plants under industrial patent laws (thus the "double protection" of the Enola under both Plant Breeders Rights and patent laws).
- The 1987 U.S. Patent Office decision that animals too are patentable.[5]

As a result of these decisions and scientific advances including the Human Genomics Project, applications for patents on life forms have skyrocketed—more than 500,000 patent filings for human genetic sequences alone by September 1998.[6] The U.S. government had issued six million patents by 1999, with a whopping three million filings for biomaterials alone awaiting review.[7] In the same year, the World Intellectual Property Organization (WIPO) received 76,023 patent filings.[8] Within the deluge of requests for intellectual property protection, biotech is unquestionably the rising star in the patentable galaxy.

However, the Enola patent has raised some serious doubts about plant patenting practices. Several bean specialists, including Gil Waibel of the Colorado Seed Growers Association, maintain that two years is far too short a time to breed a "new" bean.[9] Experts further assert that a process of natural selection for certain traits, such as Proctor used to grow the Enola, is insufficient basis for patenting since it requires no scientific innovation or invention.

The Tutuli countersuit argues that regardless of the length of the breeding process, the patent is invalid and unenforceable and maintains that there is nothing new about the Enola. The law office representing Tutuli in the case points to "prior art," indicating that the yellow beans covered by the patent have been around since at least the 1970s in Mexico, with printed publications proving their existence in the United States as early as the 1930s.[10]

Genetic tests carried out by the Mexican Institute for Forestry, Agriculture and Livestock Research indicate that the Enola is essentially the same as yellow beans grown in northwestern Mexico. Growers say the true identity of the Enola is their own *mayocoba*, the product of a combination of generations of farmer breeding and selection in the fields and three years of experimental testing in the 1970s.

Another argument against the Enola patent on scientific grounds has to do with the breadth of the protection. Since the patent covers a color range defined by color strips matched by the naked eye rather than a specific genetic make-up or distinguishable feature, Mexican farmers call it subjective and absurd. In fact, the legal brief calling for a reexamination of the patent states, "We believe it will make a mockery of the patent system to allow statutory protection of a color *per se*, especially given that the patent holder then tries to block other persons from making, selling or using beans with that color."[11]

Market Woes

Tutuli Produce began importing *peruano* and *mayocoba* yellow beans from Mexico in 1994. Today its president, Rebecca Gilliland, believes that the Enola patent is an opportunistic attempt to steal her market. When informed that she needed permission to sell the beans because it was an infringement on Proctor's patent, Gilliland's first reaction was disbelief. Pod-ners demanded six cents a pound in royalties, and included a demand for retroactive royalty payments. According to Gilliland, one proof that the patent is an attempt to conquer a ready-made market is that the bean is not marketed under the name Enola, but sold under its Mexican names of *mayocoba* or *peruano*.[12]

In the first year of the patent, the Sinaloa farmers' bean export market began to dry up. First, Pod-ners began to notify Tutuli customers that it was against the law to buy yellow beans from Tutuli Produce due to patent infringement. Then, Rio Fuerte farmers were informed that customs officials were stopping loads of yellow beans sent to the United States to sample them, in search of a single bean that fit the description of the patent. The inspections, according to Gilliland, cost $300 a load and unpredictable delays. She began to lose clients rapidly.

As a result of the controversy, Rio Fuerte growers figured they had no choice but to abandon their promising yellow-bean export market in the United States. Yellow bean production in Sinaloa dropped sixty-two percent, from 250,000 tons in 1998–99 to 96,000 in 2000. After exporting close to 4,000 tons, Rio Fuerte growers did not export to the United States at all in the 2000–2001 season. Yellow beans were sown on only thirty-five percent of the acreage sowed in 1999, and the entire harvest was sold on the domestic market. While climate and crop choices factored into the decision, Ramón Osuna, a local farmer, notes that many growers shifted to other crops or sold in the regional market because of the patent. "I didn't export in 2000 because I don't want to pay six cents a pound to Pod-ners— I want to earn that as the producer." He adds, "Besides, it's fraud. Why are we going to pay royalties on our own product?"

The Tutuli-Rio Fuerte countersuit demands punitive damages from Pod-ners, citing "trade libel and intentional interference with contractual relationships and prospective economic relations." Mexico's agricultural ministry quickly stepped in to offer advisory help, declaring the defense of the *mayocoba* a question of "national interest." Ricardo Hernández, director of foreign trade in the ministry, seconded Tutuli's complaint that Proctor was not playing fair, declaring that the basis of the patent was commercial, not scientific. The agricultural ministry has dedicated time and resources to reverting the patent in a case it deems an effort to displace successful Mexican businessmen in a growing market.[13]

Proctor admits his main objective has always been to control the market. All Enola beans cultivated and sold in the United States must go through International Bean Marketing, an affiliate of Pod-ners. While this system effectively deals with the problem of overproduction, a problem Proctor says destroyed the market for Colorado's pinto bean production, it also shuts out the Mexican export farmers who pioneered the yellow-bean market in the United States.

Science Enters the Fray

In an unusual move, on December 20, 2000, the International Center for Tropical Agriculture (CIAT) formally requested a reexamination of the Enola bean patent. The U.S. Patent and Trademark Office granted the request in February 2001. The patent reexamination request cites extensive prior publication of the yellow bean[14] and accuses Proctor of bringing the beans into the country illegally. It also challenges the patent on the basis of the wide breadth of its claim.[15]

According to Dr. Daniel Debouck, a Belgian scientist with the Cali-based research center, the Enola patent violates a U.N. agreement that plant varieties held "in trust" cannot be protected under intellectual property laws. The Food and Agriculture Organization agreement, signed in 1994, stipulates that as one of sixteen centers worldwide charged with collecting and improving varieties of basic foodstuffs, CIAT must assure that their materials remain in the public domain for research and breeding.

CIAT holds 260 varieties of yellow bean, including six that are covered under the Pod-ners claim. CIAT believes that the Enola patent presents a threat to its work because it attempts to privately patent the institution's material. In addition, the patent, according to Debouck, presents a threat to future research since it covers not only the process of producing a variety with this type of bean seed, but also research so all agricultural research and germplasm centers would have to enter into conversations with the patent-holder to continue experiments.[16]

The kind of cooperation and exchange between international institutions and farmers that originally produced the *mayocoba* has proved the basis for important advances in producing basic foods, particularly in underdeveloped countries. In a letter supporting the CIAT patent challenge, the Food and Agriculture Organization noted that the "patent may impinge upon the availability and free movement of material designated under the FAO-CIAT agreement." The agreement states that CIAT placed collections of germplasm "in trust for the international community" within the International Network of Ex Situ Collections under the auspices of the FAO. This agreement obliges CIAT to hold the germplasm for public interest and "not to claim ownership over the designated germplasm or seek any intellectual property right over that germplasm or related information." It also requires the institutions to provide samples of it to all bona fide researchers and plant breeders.[17] The letter notes that CIAT's commitment to continue to provide the bean, including in the United States if warranted, may run up against legal actions from the patent-holder, and the FAO supports all efforts to establish the preexistence of the bean and guarantee its continued circulation in the public realm.

The CIAT position is the result of some serious prodding from non-governmental groups, particularly the agricultural and biodiversity watch-dog organization the ETC Group (formerly the Rural Advancement Foundation International–RAFI). The difficulty in protecting genetic material in the public realm is among the reasons this organization has called for a ban on patenting life forms. Hope Shand, of the ETC Group, claims that "the Enola case demonstrates it is wrong for a private company or individual to claim exclusive monopoly control on genetic material developed over generations by anonymous farmers, in this case in Mexico," and warns that if the Enola patent is upheld it could raise serious questions about the rights of farmers and the right to keep knowledge in the public domain. Shand and other activists believe that the Enola case should be heard before the International Court of Justice to set a clear precedent as a "fundamental human rights issue, about where intellectual property infringes on basic human rights."[18]

International researchers are concerned that the Pod-ners patent could conceivably end not only U.S.-based research and production of yellow beans, but even CIAT's research with its own yellow beans. The patent system was originally devised to protect inventions, thus providing incentives for research and development. However, the patenting of genetic sequences and biological materials is already having a chilling effect on scientific—especially public interest—research.

In agricultural research, fundamental to solving the problems of feeding a growing planetary population in times of environmental deterioration and social inequity, the patent system would reduce the free flow of information and materials between public sector institutions that has facilitated major advances to date. Moreover it could force a switch from public-interest work to corporate-led research and development. The ETC Group warns that "surrendering to corporate R&D" would effectively terminate some of the crucial work currently being done, given that the two systems have differing priorities, capacities, and prospects.

Feeding the poor and assuring stockholder dividends are two very different goals that lead to divergent strategies and actions in the field. Corporate agricultural research in the South accounts for only ten to fifteen percent of the total, meaning that few discoveries would be adapted to the climatic and soil conditions found in the regions of greatest need. Moreover, only twelve percent of corporate research goes to farm-level technology. Lastly, the lion's share of corporate R&D goes to research on post-harvest and processing.[19] Needless to say, technologies adapted to increasing production and nutritional value for family consumption are out of the market loop and would be of very little interest to agribusiness, and yet these are precisely the subsistence farming sectors often targeted in efforts to reduce poverty and hunger worldwide.

If the health field is any indication, agricultural researchers have cause for alarm. In public health and disease prevention, the rush to patent genetic material has had a chilling effect on both scientific research and patient access to life-sustaining medications. In one instance, a University of Washington researcher announced recently that research into a colon cancer-screening test would be terminated since the gene under investigation was in the process of being patented by a private company.[20] In another case, a human gene known to be responsible for breast cancer (BRCA1) is "owned" by Myriad Genetics in Salt Lake City. To run a test that could indicate a genetic predilection for the disease and lead to monitoring and prevention activities, a patient must pay $2,500 in royalty payments to Myriad Genetics.[21]

While promoters of bioprospecting predict that Third World jungles may soon yield a cure for cancer or AIDS, patenting of life forms has led to economic barriers to health access since a patent raises consumer costs considerably. To give an idea of the "monopoly bonus" accrued to patentholders, when President Clinton extended pharmaceutical patents from seventeen to twenty years as a response to new GATT-TRIP rules, the decision cost consumers in the United States an estimated *additional* $1.2 billion in 1996 and 1997 for over-the-counter drugs.[22]

In a bold move, the FAO finally addressed the larger issues of public-domain agricultural research in its November 3, 2001, meeting in Rome. The organization approved an International Treaty on Seeds and Farmers' Rights, despite the abstentions of Japan and the United States. The treaty contains two crucial points: First, it establishes a multilateral system to ensure access to germplasm from thirty-five basic food crops (corn, wheat, rice, beans, etc.) and twenty-nine varieties of forage crops. These cannot be patented or claimed under any form of intellectual property. Second, it establishes farmers' rights to save, use, exchange, and sell saved seed on their own farms, and to protect traditional knowledge on seeds and participate in benefits derived from these resources. This treaty would apparently have a direct impact on the Enola case, although it is too soon to tell exactly how.

Tools of the Trade

Another major concern raised by the Enola case is that everyone is *not* equal in the brave new world of biological claim-stakers. In the words of a lawyer at a prominent Palo Alto biotech firm, "Patents are considered 'economic tools.' And the country with the bigger toolbox wins." While the United States has built up an enormous governmental, legal, and business infrastructure to promote its intellectual property claims, most other countries have little hope of catching up—even when the materials being patented or to be patented are found in their territory. Ninety-seven percent of all patents are held by nationals of OECD countries (of which Mexico is a nominal member) and trade in patented production makes up fully half of gross domestic product in these countries.[23]

There is wide disparity in the global race to patent potentially lucrative biological materials, whether whole plants or gene sequences. Even Mexican government officials have been forced to acknowledge inherent inequities in the system. When asked what the solution to a yellow-bean case might look like, Ricardo Hernández, Undersecretary of International Commerce in Foreign Relations, expressed concerns over the rush to patent plants. "We have to be aware that not all our producers are in condition to pay huge quantities like those paid in the U.S. to take out a patent."

For poor Mexican farmers, that is a gross understatement. Seventy percent of agricultural producers in Mexico earn less than minimum wage (about four dollars a day), while indigenous campesinos who live in some of the biologically richest and most coveted areas of the country are among the poorest farmers. It costs an average of $50,000 to take out a patent in the United States. In 1998, $100 billion were spent in patent licensing, and some predict that will reach *half a trillion dollars* by the year 2005. Costs run even higher when the patent goes to court, meaning that biotech patents have become a vastly profitable market for lawyers. The average cost of litigation for a biotech patent in 1999 was $1.5 million, and 8,200 cases were filed in that year alone.[24]

Moreover, Mexican rural organizations and advisors worry that not only does the plant patenting process cost too much, more importantly it violates Mexico's traditions of seed-sharing and collective use of biological materials. As plant varieties become patented, farmers are prohibited from sharing seed and each must purchase seed annually—a virtual impossibility in the crisis-stricken Mexican countryside. Any changeover to patented crops threatens to widen an already immense gap between Mexican farmers and their heavily subsidized U.S. counterparts, while benefiting the transnational agribusiness companies that hold the patents by requiring royalty payments and by often binding the producer to the exclusive use of their technological packages.

Another grave concern is that the new monopoly-held varieties, whether hybrid or genetically modified, may take over traditional native varieties through cross-pollination. This would lead not only to questions of legal responsibility but also to a loss of agricultural diversity. In the case of corn, beans, chilies, and squash, such a loss would have global implications, since Mexico is the place of origin of those crops and one of the richest *in situ* germ banks for the many varieties still preserved on Indian lands.[25]

The aggressive role of the U.S. Patent and Trademark Office in granting a patent on a Mexican product in the Enola case is seen by some as an oversight, or excess, in an otherwise balanced system. However, this race to patent—as analyzed further in the next chapter—reflects a long-term strategy to control intellectual property rights in a global economy where tangible goods and services increasingly take a backseat.

As intellectual property rights become the new tools of dominance in a globalized economy, developing countries are fairly assured of having a permanent, and growing, disadvantage. In the past, these countries provided the raw materials to fuel colonial and industrial world systems. Today, intellectual property rights over their newly discovered biological and agricultural wealth are rapidly accumulating in the archives of transnational and Northern companies. Once again developing countries find themselves reduced to providing the raw materials, now on a microscopic level.

Globalizing Intellectual Property Rules:
NAFTA and TRIPs

Today, judicial systems and trade agreements actively encourage the patenting of life forms. With the move to integrate intellectual property law among nations, the World Trade Organization (WTO) seeks to impose homogeneous intellectual property codes worldwide. Opposition to the new intellectual property rights (IPR) regime on life forms has focused on Article 27.3(b) of the WTO's Trade Related Intellectual Property Rights (TRIPs) Agreement. This article reads that members may exclude plants and animals and essentially biological processes for the production of plants or animals from patentability. Microorganisms and nonbiological and microbiological processes may not be excluded. It adds, "Members shall provide for the protection of plant varieties either by patents or by an effective sui generis system or by any combination thereof."

Thus, after decades in which the scope of patentability was widened by increments mandated by courts or parliaments, the TRIPs article leaps from the premise that specific rules must define what is patentable to the assumption that *everything* is patentable and specific rules must create narrowly defined categories of exceptions.

NAFTA rules follow the same pattern. Chapter 17 pertains to intellectual property and seeks to protect transnational IPR, with no reference whatsoever to community rights. Under the patents section, Chapter 17, in the words of one analyst, "defines a universal criteria for patenting, such that practically any product or process is patentable, with almost no restrictions on the basis of ethical, economic, or national sovereignty arguments."[26] Like Article 27.3 of TRIPs, Article 1709(3) establishes that plants and animals may be excluded, except microorganisms, and refers to the need to cover these under patents, or sui generis systems. It does not exclude human genes, although Mexican legislation specifically excluded them from patentability. The section on procedures for sanctioning violations is particularly lengthy and explicit.

Although many of the intellectual property reforms contained in Chapter 17 were unilaterally instrumented with the trade opening under the Salinas administration (1988–94), NAFTA's intellectual property chapter codifies them in international law. Although it ignores collective rights, especially of indigenous peoples and farmers, and excludes problems of materials in the public domain, it is already considered a model for Latin America and for a future Free Trade Area of the Americas (FTAA).

Are There Alternatives?

The intellectual property regime envisioned by the WTO has generally been presented in much the same way as globalization itself—as the only answer. But governments and organizations around the world have stood up to oppose the plans for globalized intellectual property rules and propose alternatives.[27] A summary of opposition to TRIPs can be reduced to four main points: whether life forms should be patentable at all; whether and how to harmonize TRIPs with the Convention on Biological Diversity; how to balance the rights of IPR holders with the rights of farmers, indigenous peoples, and local communities; and how to devise effective sui generis systems that go beyond the alternative suggested by International Union for the Protection of New Varieties of Plants.[28]

Countries that have taken an official position against patenting "naturally occurring plants and animals and their parts" include: the Least Developed Countries Group; Zambia, Jamaica, Kenya, Pakistan, Sri Lanka, Tanzania, Uganda, Zimbabwe, India, Brazil; and the African Group. Many others call for specific mechanisms to ensure respect for traditional farming methods and indigenous knowledge and collective rights.[29] Other countries have insisted that the new IPR rules comply with the Convention on Biological Diversity.[30]

Implicit also is the question of preserving national sovereign rights over genetic material and trade-related policies, and the right to access to socially useful products through public-interest licensing agreements. Both

TRIPs and NAFTA severely limit any possibility of licensing agreements, often leaving life-saving drugs out of reach of patients. As seen in the recent case of South Africa AIDS medications, under these conditions any settlement with pharmaceutical companies in the public interest must be based on public pressure and corporate image campaigns rather than a legal framework that would allow a nation to provide for its citizens' well-being. Likewise, by accepting the current intellectual property regime governing the patenting of life forms, the Mexican government must depend on the U.S. Patent Office's ability to recognize an "error" in the Enola case, rather than challenging the system that allows a U.S. interest to close an agricultural market to the very farmers who developed the product in the first place.

While most nations base their opposition to TRIPs on issues of national sovereignty and positions against the privatization of natural substances that could be vital to human welfare, TRIPs have also run into trouble with international human rights groups. On August 17, 2000, the U.N Sub-Commission on the Promotion and Protection of Human Rights issued a resolution stating that the right to intellectual property protection is subject to limitations in the public interest. The ground-breaking resolution charged "there are apparent conflicts between the intellectual property rights regime embodied in the TRIPs agreement (of the WTO) and international human rights law" and concluded unequivocally that "the TRIPS agreement does not adequately reflect the fundamental nature and indivisibility of all human rights, including the right of everyone to enjoy the benefits of scientific progress and its applications, the right to health, the right to food, and the right to self-determination. . . ." The resolution goes on to remind national governments of the primacy of human rights obligations over economic policies and agreements and calls for a full study of the relationship between intellectual property rights and human rights on all levels.

With Mexico as a notable exception, developing countries that boast a high level of agricultural and biological diversity have generally opposed privatization of those resources. In most cases, these resources have been preserved and fostered over the centuries precisely through collective forms of stewardship and the free circulation of genetic materials. Strong forms of cultural resistance and ties to ancestral farming methods account for the survival of crop diversity found in these countries. That diversity has increasing value in a world where the Green Revolution decimated the number of varieties of basic foods sown in most countries.[31]

India has taken a particularly strong stance against patenting life forms. More than 50,000 varieties of rice are cultivated in India, each historically adapted to its particular climate and cultural milieu. One of them, the Basmati, has already fallen prey to "biopiracy." RiceTec Company of Texas patented a strain of Basmati rice in 1997. The move so outraged Indian farmers that they mobilized against the patent and submitted a letter of protest to the U.S. Embassy stating, ". . . the persistent pressure on the Indian government to change its patent laws is an assault on Indian democracy and an encouragement to biopirates." The letter demanded that U.S. patent law be changed to "recognize the traditional knowledge system of the biodiversity-rich Third World countries in order to deny 'novelty' and 'non-obviousness' criterion to the patent clams based on such knowledge." It ended defiantly: "We will never compromise on this great civilization which has been based on the culture of sharing the abundance of the world, and will continue to maintain this trend of sharing our biodiversity and knowledge. But we will never allow your culture of impoverishment and greed to undermine our culture of abundance and sharing. . . ."[32]

In Mexico, the issue hit the newspapers again in May 2001, when Greenpeace-Mexico informed the government that Dupont had patented a maize variety native to Mexico in the European Union. The patent, obtained in August 2000, on a variety with a high fat content, potentially covers several native varieties with similar characteristics and would be used to produce oil.[33] If the patent is upheld and registered with the World Intellectual Property Organization, the same Mesoamerican farmers who developed and cultivated these maize varieties would have to pay royalties to continue to plant them.[34] Corn was first cultivated in Mexico some 8,000 years ago and Mexico is the home of "the mother of corn," *teocintle*, which still grows wild in the countryside and is revered by some Indian peoples. Dupont developed its variety based on seed from several of the 300-plus varieties found in the country. The Mexican government, under pressure from environmental groups and corn producers organized in the ANEC (see Chapter 7), filed an appeal before the European Union Patent Office.

The Andean Nuña bean and the quinoa plant, Mexican maize and cactus plants, the Indian Neem tree, kava in the Pacific and even the DNA of New Guinea tribes have fallen prey to biopirates who patented this genetic material as their property. As the list grows longer,[35] among indigenous peoples a remarkable level of organization and consensus exists against patenting life forms. International forums and conferences on biopiracy and bioprospecting have resulted in major declarations protesting the practices and the intellectual property regimes that give rise to them. In the Mataatua Declaration on Cultural and Intellectual Property Rights of

Indigenous Peoples, drawn up in June 1993, in New Zealand, indigenous delegates from fourteen countries declared their right to self-determination and proclaimed indigenous peoples as the exclusive owners of their cultural and intellectual property. On July 25, 1999, indigenous groups meeting in Geneva released a document "No to patenting of life!" criticizing Article 27.3bi of TRIPs of the WTO, stating, "It will lead to the appropriation of our traditional medicinal plants and seeds and our indigenous knowledge on health, agriculture and biodiversity conservation." It demanded that an amendment to the article disallow the use of patents to protects plant varieties; ensure that any sui generis system protect the knowledge and practices of indigenous peoples and farmers; allow seed saving and sharing and the harvesting, cultivation, and use of medicinal plants; prevent the theft and piracy of indigenous materials and knowledge; integrate the principle and practice of informed consent and the right of indigenous peoples to veto any bioprospecting activity. The Indigenous People's Seattle Declaration on the occasion of the Third Ministerial Meeting of the WTO in December 1999, again condemned patenting of life forms, including microorganisms, genetic sequences, and natural processes, stating that if the demands for respecting indigenous and farmer practices and informed consent cannot be assured, the TRIPS agreement should be removed.[36]

The Mexican government has generally supported the IPR regime outlined by the WTO and compliance with its obligations under NAFTA. But officials accept the need to seek other means of protecting the nation's genetic resources. Although little has been done in this respect, officials have suggested the formation of gene banks and registries to assure public access and to establish species as native to the country. The Agriculture Department announced in May that it will establish a national bank of phytogenetic resources to register and study genetic diversity important to agriculture. The government announced that the capital of this bank will be "the genes and diversity, which should be at the disposition of the farmers."[37] Meanwhile, Hernández says his office is also meeting with the U.S. patent office to develop mechanisms to share patent information across NAFTA borders and avoid problems such as the Enola bean.

Nongovernmental organizations have proposed alternatives that follow three basic lines: nonpatented forms of protection and recognition, publishing to establish the preexistence of biological materials, and citizen organization to monitor and expose biopiracy activities and exert public pressure on companies. Several patents have been voluntarily withdrawn so far due to public pressure and concerns over damage to corporate or institutional images. Groups directly affected, like the Rio Fuerte Growers Association, are finding unexpected allies among international agricultural and environmental groups. The publicity campaigns carried out by Internet may be the most powerful tool discovered so far to prevent acts of biopiracy.

Conclusion

The Tutuli case will eventually be heard before the U.S. District Court of Central California, but it has been repeatedly delayed. The conclusions of the patent reexamination should have been released in early 2002, but Podners has filed to add forty-three more claims to its original documentation, and the Patent Office has agreed to combine the process of renewing the patent with the reexamination request. For now, both sides are upping the ante. The Mexican government has sworn "to do everything necessary" to revert the patent, including presenting the case before a NAFTA panel. Larry Proctor recently filed suit against sixteen Colorado farmers for patent violation for growing and/or selling yellow beans.[38]

The battle will apparently be fought both in the courts and in the marketplace, where the whole thing started. In a thinly veiled dumping threat, Proctor has warned that if the patent gets thrown out he will sell all his seed and "by next October there would be about 400,000 bags of beans sitting on the border ready to go into Mexico."

Sinaloa's yellow bean farmers hope to begin to export again soon. They still have trouble believing the patent could be upheld. Standing in the middle of his bean fields just outside Los Mochis, Ramón Osuna wondered out loud, "If Larry Proctor invented this bean, how did all these plants get here?"

The Rio Fuerte growers thought they were doing everything right to fit into the new system. They used NAFTA to find a comparative advantage and to build a new market. They invested in new equipment to guarantee the export bean a high and consistent quality. They modernized facilities, developed an export-oriented product, created economies of scale by associating successful growers, and built up their own services to create horizontally and vertically integrated chains of production and marketing. In sum, it was a textbook case of an organization adapting to the world market.

As relatively privileged farmers, the Rio Fuerte Growers have the option to convert crops and maintain viability. They view the case as a matter of principle and an important test of the new rules under economic integration.[39] Rodolfo Soto put it succinctly: "The patent office is encouraging global piracy. We really want to set a precedent here. Because we have a lot of things to offer to the world but this kind of patent puts a brake on everything."[40]

Activists claim the Enola case just proves their point that biotech patenting is the next frontier for predatory trade practices. When NAFTA was signed in 1992, then-Secretary of Commerce Jaime Serra Puche stated, "The contents of this chapter (Chapter 17 on Intellectual Property), along with that of investment and access to markets, complete an ideal framework of incentives, since they provide legal security, encourage technological innovation and promote the development of modern, highly competitive projects, with the capacity to generate employment and income, and with a perspective of long-term well-being." Mexico has gone to great lengths to attract foreign investment under the new economic integration. Farmers and citizen groups worry that as U.S. companies and transnational corporations retain patents on the country's genetic and biological resources, there may no longer be a country to invest in.

Notes

1. Quoted in "Blood and Oil," *The Economist,* March 4, 2000, 68.
2. Rodolfo Soto, Rio Fuerte Growers Association, interview with author, March 15, 2001.
3. Interview with Rodolfo Soto, March 15, 2001.
4. The current law 35 USC Sec. 161 Patents for Plants, Amended Sept. 3, 1954, reads: "Whoever invents or discovers and asexually reproduces any distinct and new variety of plant, including cultivated sports, mutants, hybrids, and newly found seedlings other than tuber propagated plant or a plant found in an uncultivated state, may obtain a patent therefore, subject to the conditions and requirements of title." The 1970 Plant Variety Protection Act broadened the definition to include sexually reproduced plants. Cited in Kimberly Wilson, "Exclusive Rights, Enclosure and the Patenting of Life" in *Redesigning Life? The worldwide challenge to genetic engineering,* ed. Brian Tokar (London: Zed Books, 2001), 292.
5. Hope Shand in Tokar, *Redesigning Life,* 226.
6. Hope Shand in Tokar, *Redesigning Life,* 233.
7. Rural Advancement Foundation International (RAFI), "In Search of Higher Ground: The Intellectual Property Challenge to Public Agricultural Research and Human Rights, and 28 Alternative Initiatives," 9. Occasional Paper: http://www.rafi.org.
8. RAFI, "In Search of Higher Ground," 9.
9. Interview with Gil Waibel, Colorado Seed Growers Association, March 21, 2001. Proctor has since filed for a "broadening re-issue" of the patent that would add an additional 39 claims to the original 15, further specifying characteristics

of the Enola. He has also asked that the USPTO revise his original assertion that the beans were bought in 1994 to read 1990.

10. Interview with Jill Pietrini, of the L.A. law office of Manatt, Phelps and Phillips, March 21, 2001.

11. Request ("Re: Enola Bean Patent 5,894,079") prepared by Washington, D.C. lawyer John Dodd, of Dodd & Associates, December 18, 2000. Document in possession of the author.

12. Interview with Rebecca Gilliland, March 2001.

13. Interview with Ricardo Hernández Muñoz, March 2001.

14. The May 31, 2000, letter from the FAO legal department in an annex reads: "It is clear that the existence of these materials prior to the granting of the patent is a matter of public record. We recognize that CIAT is one of the world's premier institutes for bean breeding. It houses the world's single largest collection of *Phaseolus*. Information on these collections (including the accessions cited above) was readily available on-line, or by request, at the time of the patent application." Letter from Giuliano Pucci, Officer in Charge, Legal Office, FAO, Rome, dated May 31, 2000. Documents in possession of the author.

15. Request ("Re: Enola Bean Patent 5,894,079").

16. Interview with Daniel Debouck, CIAT, March 23, 2001.

17. Letter from Giuliano Pucci, Officer in Charge, Legal Office, FAO, Rome, dated May 31, 2000.

18. Interview with Hope Shand, ETC Group, March 14, 2001.

19. RAFI, "In Search of Higher Ground," 7.

20. Dr. Leroy Hood, of the Molecular Biology Department. Cited in *Redesigning Life*, 234.

21. Wil S. Hylton, "Who Owns This Body?" *Esquire Magazine*, June 2001.

22. Kristin Dawkins, Michelle Thom, and Carolyn Carr, "Information about Intellectual Property Rights No. 1," Institute for Agriculture and Trade Policy: http://www.iatp.org/tradeag/.

23. RAFI, "In Search of Higher Ground," 10.

24. John Barton of the Stanford Law School, cited in RAFI, "In Search of Higher Ground," 9.

25. Recently, genetically modified corn plants were found growing in the state of Oaxaca, home to scores of native varieties, despite the fact that sowing GM corn is prohibited by law due to the ecological implications. See David Quist and Ignacio Chapela, "Transgenic DNA introgressed into traditional maize landraces in Oaxaca, México," *Nature* 414, November 29, 2001.

26. Analysis in Victor Osorio, "Agenda empresarial y propiedad intellectual en el TLC," in *El Tratado de Libre Comercio Texto y Contexto*, ed. Gustavo Emmerich (México City: UAM-Iztapalapa, 1994), 257 (author's translation).

27. As early as 1990, the Third World Patent Convention issued a declaration stating: "We believe that a review of the intellectual property system should take into account the fact that the public interest of the majority takes precedence over commercial interests, and over rights derived from monopoly proposals aimed at strengthening the rights of intellectual property holders with no obligations to the interests of the people, as consumers and producers." "New Delhi Declaration," in *GATT Briefing on Trade-related Aspects of Intellectual Property Rights, No. 2,*

European Network on Agriculture and Development, July 1990, cited in Emmerich, *El Tratado de Libre Comercio Texto y Contexto,* 253.

28. Genetic Resources Action International (GRAIN), "Update on the Review of TRIPs Article 27.3(b), July 2001: http://www.grain.org.

29. GRAIN, "Update."

30. The Convention on Biodiversity states a commitment to "the conservation of biological diversity, the sustainable use of its components and the fair and equitable sharing of the benefits arising out of the utilization of genetic resources" and seeks to ensure "appropriate access to genetic resources and by appropriate transfer of relevant technologies, taking into account all rights over those resources and to technologies, and by appropriate funding." Benefit sharing is discussed in the next chapter of this book.

31. See, for example, GRAIN, "Investing in Destruction: The World Bank and Biodiversity," November 1996, http://www.grain.org.

32. Cited in Vandana Shiva, "Seed Satyagraha: A Movement for Farmers' Rights and Freedoms in a World of Intellectual Property Rights, Globalized Agriculture and Biotechnology," in Tokar, *Redesigning Life,* 357.

33. *La Jornada,* May 16, 2001. The fat content covered in the patent is from six to fifty-five percent oleic acid. Greenpeace reports that the native varieties similar to the patent are: *dulcillo, tabloncillo, dulce, onaveño, jala* and *nal-tel.*

34. Ernesto Camou Healy, researcher with the Centro de Investigación en Alimentación y Desarrollo, A.C., calls it "one more case of commercial and genetic piracy against the interests of countries with fewer resources." Article published in *El Imparcial,* Sonora, Mexico, May 18, 2001. ANEC calculates that the patent could affect some three million producers (*La Jornada,* May 17, 2001).

35. Examples of biopiracy can be found on the RAFI web site: http://www.rafi.org. The Papua New Guinea patent was taken out by the major public-sector biopirate, the U.S. National Institutes of Health, on March 14, 1995. It was subsequently withdrawn due to protest. See Victoria Tauli-Corpuz, "Biotechnology and Indigenous Peoples," in Tokar, *Redesigning Life,* 264.

36. Statement by the Indigenous Peoples' Caucus convened and sponsored by the Indigenous Environmental Network USA/Canada, Seventh Generation Fund USA, International Indian Treaty Council, Indigenous Peoples Council on Biocolonialism, the Abya Yala Fund, and TEBTEBBA (Indigenous People's International Centre for Policy Research and Education), December 1, 1999, Seattle, Washington.

37. Matilde Perez, "Empieza México gestiones para evitar que Dupont patente el maíz," *La Jornada,* May 18, 2001.

38. Angela Enciso, "Dueño de patente de frijol mexicano demandó a productores de Colorado" *La Jornada,* Dec. 19, 2001. See also the Dec. 18, 2001 press release from ETC Group: www.etcgroup.org.

39. Interview with Martín Robles, Los Mochis, Sinaloa, March 15, 2001 (author's translation).

40. Interview with Rodolfo Soto, March 15, 2001.

6

Biopiracy, Bioprospecting, and Resistance: Four Cases in Mexico

Andrés Barreda

BIOPIRACY IN MEXICO IS NOT NEW. FOR SEVERAL DECADES PHARMACEUTICAL companies, botanical gardens, and universities from various parts of the world have been involved in the direct extraction of Mexico's biological riches. In addition, national and international mafias have long collected wild animals for sale on the black market. More recently, food and seed companies have joined in, as well as those linked to biotechnology and genetic engineering. This plunder has been accomplished with little regard for Mexican law and often through bribery.

Mexico is one of the world's five wealthiest countries in terms of biodiversity.[1] It is estimated that Mexico has between eight and twelve percent of all the species on earth within its borders. It has the most reptile species, second-most terrestrial mammals, and ranks fourth in the number of amphibians. Mexico has thirty percent more bird species than the United States and Canada combined. More than 2,000 species of fish, 25,000 species of butterflies and moths, and 1,500 species of bees are native to Mexico. Although knowledge about Mexico's flora is incomplete, experts estimate that the country stands fourth in the world in the number of vascular flora. There are fifty-four genera and 850 species of cacti—more than in any other country in the western hemisphere—and over two-thirds of the 375 known species of agave.[2] Furthermore, the part of central and southern Mexico and much of Central America known as Mesoamerica is a principal center for plant domestication. This is why the country holds such an irresistible attraction for biopirates and bioprospectors.

Mexico's unique biological wealth comes from its favorable location, where temperate and tropical biotic zones meet. In addition, Mexico's coastline includes maritime bands of coral reefs, mangrove forests, and kelp forests—the areas of greatest marine biodiversity. It also features regions that overlap with the deserts of the northern hemisphere (23–24 degrees latitude), giving the country some of the most important desert plant life on earth. Mexico possesses extraordinary biological abundance, which endures despite the high rates of environmental destruction over the past few decades.

Mexico also has the largest indigenous population in Latin America. Of the many indigenous peoples that existed in Mexico at the time of the Spanish conquest,[3] fifty-two still exist. They speak 280 original languages, which places Mexico in fifth place worldwide in the number of living languages.[4] Studies in the last ten years show that maps of cultural diversity follow the contours of the maps of biological diversity.[5] This overlap is not coincidental. Mexico is one of the regions of the world where indigenous peoples have kept their cultural practices alive and passed on knowledge accumulated over hundreds of years. These practices include the domestication, diversification, and adaptation of a great variety of edible plants, animals, medicinal plants, trees, mushrooms, and insects found in their territories. In the new industry of bioprospecting, this ancient knowledge has become an indispensable guide in the search for a strategic share of the "green gold" of biodiversity.

To date, four cases of bioprospecting-by-contract have come to light in Mexico. Two involve the National Autonomous University of Mexico (UNAM) and counterparts in the United States for bioprospecting in Protected Natural Areas and desert zones. One involves indigenous communities in Chiapas, and the other is between an indigenous organization and the transnational company Novartis. While the cases vary in their specific issues, each has stimulated regional and national resistance to bioprospecting, contributing to a growing call for a moratorium on bioprospecting contracts in Mexico. The cases reveal some of the ways in which bioprospecting is practiced and some of the contradictions that result from this use of Mexico's rich biodiversity.

The Bioprospecting Boom

An international race is underway to patent the chemical sequences of active substances (such as proteins, hormones, enzymes, secondary metabolics).

Any live organism can turn out to be lucrative to a transnational corporation. Intellectual property rights can be applied to samples of species of plants, animals, fungi, or microorganisms that may contain strategic substances such as genetic segments, genetic sequences of modified biological organisms, or complete genomes of species or varieties of interest.

Another focus of interest for bioprospectors is agricultural products, the majority of which are the result of centuries of cultivation and selection by indigenous peoples and peasant communities. These include the multiple varieties of native corn, chile, bean, and squash. As the place of origin of these plants basic to the human diet, Mexico is an *in situ* reserve of varieties lost in other parts of the world, attracting renewed interest in some of their genetic characteristics.

Living beings are now seen as the raw material for new forms of production. Two principal factors have unleashed this global race to gain exclusive access to these forms of life. The first is the unprecedented technical capacity to identify genetic structures. The second is intellectual property laws that have given a green light to the patenting of life forms all over the world, making possible their conversion to private property. The patenting of life is leading toward the privatization of existing reserves of germplasm, both *ex situ*—the extensive plant collections found in seed banks, botanical gardens, hospitals, research centers, universities, and libraries—and *in situ*—the biological reserves located in Mexico's Protected Natural Areas as well as in the biological corridors that link them and keep them genetically renewed.

Another key to understanding the new interest in bioprospecting is the ongoing merging of the food and pharmaceutical monopolies. Until a few years ago these areas remained quite separate. Food was largely controlled by large corporations that had interests in all levels of its production—land, the sale of agrochemicals and machinery, and the global distribution of basic grains. In a similar fashion, health care depended to a growing extent on the pharmaceutical industry. Now, however, the growth in the industries producing biotechnology or transgenic organisms has catalyzed the merger of those who design foods and drugs. The concentration of—and competition among—these economic giants, and the prospects for super-profits, has set off an unprecedented effort to privatize the genetic sequences of the active chemical substances found in live organisms.

The huge biotech transnationals—the so-called "gene giants"—seek to control the codes of chemical and biological substances (as "intellectual property") to guarantee their monopoly in agricultural production and in food and medicine. The design of patented, "improved" foods with exclusive rights allows them to monopolize markets for seeds and other products, while the patent system for medicines facilitates the monopoly of the chemical base of health care processes.

In the search for nature's winning formulas, transnational corporations have entered an entirely new area for exploitation: biodiversity. In 1998, ten of the thirty most popular medicines were derived from natural substances, and forty-five percent of the global market was directly based on biological products and processes.[6] In addition, many seeds have been developed using genetic material derived from native plant varieties *in situ* or in germplasm banks elsewhere.

In this context biodiversity, especially in the countries of the South, has become the new sphere of research and prospecting for the development of biotechnological products.[7] It is estimated that the biological riches of the world's meridional zone contribute tens of billions of dollars a year to the pharmaceutical industry in the North. In 1980, the U.S. pharmaceutical industry had no budget for biotechnological plant research. By the mid-1980s, pharmaceutical industry analysts were warning that each medicinal plant from tropical forests that becomes extinct represents a potential loss of more than $200 million.[8] Currently, 1,300 research companies, seventy-five percent of which have their headquarters in the United States, search the world over for plant- and animal-based compounds with medicinal properties.[9]

For the U.S. pharmaceutical industry alone, the value of these natural products for research (either as samples or extracts of biological materials) was estimated at $68 million for 1997.[10] The stock market value of the biotechnology industry as a whole rose from $97 billion in 1998, to $350 billion in 2000. These figures are astonishing for an industry that to date is primarily speculative. Most of biotechnology companies' resources are generated through a combination of venture capital, government subsidies, and stock appreciation, even though many have yet to sell a single product. Nonetheless, biotechnology is a huge and growing business, and it is easy to see why these prospectors for "green gold" are so interested in areas of megadiversity like Mexico.[11]

In the 1990s the technological revolution, led by biotechnology, engineering—materials as well as genetics—and geographic information systems, transformed biological wealth into an extraordinary strategic resource. The regions of the world with the greatest biodiversity, already important because of the global environmental crisis, acquired further economic and geo-political significance as strategic gene reserves for those who control the new engineering of plant and animal life.

The Convention on Biodiversity
and Bioprospecting Contracts

Because of the increasing technological sophistication of genetic engineering and the growing number of companies interested in bioprospecting, as well as pressure from civil sectors concerned about the plunder of biological resources, government representatives from all over the world met in 1992, in Rio de Janeiro to establish norms that would protect biodiversity globally and regulate the flow of transnational capital dedicated to exploiting these resources. The result of the meeting is the Convention on Biodiversity (CBD), under which the first national standards for bioprospecting and conservation were established.

The agreement represents a paradigm shift in biodiversity management, in two senses. First, by establishing criteria for the extraction of genetic and biological resources, the agreement obligates companies and bioprospecting institutions to comply with certain requirements for consultation and distribution; at the same time, the treaty gives approval for such activities to go on. Second, the agreement requires companies and international environmental organizations to recognize the sovereignty of governments over their biological resources. The result was, in the words of the international organization Genetic Resources Action International (GRAIN), that "overnight, national sovereignty over biodiversity replaced the previous concept of 'common patrimony of humanity.'"[12] Both changes have major implications for the local, national, and global treatment of biodiversity.

The new paradigm established by the CBD revolves around the distribution of benefits that transnational corporations offer directly to indigenous communities or to the national institutions that offer biological resources and traditional knowledge on behalf of these communities. The means for establishing the terms of the exchange is the bilateral contract.[13] The contract is typically based in complex formulas that include the establishment of set fees or royalty rates (in general, extremely low), or on the hiring of employees from the communities themselves for the bioprospecting work. Contracts often include promises of employee training, research projects, the purchase of relatively sophisticated equipment for the prospecting work, and other types of institutional support. What they do not concede or share is the intellectual property of the species collected.

Soon after the Rio Summit, the first contract was signed in Costa Rica between a transnational corporation (Merck) and a group representing itself as the local managers of biological resources (Institute of Biodiversity, or

InBio).[14] The one-million-dollar contract, which allowed for the collection of species throughout the country, has become the model for the new bioprospecting industry. To date, InBio has yet to receive any benefits because the products have yet to be developed for the market.[15]

During the 1990s, this new form of resource extraction from Southern countries and indigenous communities became more prevalent, as the CBD did not take effect until 1994, and the new standards it established were very slow to be applied to bioprospecting projects. As the model has expanded throughout the world, research institutions (universities, botanical gardens, seed banks, etc.) as well as nongovernmental organizations have sought to gain short-term benefits based on the potential profits of bioprospecting contracts.

How does bioprospecting work? The first step is the meticulous extraction of the collective knowledge inscribed in the memory of community members, in the language or other types of symbols present in the culture of indigenous peoples. This knowledge saves corporations millions of dollars if they can focus their prospecting on plants used in traditional medicines and foods, testing and evaluating the key chemical substances contained within them.[16]

By understanding the key relationships between cultural and biological diversity, bioprospectors are able to exploit traditional knowledge. For example, endemic species are identified by detecting linguistic variations that are equally endemic. Information is gathered from healers or women and children through the reconstruction not only of discursive memory but also of olfactory, visual, or geographic memory. Samples are generally collected based on healers' precise geographic and seasonal knowledge. Bioprospectors will also take full advantage of existing scientific networks, research centers, and gene banks, and often facilitate the creation of new ones.

The typical mode of operation is to form a local partnership with an indigenous group, which shares its knowledge of medicines and foods and directly assists in collecting samples. In exchange, a modest payment is offered or future compensation is promised. In some cases, the offer consists of ownership of patents that the recipients themselves can license to third parties.[17]

The method of extraction is not significantly affected by the presence or absence of a contract, and neither is the transaction's net effect: biological resources are transferred from a system of collective ownership and use to one of private property. For this reason many environmentalists, indigenous organizations, and researchers insist that bioprospecting is, in effect, a form of biopiracy. The benefits-sharing provisions in bioprospecting contracts seek to eliminate the unlawful forms of biopiracy without questioning the underlying system of intellectual property rights. Vandana Shiva, a recognized leader of movements against biopiracy both in her native India and worldwide, defines the benefits-distribution system as "a crumb-sharing model established to hide the theft of the loaf."[18]

Four Bioprospecting Contracts in Mexico

Bioprospecting contracts are not made public in any part of the world, and in Mexico the directly affected populations usually do not know of their existence. Four of these contracts, however, have recently come to light. They form the tip of a large iceberg:

- the contract between Diversa and the National Autonomous University of Mexico (UNAM);
- the contract involving the Organization of Traditional Indigenous Doctors of Los Altos de Chiapas (Omietch), the Colegio de la Frontera Sur, the University of Georgia, and Molecular Nature Limited;
- the contract involving the Sandoz Corporation and the Association of Zapotec and Chinantec Forest Communities (Uzachi);
- the contract involving American Cyanimid and American Home Products, the University of Arizona, and the Botanical Gardens of the Biology Institute and the Department of Chemistry of the UNAM.

These cases show some of the ways bioprospecting contracts can be carried out, ranging from high-level agreements between a transnational corporation and a government institution that bypasses the local population, as seen in the UNAM-Diversa contract, to agreements that include a part of the affected population, as with the Uzachi case. All these contracts have elicited protests from civil society and resistance movements against the privatization of biodiversity, including a national call for a moratorium on bioprospecting contracts.

The UNAM–Diversa Contract

The contract between the UNAM and the biotechnology corporation Diversa, with headquarters in San Diego, California, authorized the extraction of extremophile bacteria that endure extremes of temperature, salinity, sulfur, and pressure in all of the country's Protected Natural Areas. The contract was formalized in November 1998, with the active intervention of Mexico's National Commission for Knowledge and Use of Biodiversity (Conabio).

In the three-year contract, UNAM agreed to collect samples, send them to Diversa, and provide Diversa a list of every sample collected. For its part, Diversa agreed to pay fifty dollars per sample and, at the end of the contract, turn the technology used in the project—with an estimated value of $5,000—over to UNAM to establish a Center for Microbial Diversity. Furthermore, Diversa agreed to give UNAM a percentage of the royalties on net sales (0.3–0.5%) if it develops a product based on the samples. These revenues would be transferred to a trust called the Fund for Biodiversity, under the auspices of the National Ecology Institute (INE).

Diversa is a U.S. corporation that develops biotechnology products for the agricultural, pharmaceutical, chemical, and industrial markets[19] and presents itself as a scientific research organization to public institutions in countries known to contain significant biological wealth. However, due to its commercial nature, Diversa's structure is very attractive to large transnational corporations. Among its strategic partners are Novartis, Aventis, Danisco, Celanese Limited, Celera Genomics, Glaxo-Smith Kline, Invitrogen Corporation, and Syngenta Agribusiness Biotechnology Research, Inc. Diversa has joint venture projects with Dow Chemical Company (Innovase LLC) and Syngenta Seeds AG (Zymetrics, Inc.). It has fifty-two patents, with more than 200 pending.[20] The company has contracts similar to the UNAM contracts for collecting samples in Yellowstone National Park[21] as well as in Alaska, and in Russia, South Africa, Indonesia, Bermuda, and Costa Rica.

In the case of prospecting for extremophile bacteria in Mexico, groups have protested that the contract represents an unconstitutional transfer of property rights from the genetic patrimony of Mexico's Protected Natural Areas. It surrenders national sovereignty over part of the country's strategic resources to an important transnational corporation that specializes in the commercial exploitation of extremophile enzymes.[22] Ceding the rights to these materials will have profound implications for Mexico's long-term development.

Another problem with the contract is that it left very unclear the role that indigenous and peasant communities play when samples are collected in their territories. The local populations knew nothing about the bioprospecting contracts. Similarly, the criteria that determine the terms of the exchange, such as how the price per sample or the percentage of royalties was determined, were not made explicit. The total amount of money offered by Diversa in this contract was also very low.[23] By comparison, Diversa's comparable project in Yellowstone National Park provides much more favorable terms.

The contract became a public controversy when, in 1999, researcher Alejandro Nadal made the deal public in the Mexican City daily newspaper *La Jornada*,[24] claiming that the people living in the biosphere reserves where the sample gathering took place were not informed. He also questioned the legality of the university bestowing upon itself the power to trade a strategic good owned by the nation, as well as the limited rewards promised in exchange.

As a result of Nadal's efforts, a wide and impressive range of organizations came together to demand that the agreement be nullified, among them the National Association of Democratic Lawyers (ANAD), the Environmental Studies Group (GEA), the National Union of Autonomous Regional Peasant Organizations (UNORCA), the National Association of Commercializing Enterprises (ANEC), the Network of Mexican Permaculture, the Research Center for Change in Rural Mexico (CECCAM), the Citizens Council for the Defense of Cultural and Natural Patrimony, Greenpeace, and various academics. They also demanded that INE intervene to stop similar agreements from being carried out until adequate legislation was in place. On June 8, 2000, many of these same organizations filed suit with the Federal Environmental Protection Commission (Profepa).[25]

The management of Profepa, under the administration of President Ernesto Zedillo (1994–2000) recognized, as the last act of the Zedillo government, that the contract was illegal. In effect, the Mexican government admitted that the consultation with affected communities required by the CBD never took place. INE says (using ambiguous language) it will respect the judgment. UNAM, for its part, has not commented on the matter, though it is developing a new contract with the same corporation.

The Omietch–Colegio de la Frontera Sur–
University of Georgia–Molecular Nature Limited Contract

The second contract presented here involves the Organization of Traditional Indigenous Doctors of Los Altos de Chiapas (Omietch), the Colegio de la Frontera Sur (ECOSUR), the University of Georgia, and Molecular Nature Limited. This contract entails the collection of thousands of varieties of medicinal plants to be tested for commercially exploitable active compounds. In this case, the foreign institutions attempted to get the consent and participation of the indigenous communities of Los Altos in order to carry out the project. The contract has been suspended, however, due to complaints about lack of information and transparency, and deeper concerns over the propriety of privatizing these resources.

The researchers at the University of Georgia belong to the International Collaborative Biodiversity Group (ICBG), a consortium of U.S. government agencies formed to coordinate the global search for new medicines in strategic biodiversity areas.[26] ICBG makes grants to public and private research institutions in the United States which serve as project coordinators; these, in turn, make grants to partner institutions in host countries.[27]

The Omietch–University of Georgia–Molecular Nature Limited project, known as ICBG-Maya, follows the model established by the CBD, InBio, and the very same ICBG. Omietch gives its permission to carry out the bioprospecting in its territories. The Mexican national institution in charge of supervising the sample collection is ECOSUR. The ICBG researchers are from the University of Georgia, and the interested corporation is Molecular Nature Limited (MNL), a Welsh biotechnology company. The plant samples are first delivered to the University of Georgia's botanical gardens for study. Later they are transferred to MNL for analysis of the chemical components responsible for the plants' medicinal properties.

Omietch is part of a larger federation of eleven indigenous organizations, the Council of Traditional Indigenous Doctors and Midwives of Chiapas (Compitch), with representation from the principal Mayan peoples of Chiapas (Tzeltales, Tzotziles, Tojolabales, Choles, and Zoques). The Council, headquartered in the city of San Cristóbal de las Casas, promotes the use, exchange, and development of all types of traditional medical knowledge. With the intention of expanding and advancing the project, the ICBG researchers invited Compitch to participate in the medicinal plant identification program.

At the beginning, Compitch saw the invitation as a chance to obtain a source of income for the communities. Nonetheless, in accordance with its traditional practices of community consultation and decision-making (*usos y costumbres*), it requested more background information for community discussion about the project's merits. In fact Compitch proposed that the project not begin until this information was released and discussed.

The project, however, began before consultation with the indigenous communities was completed. Plant samples already collected were processed, and new samples were clandestinely gathered and sent to Georgia. Botanical gardens were also established in some communities in Los Altos that were not a part of Compitch and not part of the agreement. ICBG initiated these activities without regard for Compitch's request for time to consult with the communities.

When Compitch became aware of the project's unapproved progress, it raised the issues in the national and international press. Only then did project coordinators begin to deliver partial information. Federal environmental officials from Semarnap (Secretariat of Environment, Natural Resources, and Fishing) began to play a role in the affair, counseling Compitch to move quickly to begin a phase of negotiations. Compitch agreed, but after a few meetings the group suspended talks because it felt the negotiation process did not respect its traditional forms of self-governance. More fundamentally, Compitch believed that bioprospecting as a whole deserved a more profound discussion within indigenous communities in Chiapas and in the entire country.

Meanwhile, Semarnap pushed forward in the effort to create a framework for new national norms for bioprospecting contracts within indigenous regions. For its part, Compitch declared that it would not be used as an "Indian guinea pig" and vowed not to continue with the project. It viewed Semarnap's attempt to devise a national regulatory framework as flawed given the absence of relevant legislation, a legal vacuum that even Semarnap acknowledged.[28]

Compitch's refusal to act under pressure, at a time when the discussion was heating up in the media, allowed time for the discovery that ICBG-Maya had already extracted 6,000 plant samples from Chiapas. The negative publicity obliged ICBG-Maya researchers to announce that they would not carry out the analysis of active compounds on the samples, the so-called bio-assays. These tests were going to be conducted by MNL and the University of Georgia even though the official permits for the samples specified they were for "scientific collection" by ECOSUR, not for bio-assays or commercial ends of any kind. Amid the controversy, on September 25, 2000, Compitch received a letter from Semarnap stating that it had denied ICBG-Maya the permit to collect samples for biotechnological uses.

These problems prompted Compitch to ask that the project be suspended, and to join the call for an active moratorium on all national bioprospecting projects, consistent with the lawsuit over the UNAM-Diversa contract.

The ICBG-Maya project was suspended, but it was not dead. After sharp accusations that Compitch was trying to sabotage the project, ECOSUR stated in December 2000, that it would not continue its bioprospecting activities until it found "valid interlocutors" among the indigenous communities. Only in November 2001, was the contract formally suspended, and Compitch declared a moratorium on bioprospecting in its territories.

Compitch is still working to open a broader debate about bioprospecting in its territories. It is offering workshops and conferences in all the indigenous zones that were part of the ICBG-Maya plan. These events are being carried out by a network of healers, midwives, and community representatives who lead all aspects of the discussion—from the general problems with bioprospecting to the details of Compitch's negotiations with the institutions, universities, and federal environmental authorities—even in some of the most remote villages in its area of operation.

The Uzachi–Sandoz Contract

The third contract—concluded in 2000—was signed between the Swiss pharmaceutical giant Sandoz (later known as Novartis and now as Syngenta after mergers and other changes in its corporate structure) and the Association of Zapotec and Chinantec Forest Communities of the Sierra Juárez of Oaxaca (Uzachi). In the two years of the contract, thousands of microbial samples were extracted from Oaxaca's northern mountains for studies of their medicinal potential.

As with other bioprospecting contracts, the specific clauses of the Uzachi–Sandoz contract are confidential. However, according to Francisco Chapela, of Rural Studies and Peasant Support (ERA), a nongovernmental organization that advised Uzachi during contract negotiations, the communities put several conditions on their participation: that their own Uzachi technicians carry out the fieldwork; that the collaboration not involve traditional indigenous knowledge; that Sandoz pay for the installation of a laboratory that would become the property of Uzachi at the end of the contract; that Sandoz provide training to Uzachi technicians; that Sandoz pay a fixed annual fee and another payment based on productivity; and finally, that if a compound of pharmaceutical interest was discovered, Sandoz make to Uzachi "a payment that would be sufficient to establish a patrimonial fund large enough to keep its team of technicians operating in perpetuity."[29] For its part, Sandoz stipulated that it have exclusive use of information generated by the project for a period of two years, receive at least 2,000 samples a year, and that confidentiality be maintained by both parties. The extraction of samples began in 1999; it is estimated that more than 10,000 samples were sent to Switzerland.[30]

Uzachi is an association of four Zapotec and Chinantec communities formed at the end of the 1980s.[31] From its inception it has received technical assistance and training in the use of natural resources from ERA. After a study of biodiversity management schemes carried out by ERA between 1990 and 1992, Uzachi decided to allow bioprospecting in its forest areas, as "a way in which the communities could receive the greatest possible benefit from its biological diversity."[32]

Sandoz-Novartis-Syngenta, as its name changes suggest, is a transnational corporation on the forefront of the fusion of the pharmaceutical, biotech, and agricultural industries. With sales of more than $34 billion in 2000, it ranks at the top of the list of "gene giants."[33]

Due primarily to ERA's position, which strongly favors bioprospecting, the Uzachi–Sandoz contract has become very controversial. It has received a great deal of attention on a new Internet site on the topic[34] and the debate has also received extensive coverage in the Oaxacan and national press. In the region itself, two meetings were organized by the Zapotec Union of Organizations of the Sierra Juárez of Oaxaca (UNOSJO) in Guelatao to provide information and forums for discussion. The meetings brought together diverse sectors of society: municipal presidents, *ejido* authorities, other organizations from around the country that had experienced similar problems (among them Compitch and Tohono Odhom of Sonora and Arizona) as well as specialists on the subject. Both meetings were transmitted live by the regional community radio station.

The organizers of these meetings aimed to achieve a broader and deeper understanding of current bioprospecting programs and biopiracy activities around the world, and what these mean for the future of indigenous peoples. The discussions, open to all participants, were intense, due in part to the attention that this contract had received as a model for "equitable bioprospecting" that could be applied in other indigenous communities in Mexico.[35]

The debate revolves around two opposing positions. On one side, the Uzachi–Sandoz contract, with its distribution of benefits, is seen as a legitimate solution to the problems of poverty in the communities. In contrast, critics of the contract question the model in which an organized indigenous community sells samples to a transnational corporation in return for a share of benefits, regardless of whether or not this particular exchange is just and fair. These critics point to the lack consultation with other communities in the same region as well as with national groups. Aldo González, municipal president of Guelatao, has voiced this position: "The four communities that make up Uzachi are not the only ones in which these types of [biological] organisms are found. There are outlying communities that share the same climate and the same biodiversity, but because they do not belong to Uzachi, they do not receive the royalties that were agreed upon with Sandoz. This contract has left the communities in confrontation."[36]

The Uzachi–Sandoz contract expired in 2000. However, the debate ranges on about the complex consequences such a contract has for the indigenous communities.

UNAM–Botanical Gardens, American Cyanamid-American Home Products, and the University of Arizona/ICBG Contract

The fourth contract is between the transnational pharmaceutical corporation American Home Products and its subsidiary American Cyanamid, the University of Arizona, the UNAM Department of Chemistry, and the Botanical Gardens of the Institute of Biology. This contract, which is still in force, covers the collection of cacti, xerophytes, and other plants from deserts all over Mexico. The research on the samples will determine the key chemical substances that enable these plants to survive harsh desert conditions.

Although this is the oldest of the four contracts, the dealings between UNAM and the pharmaceutical company remain the least known and have generated the least overt opposition. We do know, however, that this contract follows the ICBG model. The University of Arizona, in fact, is part of ICBG. From what is known, the indigenous communities living in the areas where the sample collection is taking place did not participate in the contract, and there is no evidence that they were consulted at any time. As with the UNAM–Diversa contract, the Mexican national partner is UNAM. American Home Products (AHP), with headquarters in New Jersey, is one of the largest pharmaceutical companies in the world, with sales of $13.3 million in 2000. AHP has developed an aggressive biotechnology strategy, dedicating an annual budget of $2 billion to biotech research and development.

There have been many requests for information, based on the fact that UNAM is a public institution, but they have received no response. Currently, the Mexican Society of Ethnobiology is collecting signatures to stop the project.[37]

The Moratorium Campaign

The public controversies about these contracts have generated a broad movement to suspend existing bioprospecting contracts and establish an active moratorium against future contracts until the legal and policy issues are clarified.

On September 14–15, 2000, the Research Center for Change in Rural Mexico (CECCAM), the Rural Advancement Foundation International (RAFI), and the Center for Social Information Analysis and Popular Education organized a seminar in Mexico City entitled Biopiracy or Bioprospecting? Biodiversity and Indigenous and Peasant Rights. The event proved critical to mobilizing opposition to bioprospecting contracts. The seminar was very well attended, bringing together civil society organizations (indigenous, peasant, environmental, and nongovernmental organizations from all over Mexico), academics (university students, professors, biologists, sociologists, economists, and chemists), and experts on rural issues, economics, and biodiversity. Highlighting the seminar were testimonies about struggles with and resistance to biopiracy/bioprospecting and proposals to organize an independent strategy to address the problem.

The seminar took up a number of critical themes:

- The current context in which bioprospecting is taking place: indigenous communities and the privatization of biodiversity in the Protected Natural Areas and the Mesoamerican Biological Corridor.
- The characterization of bioprospecting itself: What ethical issues does biopiracy present for scientists? Who decides what to do with genes? Who decides who owns genetic material? How can discussions about biopiracy be democratized? How can scientific progress continue if bioprospecting is stopped?
- The consequences of patenting living beings for communities, the country, and humanity in general: What are the links between the privatization of genetic and chemical codes and the privatization of Protected Natural Areas? What are the social, economic, and political effects of these processes over the long term?

Participants also discussed the increasing popular resistance to biopiracy throughout the world and how this resistance is being organized in Ecuador and Brazil, among other countries. What are the relationships between this struggle and other social movements, such as the opposition to transgenic products and the fight for the defense of indigenous rights?

The seminar provided a deeper understanding that Mexico—as one of most important centers of natural, cultural, and agricultural diversity—is among the countries most besieged by transnational biotechnology companies in search of genetic resources and the traditional knowledge associated with these resources. The gathering also clarified that bioprospecting activity to date has been carried out in a legal and political vacuum.

In spite of the diverse viewpoints at the seminar, participants agreed on a campaign to demand a moratorium on all bioprospecting contracts under development in Mexico, at least until information about potential projects is freely available and there is broader national consensus exists about the best way to use these biological and cultural resources. The call for an active moratorium has three main components:

1. A worldwide moratorium on current or proposed bioprospecting projects, agreements, or contracts until the parties involved provide sufficient information about the projects in a timely manner to the population—especially indigenous communities and peasant organizations—and there is an open public debate about biosprospecting and the scope of biotechnology that allows a realistic assessment of the consequences of accepting or rejecting the project in question. Participants also demanded that all patents of living beings or their components, at any level of life on the planet, be revoked, and that no new patent of living beings or their components be granted.
2. A timely, serious, truthful, and egalitarian debate at the national and international levels regarding these matters.
3. The fulfillment of the San Andrés Accords on indigenous rights and culture, which were the expression of an inclusive dialogue and effective participation, and based on Convention 169 of the International Labor Organization. This statement is directed in particular to the Mexican government.[38]

More than one hundred organizations, nongovernmental organizations, and individuals signed the document. It was not formally presented to government officials, but the Mexican government has made its opposition clear, arguing for better regulation of bioprospecting rather than a halt to such activities.[39]

According to its backers, the moratorium strategy for protecting biological wealth goes hand-in-hand with the defense of indigenous and peasant rights. They argue that the goal is to protect not just natural resources, but also the right to land, culture, and knowledge for those who have nurtured and conserved these resources for thousands of years. They also see it as a means of recovering local knowledge about biodiversity, to prevent it from becoming private property. Similarly, they emphasize that the opposition to bioprospecting is a central part of the national struggle against the privatization of the nation's strategic resources.[40]

The moratorium is more than just a petition campaign. It also involves exchanging information among concerned groups and individuals, studying and discussing the phenomenon, disseminating findings among affected communities and organizations, and creating educational materials such as pamphlets, posters, and videos. The campaign also promotes creating networks to monitor bioprospecting and biopiracy activities, participation in international initiatives against biopiracy (events, publications, Web pages), and even the possibility of organizing international days for the free exchange of genetic resources, without patents, in order to break the patterns established by the market.

Government Complicity

The strategy of the probusiness government of President Vicente Fox in the management of natural resources is to open the biodiversity market and attract foreign investment.[41] Expressed in its clearest form in the government's Plan Puebla-Panamá, the proposed megadevelopment project for southern Mexico, this approach requires two preconditions. The first is the denial of basic indigenous rights, something the government already achieved with its May 28, 2001, approval of an indigenous rights law that neither guarantees fundamental indigenous rights nor complies with Convention 169 of the International Labor Organization. This leaves Mexico's indigenous peoples with no legal basis to defend their collective rights and self-determination.[42] Without basic rights pertaining to land and territory, natural resources, culture, and the forms of autonomous decision-making, a corporation or university can negotiate a contract with an isolated community without having to deal with a consensus by a larger body or an intercommunity consultation.

The second condition, complementing the limitations on indigenous rights, is the gradual privatization of the Protected Natural Areas. The environmental law sent to Congress in 2001, seeks to transfer Protected Natural Areas to the states and nongovernmental organizations associated with corporations such as Ford, Bimbo, AHMSA, Nestlé, and Pemex. Federal budget problems are cited as the rationale for the law.[43] The Fox administration expects that by the end of its term in 2006, one-third of the Protected Natural Areas' budget will be covered by sources other than the federal government.[44] Greenpeace-Mexico is opposed to this plan, warning that management by nongovernment organizations with private funds could "greenwash" the business sector's attempt to use the Protected Natural Areas for its own benefit. In the absence of clear laws regarding the use of biodiversity, greater participation by corporate interests could lead to perfectly legal contracts that allow the massive exploitation of genetic resources.[45] Both the Plan Puebla-Panamá and the Mesoamerican Biological Corridor promote privatization of protected areas under the guise of conservation.[46]

There is evidence that the Fox administration, along with the Congressional majority from Fox's National Action Party and the Institutional Revolutionary Party, will introduce legislation that would allow access to genetic resources and provide a legal framework that favors bioprospecting operations.[47] Semarnat will hold a series of public hearings as a first step in elaborating new laws. In the meantime, organizations such as UNOSJO and Compitch are carrying out independent hearings of their own. Their past experiences with Semarnat have left them wary, as they have seen government hearings used as little more than a pretense to legitimize decisions that have already been made.

In the last year, many Mexican organizations have realized that bioprospecting affects them directly. At the Third National Indigenous Congress, which met in Nurío, Michoacán, to debate the future of indigenous rights as a part of the Zapatista Caravan to Mexico City, the closing statement was clear: "We demand a moratorium on all prospecting (exploration) for biodiversity (biological resources), mining, water, etc., and on all biopiracy activities that are being carried out in our territories and in our country, until indigenous peoples have discussed in their own time and conditions the issues related to the control of their resources."[48]

Bioprospecting contracts were also discussed in a May 2001 conference in Tapachula, Chiapas, that called for the disclosure of information about the Plan Puebla-Panamá.[49] These meetings were attended by a wide range of Mexican and Central American organizations. Attendees representing indigenous peoples, peasant organizations, and nongovernmental organizations voiced support for a moratorium. Meetings such as these could make it possible to build a regional alliance against biopiracy, while strengthening resistance through the sharing of experiences and educational linkages.

Conclusion

The four cases presented here and the public debate on the subject suggest some conclusions about the consequences of these contracts for indigenous peoples and peasant communities, as well as for Mexican national sovereignty. There are four problematic areas:

1. *The privatization of life and the commodification of biodiversity.* Bioprospecting transforms biological and cultural diversity zones into private property. The main signs of this transformation are the identification and patenting of life forms and the expulsion of indigenous peoples who live in these areas. By allowing collective ownership of living things and knowledge to be made into marketable goods, biological and cultural wealth becomes part of the private monopoly of transnational corporations. This happens thorough a process in which live organisms and knowledge—after being submitted to scientific investigation of its cultural uses, geographic distribution, and the chemical or genetic components—end up being treated as the inventions of the transnational corporations. The companies then patent this invention, giving them the exclusive right to profit from the sale of the resulting products.[50]

2. *Intercommunity conflicts.* The exploitation of biological resources involves indigenous communities in the sale of their ecosystems and age-old knowledge. These resources had never before been considered as property, much less the sole property of any single community. Communities are placed in competition with one other, destroying the complex fabric of collective ties that still exist in many regions of Mexico, and threatening the survival of the very cultures responsible for the care and development of biodiversity. Because the contracts are offered to extremely poor communities, the benefits, however meager, can seem attractive. Once the word spreads in a region that collective goods are being sold to transnational corporations, conflicts arise within the communities themselves, between communities in a region, or between contracting communities and the interests of national sovereignty. In the case of the contracts with Uzachi, in Oaxaca, and to a lesser extent in Chiapas, the divisions between communities are already evident.

3. *Loss of agricultural biodiversity.* Many native varieties of domesticated food plants in Mexico are being lost, and the activities of transnational corporations reduce the chances that these goods will remain an important part of the country's biological wealth. The practice of saving and sharing seeds is becoming less common, which has a strong impact on the rural economy and on the evolution of varieties adapted to specific ecosystems. The agricultural

products of biotechnology such as transgenic seeds contaminate native varieties, decreasing the diversity so carefully conserved over the centuries.

4. *Threats to the scientific research process and the free flow of knowledge.* In the process of converting biodiversity into intellectual property rights, indigenous and peasant communities, as well as research institutions in Southern countries, are incorporated into the technical and commercial logic of globalization. In this way, the biosprospecting contracts foster the destruction of prevailing ethics regarding the free flow of agricultural and medicinal knowledge among indigenous and peasant communities. Because patented materials cannot be used in research without permission and the payment of royalties, public research directed toward humanitarian ends is severely curtailed.

There is an enormous knowledge gap about the privatization of biological wealth and its importance as a strategic resource. A new dialogue on these issues is urgently needed among those interested in national development, however divergent their points of view. Research and discussion must be deepened in several areas:

- the implications of bioprospecting projects and exportation of genetic samples that lead to the expropriation of biodiversity and the patenting of life forms;
- the power and scope of the transnational corporations that monopolize these resources;
- the role of Mexican public institutions involved in bioprospecting activities;
- the exploration of legal mechanisms for the collective patenting of Mexico's biological wealth, as well as alternative mechanisms.

One of the most important challenges is to direct scientific investigation to advance human capabilities without promoting the expropriation and privatization of natural resources and community knowledge by transnational corporations. Similarly, the challenge is to create a national scientific research program that permits Mexico's natural resources to be used for the common good. Mexico would also benefit from the institutional recognition of traditional healers and progress toward their independent economic organization.

The management of biodiversity is inextricably related to indigenous and peasant rights. Traditional farmers' access to seeds, knowledge about traditional medicine, and biodiversity itself should be the focus of the debate, with the objective of maintaining or restoring free access to biological wealth.

The proposal for an immediate moratorium on bioprospecting in Mexico is part of a global effort to oppose the patenting of life forms. This is the only way scientific investigation of life forms and traditional knowledge can be prevented from becoming a new mechanism to control humanity and an unprecedented threat to the environment. Such wealth should remain public and collective, for the benefit of indigenous peoples and everyone else who needs it. With free access to all genetic resources, without privatization or patents, no one will be able to earn a profit from such wealth.

Notes

This chapter is in part based on the article "La punta del iceberg," which colleagues Rolando Espinosa, Gonzalo Flores, Alaín Ramos, Silvia Ribeiro and I wrote for the Rural Advancement Foundation International (RAFI), recently renamed the ETC Group (Action Group on Erosion, Technology, and Concentration, www.etc.org). Other ideas found here are due to the excellent research posted regularly to the RAFI web site (www.rafi.org), but above all to the teaching and discussion generously offered to me by Silvia Ribeiro.

1. Víctor Manuel Toledo, *La Paz en Chiapas. Ecología, lucha indígena y modernidad alternativa* (Mexico City: Instituto de Ecología-UNAM/Ediciones Quinto Sol, 2000).

2. Salvador Arias Montes, "Distribución general," in *Suculentas mexicanas Cactáceas* (Mexico City: Conabio, Semarnap y Profepa, 1997), 22.

3. There is a debate about the number of indigenous groups that existed at the time of the Spanish conquest. Some speak of 182, others of 147, and still others of 113. In any case, researchers recognize that in the colonial period and later during the first independent governments, the Spanish and *mestizo* population was responsible for the obliteration of more than half of the original peoples. Bárbara Cifuentes, *Letras sobre Voces, Multilingüismo a través de la Historia* (Mexico City: CIESAS/INI, 1998).

4. The best way of distinguishing the cultural diversity in a country is through the diversity of its languages. Of the 102 million inhabitants of Mexico in 2002, approximately eight percent still speak an indigenous language (Instituto Lingüístico de Verano http://www.ethnologue.com). See also D. Harmon "The Status of the World's Languages." *Ethnologue: Southwest Journal of Linguistics* 14 (1996): 1–13.

5. For a study of the relationship between indigenous cultural diversity and biodiversity, see the Web site of the Indigenous Peoples Biodiversity Information Network: http://www.ibin.org. This relationship has been elaborated by Nietshmann in his study of the connections among cultural, linguistic, and environmental variety. See B.Q. Nietshmann "The Interdependence of Biological and

Cultural Diversity." *Occasional Paper* #21, Center for World Indigenous Studies, December 1992. Luisa Maffa synthesizes the relationship between linguistics and cultural and biological diversity. See Luisa Maffi *Terralingua: Partnerships for Linguistic and Biological Diversity,* available at http://cougar.ucdavis.edu/nas/terralin/home.html. See also "Linguistic Diversity." In *Cultural and Spiritual Values of Biodiversity: A Complementary Contribution to the Global Biodiversity Assessment,* ed. Darrell Addison Posey (London: United Nations Environment Program, Intermediate Technology Publications), 2000: 21–57.

6. Hope Shand, "Gene Giants: Understanding the Life Industry," in *Redesigning Life? The Worldwide Challenge to Genetic Engineering,* ed. Brian Tokar (London: Zed Books, 2001), 225.

7. Latin America is the region of the world with the greatest presence of these transnational corporations and organizations, including American Cyanamid (USA), Bristol Meyers (USA), Caopi Associates (USA), Ethno Medicine Preservation Project (Peru), Foundation for Ethnobiology (UK), Glaxo Group (USA), InBio (Costa Rica), International Plant Medicine Corp. (USA), International Organization for Chemical Sciences in Development (Belgium), Inverni della Beffa (Italy), Ix Chell Tropical Research Project (Belize), JICA (Japan), Knowledge Recovery Foundation International (USA), Maxus Ecuador (USA-Argentina), Merck and Co. (USA), Monsanto Co. (USA), Pfizer Inc. (USA), Pharmaco Genetics (USA), Pitón Catalytic Inc. (USA), Phyto Pharmaceuticals Corp. (USA), Pulsar/Savia (Mexico), Research Corporation Technologies (USA), Shaman Pharmaceuticals (USA), Syngenta (previously known as Novartis and Ciba-Geigy), Rhone-Poulenc Rhoer (France), Smithkline Beecham (USA), Upjohn Co. (USA), and Xenova Ltd. (USA).

8. "Medicinal Plants Lost?" *Scrip-World Pharmaceutical News,* October 1, 1986, 22. Ironically, of course, the new interest in biological wealth and indigenous knowledge on which much of it is based is one of the reasons many species, their genetic material, the ecosystems of which they form a part, and the cultures that have learned to manage them are rapidly disappearing. See also E.S. Hunn "What is Traditional Ecological Knowledge?" In *Traditional Ecological Knowledge: Wisdom for Sustainable Development,* ed. N. Williams and G. Baines. (Canberra: Center for Resource and Environmental Studies, ANU, 1993): 11–17. E.S. Hunn "Size as Limiting the Recognition fo Biodiversity in the Folk Biological Classifications. One of the Four Factors Governing the Cultural Recognition of Biological Taxa." In *Folk Biology,* edited by D.L. Medin and S. Atran (Cambridge, Mass.: MIT Press, 1999): 47–69. E.S. Hunn "Columbia Plateua Place Names: What Can They Teach Us?" *Journal of Linguistic Anthropology* 6, no. 1 (1996): 3–26. G.P. Nabhan "Discussion Paper for the Colloquium: Losing Species, Languages, and Stories: Linking Cultural and Environmental Change in the Bi-national Southwest," Arizona-Sonara Desert Museum, Tucson, AZ, April 1–3, 1996. G.P. Nabhan and J.L. Carr (eds.), *Ironwood: An Ecological and Cultural Keystone of the Sonoran Desert.* Washington, D.C.: Conservation International, 1994.

9. Brian Tokar (ed.) *Redesigning Life? The Worldwide Challenge to Genetic Engineering,* 9.

10. Hope Shand, *Human Nature: Agricultural Biodiversity and Farm-Based Food Security* (Rome: FAO, 1997), 13.

11. The typical pharmaceutical product takes, on average, ten years and an investment of $500 million before it can be brought to market. With bioprospecting, companies can save time and money by exploiting millenarian indigenous knowledge that has already identified regions, plants, and substances with medicinal and nutritive properties. Julie Dulude, "La floresta renace," *Latin Trade,* February 2001, 48.

12. Genetic Resources Action International (GRAIN), "Desenmascarando la quimera de la participación en beneficios," www.grain.org.

13. Genetic Resources Action International (GRAIN), "Desenmascarando la quimera de la participación en beneficios."

14. The contract between Merck and the nongovernmental organization Instituto de Biodiversidad de Costa Rica (InBio) was canceled in 1999, after Merck had in its possession more than 500,000 samples of species from Costa Rican forests. The contract specified that half of the royalties be divided between InBio and the government, for environmental protection. The InBio-Merck contract continues to be the preferred model of transnationals for the collection and delivery of large quantities of samples. "The universities have the biological knowledge, but that's not enough. People recognize that bioprospecting should be done InBio way." Sunil Kadam, of Eli Lily and Company, quoted in Dulude, "La floresta renace."

15. Dulude ("La floresta renace") reports, "The long wait and the relatively slow progress of InBio raise the question of whether it will accomplish one of its principal goals: saving the forests. By the time the royalties begin to flow, it's possible that the forests will have already disappeared."

16. For information on cases of biopiracy of traditional medicines, such as ayahuasca and tepescohuite, see Asha Sukhwani, *Patentes Naturistas* (Madrid: Oficina Española de Patentes y Marcas, Departamento de Patentes, 1995).

17. Sukhwani, *Patentes Naturistas.*

18. Vandana Shiva, "Biopiracy: The Theft of Knowledge and Resources," in *Redesigning Life? The Worldwide Challenge to Genetic Engineering,* 288.

19. To date, Diversa has commercialized only two products.

20. www.diversa.com.

21. The legality of this contract was disputed by the Edmonds Institute. The U.S. Supreme Court, however, ruled in favor of Diversa. The precedent is one of the most important for the industry.

22. Diversa describes itself as "the leader in the gene discovery industry" on its Web page www.diversa.com.

23. Matt Potter, "Drugs and Dollars," *The San Diego Reader,* October 7, 1999. Potter reports that Mexican bureaucrats also complained that Diversa was not paying enough for the microbes taken from Mexican locales.

24. *La Jornada,* March 11, 1999.

25. The coalition filing suit also points out that the UNAM–Diversa contract violated several existing Mexican laws. For example, Article 27 of the Mexican constitution states: "The land and waters within the limits of national territory is property of the Nation, which has had and continues to have the right to transmit the ownership of these to private parties, thus constituting private property [. . .]." "The Nation will have at all times the right to impose upon private property the modalities and the public interest dictate, such as regulation for social

benefit, the use of natural elements susceptible to appropriation, with the object of achieving an equitable distribution of wealth, conservation, the balanced development of the country, and improving the conditions of life for the rural and urban population." UNAM's signing of the contract, without due authority, also violated a clause in Article 87 of the *Ley General del Equilibrio Ecologico y la Proteccion al Ambiente (LGEEPA)* and Article 1801 of the Civil Code for the Federal District and Federal Territories.

26. ICBG includes six divisions of the National Institutes of Health (NIH) and the Foreign Agriculture Service of the U.S. Department of Agriculture. The six institutes of the NIH are Fogarty International Center, the National Cancer Institute, the National Institute of Allergy and Infectious Diseases, the National Institute of Mental Health, the National Institute on Drug Abuse, and the National Heart, Lung, and Blood Institute. Information about this program is available at http://www.nih.gov/fic/opportunities/icbg.htm.

27. The ICBG program has been criticized on two main points: 1) The contracts subsidize bioprospecting activities of transnational corporations with public funds; 2) They foster biopiracy in third countries through government coordination of these activities in order to place a significant portion of the productive and reproductive knowledge of the world's indigenous people in genetic information banks and U.S. patent offices. See Silvia Ribeiro, "Biopiratería: la privatización de los ámbitos de comunidad," in *De quién es la Naturaleza, conflictos sobre recursos genéticos en América Latina,* ed. Ulrich Brand (Frankfurt: University of Frankfurt, forthcoming).

28. "El Compitch denuncia biopiratería en Los Altos de Chiapas. Nuestros recursos, nuestro saber, inalienables" *Ojarasca,* supplement to *La Jornada,* August 14, 2000.

29. Francisco Chapela, "Aprovechar la farmacia-selva," *Masiosare,* supplement to *La Jornada,* October 1, 2000.

30. Francisco Chapela, "Aprovechar la farmacia-selva."

31. The four communities are La Trinidad, Capulalpam, Comaltepec, and Xiacuí.

32. Francisco Chapela, "Aprovechar la farmacia-selva."

33. Action Group on Erosion, Technology, and Concentration (formerly RAFI) Communiqué, July/August 2001, www.etcgroup.org.

34. Corsario is a site begun and maintained by the Research Center for Change in Rural Mexico (CECCAM). It has received more than 100 contributions since it first appeared last year.

35. For example, the World Bank is currently working on a project within the Mesoamerican Biological Corridor that treats bioprospecting as a local source of income. See the World Bank's Central America Environmental Projects web page at www.worldbank.org/ca-env.

36. Aldo González, "La guerra por los microorganismos," *Masiosare,* supplement to *La Jornada,* October 1, 2000.

37. "A los miembros de la Asociación Etnobiológica Mexicana, AC." Document presented in the auditorium of the Templo Mayor Museum, Historic Center of Mexico City, November 30, 2000.

38. Editors' note: The San Andrés Accords are a set of principles and actions on indigenous rights and culture agreed to by the Mexican government as part of

its peace process with the Zapatista National Liberation Army. The government never implemented the agreement, instead passing a set of constitutional reforms in 2001 that have been widely rejected by indigenous groups and Zapatista representatives. Convention 169 of the International Labor Organization affirms commitments to indigenous rights.

39. "Rechaza la Conabio moratoria a proyectos de bioprospección," *La Jornada,* October 13, 2000.

40. Andrés Barreda, "Biopiratería y Bioprospección," *Cuadernos Agrarios,* Mexico City: Nueva Época, no. 21, 2001.

41. Andrés Barreda, "Los peligros del Plan Puebla-Panamá," in *Mesoamerica, los ríos profundos: Alternativas Plebeyas al Plan Puebla-Panamá,* ed. Armando Bartra (Mexico City: Ediciones El Atajo, 2001).

42. This was good news for the defenders of bioprospecting contracts, since the National Indigenous Congress and other indigenous groups had taken positions in favor of the moratorium.

43. "Busca el gobierno transferir las áreas naturales protegidas a estados y ONG," *La Jornada,* November 12, 2001.

44. "Busca el gobierno transferir las áreas naturales protegidas a estados y ONG," *La Jornada.* The statement is attributed to Ernesto Enkerlin, director of the National Commission of Protected Natural Areas, of the Secretariat of Environment and Natural Resources. The program "Conservemos México" ("Let's conserve Mexico") involves the participation of forty-three corporations with a budget of about 30 million pesos (over $3 million).

45. The new head of the Protected National Areas commission, in his first statement to the press, spoke of "voluntary expropriations of valuable natural areas."

46. See Laura Carlsen, "El Corredor Biológico Mesoamericano: La nueva inserción de la biodiversidad en el mercado global," in *La Vida en Venta: Transgénicos, Patentes y Diversidad Biológica,* ed. Corinna Heineke (San Salvador, El Salvador: Ediciones Heinrich Boll, 2002.)

47. For example, the "Legal Initiative for Access and Use of Biological and Genetic Resources," presented by Senator Jorge Rubén Nordhausen González on April 26, 2001 in the Senate of the Republic of Mexico.

48. Declaración de Nurío, National Indigenous Congress, March 8, 2001.

49. In Tapachula, Chiapas, May 2001, organized by the Mexican Network for Action Against Free Trade (RMALC) and Centro de Investigaciones Económicas y Políticas de Acción Comunitaria (CIEPAC).

50. See Vandana Shiva, "Biopiracy: The Theft of Knowledge and Resources," in *Redesigning Life? The Worldwide Challenge to Genetic Engineering,* 285.

PART 2

THE CRISIS
IN THE COUNTRYSIDE:
SMALL PRODUCERS FIGHT BACK

7

Toward an Equitable, Inclusive, and Sustainable Agriculture: Mexico's Basic Grains Producers Unite

Olivia Acuña Rodarte

With all the changes [in the market], it was as though they sent us to war without any weapons, but the war taught us we had no other choice but to get organized.

—Manuel Morales, peasant farmer from the
state of Tamaulipas and president of ANEC

In Mexico, the production of basic grains is strategically important. One single product—corn—is the foundation of the national culture, the key component in the Mexican diet, and the principal source of livelihood for more than four million families.

The basic-grains sector is made up primarily of small- and medium-size producers with limited resources. They combine production for subsistence with the sale of what remains on the market. The smaller producers farm plots of less than five hectares, producing rain-fed crops using traditional production techniques. Medium-size farms are typically around ten hectares, are usually rain-fed, and use some modern inputs such as tractors and agrochemicals.[1] Grain production in Mexico is regionally distinct, with northern producers generally working larger irrigated farms while farmers in central and southern regions cultivate more traditional *milpas*—small plots of inter-cropped corn, beans, and other subsistence foods. Despite the lack of inputs, these smaller farms produce three-quarters of the national basic grains harvest. Most producers are *mestizos,* but a significant number are from indigenous groups.

The livelihoods of the country's peasant producers have always been precarious. They face the same climatic factors that affect all farmers, but which are particularly difficult for those who are poor and marginalized. Nonetheless they have proved capable of dealing with the capricious forces of nature, surviving droughts, floods, plagues, and diseases. Many have not coped as well with the forces of economic integration, however, which have unleashed a flood of imports from the United States. In the last fifteen years, "free-trade" policies have destroyed the livelihoods of an estimated 300,000 corn farmers, many of them from families that had cultivated their lands for generations.

In response to the crisis produced by these policies, thousands of small- and medium-size producers across the country created the National Association of Commercializing Enterprises (ANEC) to defend their livelihoods and create a more equitable, inclusive, and sustainable agricultural market.

Global Crisis, Structural Change

ANEC emerged in response to structural changes in the country's basic grains markets, prompted by an international agricultural crisis that began in the late 1970s. In Mexico these changes coincided with the rise of neo-liberalism in 1982, and intensified with the 1994 implementation of the North American Free Trade Agreement (NAFTA). The features of the global crisis were stark. Stagnant demand and global overproduction resulted in a rise in international grain reserves and a precipitous drop in grain prices and in the value of agricultural assets. Governments responded with strong state intervention to maintain farmer incomes and support prices. Developed countries increased their protectionist policies. Meanwhile, most less-developed countries suffered high levels of malnutrition, and some regions were plagued by famine.

The global crisis was rooted in the U.S. agricultural crisis. The world's leading agricultural exporting country saw a drop in exports and, equally troubling, a fall in its share of world agricultural exports, indicating a serious loss of competitiveness.[2] In response, U.S. agribusiness corporations called for a series of reforms in U.S. agricultural policies. The agribusiness lobby proposed a Farm Bill for 1986–90 that did away with the traditional policies—in effect since the New Deal—of supply management and agricultural subsidies based on target prices.

When Congress refused to pass these reforms, the corporate strategy shifted to the international sphere in hopes of influencing national policy from the outside. At the Uruguay Round of General Agreement on Tariffs and Trade (GATT) negotiations in 1986, the United States made agricultural trade liberalization one of the central themes of the agenda.[3] Although U.S. proposals were not fully accepted in the Uruguay Round, negotiations produced some agreements to open markets and reduce subsidies. These were important first steps toward liberalizing international agricultural markets.

Within this context Mexico, Canada, and the United States began negotiating NAFTA, signing the trade pact in 1993. For Mexico and its agricultural sector, greater integration into the global market implied a process of modernization in which low-yield crops such as basic grains were supposed to give way to more competitive export crops, such as winter fruits and vegetables.

To promote this transition, the Mexican government initiated a series of its own reforms, passing the 1992 reform of Article 27 of the Mexican Constitution to allow the private sale and lease of rural collective properties known as *ejidos,* which opened the door to the privatization of lands held outside the market since the Mexican Revolution. As part of its broader effort to withdraw from direct management of economic activities, the government undertook the sale and transfer of state-owned enterprises linked to small-holder agriculture. The government also cancelled price guarantees on all agricultural products except corn and beans and removed most agricultural subsidies. Finally, tariffs were reduced or eliminated on most rural products.

Mexico's incorporation into several international agreements hastened the privatization of agricultural markets and the general liberalization process begun in 1982. NAFTA took effect January 1, 1994, accelerating agricultural trade liberalization with the negotiated phase-out of agricultural import tariffs over five, ten, and fifteen years. In practice, the process was even more accelerated, as the Mexican government quickly moved to reduce or eliminate agricultural tariffs ahead of schedule. Corn, beans, and barley were heavily impacted. This prompted a rapid surge in imports of grains and oilseeds from the United States and Canada, further pressuring the government to eliminate price supports and accelerate its withdrawal from the countryside.

NAFTA was not the only agreement promoting the liberalization of agriculture. The Uruguay Round of the GATT took effect January 1, 1995 (Marrakech Agreement), mandating measures to liberalize agriculture, including tariff reduction, privatization of markets, reductions in indirect subsidies, replacement of price supports with more market-friendly income-support measures, and the privatization of public enterprises. Mexico's incorporation in the Organization for Economic Cooperation and Development (OECD) in May 1995, obligated the government to take similar measures.

The pressure to reduce agricultural subsidies and privatize public enterprises only heightened with Mexico's December 1994 financial crisis. As the recession rippled through the economy in 1995, the government faced severe fiscal constraints, deepening the crisis in the countryside.

Meanwhile the United States and the European Union—and to a lesser extent Canada, Argentina, and Australia—sought to take advantage of the opening to expand their shares of the international agricultural market. This newly liberalized "global supermarket" gave these countries new markets for their food exports, alleviating the oversupply crisis they had confronted since the 1980s. For the United States and Canada, the opening of the Mexican market, guaranteed through NAFTA, offered an important outlet for basic grains.

The Withdrawal of the State

Since 1982, four different Mexican administrations have worked to liberalize the basic grains market.[4] As part of this process, the government has increasingly pulled back from its direct role in the production and commercialization of basic grains. The government traditionally played a key role in domestic grains production through its system of price guarantees[5] and the construction of storage infrastructure. The price guarantees had two fundamental objectives: promoting production and assuring a minimum income for rural producers. The price guarantees also allowed for a better distribution of the national product, which brought higher prices and increasing purchasing power in the countryside. This stimulated demand in local and regional markets, which was considered indispensable in promoting industrialization.

The government had also established a new and visionary institution, known by its Spanish acronym Conasupo. This important state enterprise, which was responsible for collecting and storing agricultural goods, gave the government the operational capacity to intervene and regulate markets. It purchased very large volumes from producers at guaranteed prices, and it established and administered the country's strategic food reserves. Conasupo also played a key role in distribution, moving harvested crops from production to consumption zones, importing needed goods, and distributing both food and raw materials to the thousands of tortilla mills around the country, and to the majority of the urban centers and markets serving the rural population. Conasupo gave coherence to broad networks of programs and institutions involved in both production support and social welfare.

With the adoption of NAFTA and the related policies from the agricultural negotiations of the GATT Uruguay Round, the government abandoned price supports for producers in favor of direct payments to them. Conasupo's demise was precipitous. In 1993, Conasupo purchased a record 8.3 million tons of Mexican grains, sixty-nine percent of the volume traded that year. By 1998, Conasupo's system of price regulation and supply guarantees had come to an end. In December the enterprise was liquidated, having lost all of its subsidiaries and eliminated its subsidy programs for the corn-tortilla production chain.[6]

NAFTA and Basic Grains

The inclusion of basic grains (corn, beans, rice, wheat, sorghum, soya, and barley) was one of the most contentious issues in NAFTA negotiations. For Mexico the basic grains sector—particularly corn—held strategic importance and had always served as an important source of social stability. It is a critical source of food security, providing one of the most important nutritional sources for the country's people, including an estimated seventy percent of caloric intake for rural families. It provides needed employment, serving as the principal livelihood for some four million peasants and their families, the largest single source of employment (twenty percent) in the national economy. It represents the country's most important agricultural product, accounting for sixty-five percent of agricultural production. It also retains enormous cultural significance, serving as the foundation of ancient Mesoamerican cultures and the basis for the subsistence and identities of the country's fifty-six indigenous groups.[7] Traditional farmers also serve as the unpaid stewards of Mexico's wealth of genetic diversity in seeds. Grains farming also contributes to soil and water management on some sixteen million hectares of land.

In addition to these factors, critics of agricultural trade liberalization pointed to the profound asymmetries between Mexico's more traditional grains sector and its industrialized high-yield counterparts in the United States and Canada. Corn is produced in the United States at roughly forty percent of the cost of corn produced in Mexico, with average yields in Mexico less than one-quarter of U.S. yields (1.8 tons versus 8 tons per hectare).[8] Some experts recommended that grains be excluded from NAFTA, or at the very least that corn and beans, the basic Mexican staples, receive continued protection.

Most independent peasant organizations, large segments of civil society, and many universities and research centers opposed the Mexican government's agreement to include basic grains in the NAFTA negotiations, with even greater opposition to the total elimination of tariffs. Nonetheless, Mexican President Carlos Salinas agreed to sacrifice the sector and, along with it, peasant agriculture and national food security, all under the guise of his fundamental commitment to trade liberalization. Guided by the logic of comparative advantage, he promised major benefits for the agricultural sector and for the national economy as a whole.

The government came out of the NAFTA negotiations claiming it had won important concessions for the grains sector, including the long-term phase-out of tariff protection (ten and fifteen years), reduced quotas for tariff-free imports, and extremely high tariffs for imports above quota. The government promised to implement a gradual transition and production-conversion program for peasant producers of basic grains. In effect, the government claimed, there was nothing to worry about: The negotiations had been excellent, with peasant and national interests fully taken into account.

The Negative Balance

Seven years after NAFTA, it is clear that even the most pessimistic predictions about the consequences of including basic grains in the agreement pale in comparison to the reality of actual results. For almost every product, Mexican producers have suffered from a flood of imports induced not only by NAFTA itself but by the Mexican government's willingness to forego import duties on above-quota imports. This effectively eliminated the long-term, staggered phase-out of tariff protection, leaving producers on their own to compete with U.S. and Canadian exports.

NAFTA set out a so-called tariff-rate quota system in which an agreed-upon volume of a given product could be imported duty-free, but above that quota very high tariffs would be applied to limit an import flood. NAFTA set initial quotas and above-quota tariff rates, and called for the gradual elimination of tariffs through annual three-percent increases in the quotas. So, for example, 2.5 million tons of corn was approved to enter Mexico duty-free from the United States at the start of NAFTA, with a duty of 215 percent on any corn imports above that. The quota would go up three percent per year, resulting in the gradual phase-out of tariffs over fifteen years.[9]

The Mexican government's refusal to collect above-quota tariffs had a dramatic impact on producers. The story was similar for major crops:

Corn. From the first year of the agreement, U.S. exports of corn to Mexico—over three million tons—exceeded the NAFTA import quota of 2.5 million tons.[10] According to Mexican government data, between 1994, and 2000, 10.5 million tons of corn were imported from the United States and Canada above the import quota without paying a single cent of the agreed-upon tariff. This amounted to *more than $2.3 billion* in uncollected duties. In four different years (1996, 1998, 1999, and 2000) the tariff-free import quota was exceeded. In effect, corn was fully liberalized by the third year of NAFTA (1996), not the fifteenth year (2008).

Beans and barley. Beans and barley have seen similar results. In seven years under NAFTA, Mexico has imported more than 700 million tons of beans from the United States and Canada, half of it above quota and without tariff payments. The agreement was not observed in six of the seven years, with the bean market effectively liberalized by 1996, instead of 2008. For barley, the quotas have been exceeded in every year, with 481,953 tons imported from the United States and Canada without tariff payments.

Wheat, rice, soy, and sorghum. For the first three products, tariffs were dramatically reduced ahead of schedule in the first five years, with tariffs falling from fifteen to six percent on wheat, twenty to eight percent on rice, and ten to four percent on soy. In the case of sorghum, tariffs were completely eliminated from the first year of NAFTA.

The government argued that it was necessary to forego import tariffs to avoid national shortages resulting from insufficient domestic production, which could have caused price increases in foodstuffs. The drop in national production of basic grains, however, was not the cause of the import flood but rather its consequence, with imports coming in at prices tantamount to dumping. NAFTA's abrupt and total liberalization of basic grains has created unfair competition for Mexican producers, particularly for traditional farmers. Domestic production has thus fallen from 326.7 kilograms per capita in 1990, to 297.6 kilograms in 1998, a drop of nearly nine percent.

At the same time, imports have risen precipitously, as seen in Tables 7.1 and 7.2. The volume of imported grains has increased for most grains, but particularly for corn, beans, and soy. In the seven years under NAFTA,

Table 7.1 Volume of Basic Grains Imports, 1994–2000 (tons)

	Corn	Beans	Sorghum	Wheat	Barley	Rice	Soy	Total
1994	2,263,253	57,510	3,487,157	1,465,066	184,207	284,971	2,634,939	10,377,103
1995	2,661,446	26,062	2,109,696	1,243,444	189,535	248,929	2,207,572	8,686,684
1996	5,844,002	130,780	2,010,071	1,957,932	357,196	328,313	3,172,504	13,800,798
1997	2,500,776	90,161	2,213,063	1,881,265	258,756	303,498	3,534,232	10,781,751
1998	5,331,075	172,588	3,109,912	2,468,133	248,396	420,610	3,485,512	15,236,226
1999	5,498,846	61,309	4,566,257	2,656,086	214,123	549,660	4,067,280	17,613,561
2000	5,218,572	172,760	3,109,912	2,448,832	169,766	402,716	3,485,513	15,008,071
Total	29,317,970	711,170	20,606,068	14,120,758	1,621,979	2,538,697	22,587,552	91,504,194

Source: Banco de Comercio Exterior, México.

Table 7.2 Value of Basic Grains Imports, 1994-2000 ($millions)

	Corn	Beans	Sorghum	Wheat	Barley	Rice	Soy	Total
1994	369,528	38,512	394,815	189,255	6,736	104,074	640,472	1,373,864
1995	402,033	15,551	269,965	227,071	16,634	79,638	573,800	1,584,692
1996	1,063,480	88,732	331,292	427,170	69,106	123,298	897,558	3,000,636
1997	379,525	55,462	280,229	322,975	38,478	129,127	1,077,546	2,283,342
1998	624,134	130,130	348,928	339,441	40,575	111,486	861,475	2,456,169
1999	594,659	35,548	426,918	336,371	33,075	145,692	1,002,264	2,574,527
2000	620,967	112,072	348,929	336,199	29,979	107,048	861,472	2,416,666
Total	4,054,326	476,007	2,401,076	2,178,482	233,883	800,363	5,914,587	16,058,724

Source: Banco de Comercio Exterior, México.

this amounted to more than ninety million tons of imported grains. The price tag was not low for these imports. It is estimated that by the fifth year of NAFTA the value of grains imports were nearly twice as much as they had been in the previous nine years. In the seven years under the agreement, Mexico imported more than $16 billion of basic grains.

The massive imports have combined with other government policies—particularly price system reforms, subsidy regimes, and the government phase-out of Conasupo—to drive down prices for basic grains. For example, the real price of corn fell twenty-seven percent in the seven years under NAFTA. This decrease in real prices has provoked an unprecedented profitability crisis for basic grains producers throughout the country.

That national production did not collapse even further is due to the peasant economy's multiple survival strategies. Peasant households coped with the crisis by cutting consumption, even on necessities such as food, clothing, housing, education, and health while stretching their productive assets and taxing the fertility of the soil. They have survived by having more family members earn money in paid labor, by relying on remittances from those who have migrated, and even by growing and selling drugs.

Currently, grains producers in Mexico face production and marketing issues shared by no other OECD country. Mexico's small- and medium-scale producers do not know before they plant what prices they can get for their products, or if they will be able to sell them at all. Every growing cycle, producers have to mobilize, protest, and negotiate—for weeks or even months—to try to achieve better market conditions.

While Mexican producers face decreasing government support, subsidies in the United States have increased substantially. Mexico's federal budget for agriculture has decreased from 6.4 percent of the total budget in 1994, to just 4.3 percent in 2000—some $2.7 billion. By contrast, U.S. government support for agriculture increased consistently from 1994 to 2000, rising a remarkable 350 percent over the period, from $7.9 billion in 1994 to $28 billion in 2000.

The winners in this global restructuring are the local intermediaries, the big agricultural processing companies, and the large, multinational corporations. In Mexico three large, multinational associations control the chain of production, processing, and commercialization for basic grains. Monsanto (biotechnology and agrochemicals, seeds) is associated with Cargill and Continental, which take care of marketing, distribution, transport, and contract agriculture. The second chain is Novartis–ArcherDanielsMidland–Maseca. A Mexican transnational, Maseca controls seventy percent of the corn-flour market, while ArcherDanielsMidland (ADM) controls the wheat market. The third, Novartis produces and distributes ethanol and sweeteners, includes Minsa, Arancia, and Corn Products.

Despite falling producer prices, consumers have seen a significant rise in prices due to the near-monopoly in the food industry, inefficient distribution systems, and inadequate regulations to protect consumers. From 1994 to 1998, the cost of the basic market basket increased by almost 240 percent. With respect to corn products, the price of tortillas increased by 350 percent from January 1994 to December 1998. In addition, the quality of imports has been poor. Yellow corn has displaced the locally favored white corn, transgenic corn has been mixed in without separating or labeling it, grains have been tainted with aflatoxins and mushrooms, and many imported grains have been stored for overlong periods of time.

The overall impact on the Mexican economy has been negative as well. Even though agricultural trade grew 44.3 percent during the NAFTA period, agricultural output declined and the agricultural trade balance has worsened. From 1994 to 1999, the accumulated agricultural trade deficit was $939 million.[11]

Indiscriminate trade liberalization and the Mexican government's withdrawal from its economic role in the countryside have abandoned millions of peasant farmers who depended on government programs. Because of this structural change, Mexican producers suddenly faced not only the uncertainty of the climate, exchange rates, and shifting government policies but also the uncertainty of the international market. In such conditions, grains producers were left with only the tools of mobilization, protest, negotiation, and pressure to defend themselves. The crisis, however, did not automatically result in abandonment, migration, or the ruin of the countryside. Instead it generated a unique set of producer-led economic and organizational initiatives to meet the challenges of economic integration.

The Rise of ANEC

"We do not and will not accept that we are mere surplus, that we are not productive, not competitive, that we are a burden for the country. . . . We will not accept that only large foreign agricultural enterprises have and deserve a place in the countryside, as the federal government has maintained for the last eighteen years. . . . We have been productive in the past; the country has been built through our work. We are productive now despite the unfair competition from imports, and we can be more productive in the future, but only if the policies that favor just a few are abandoned, only if the role of the small and medium peasant producers is revalued,

*only if policies toward the countryside are established for everyone, with-
out exclusions or privileges."*
—From the opening speech at ANEC's Fourth
General Assembly, December 8–9, 2000, Mexico City

The structural changes in rural Mexico have compelled farmers to develop new forms of organization—structures capable of addressing not only farmers' socioeconomic needs but the market's demands for efficiency. Producers needed a strategy that combined successful economic projects with new public policies, and that could foster producers' capacity to work together effectively.

Two factors stood in the way of producer efforts to increase competitiveness. On the one hand, government intervention had brought many tangible benefits, but also fostered a paternalism and corporatism that limited farmers' active participation. The other related factor was the prevalence of corporatist peasant associations allied with the ruling political party and thus more responsive to the whims of party bosses than to the needs of their members. For producers, having a truly representative organization that could fight for improved conditions seemed a distant dream.

The harsh conditions in which trade liberalization and government withdrawal from the countryside took place forced producers to develop a new model of peasant organization that made the peasant farmer the central actor in rural development. Since the 1980s, some organizations had experimented with new organization forms, but it was these new processes of globalization in agriculture, combined with the peso crisis of 1994, that brought them about. Producers were forced to develop their own enterprises for production and commercialization, which gave smaller producers lower production costs, greater negotiation powers, increased productivity, and a broader range of choices. Several peasant organizations of basic grains farmers appropriated the production process for themselves by directly marketing their crops and implementing their own form of supply management to improve market conditions.

One of the new models of specialized economic organization is the Peasant Commercializing Enterprise (known by its Spanish acronym, ECC). ECCs' most important feature is its integration of social, economic, and environmental goals. Social objectives include collective survival and mutual support, democratic participation and control, and the social appropriation of the process and benefits of self-managed integrated development. The economic objectives include adaptation to market prices and interest rates, efficiency, competition, and professional managerial administration.

The environmental objectives are to recover and maintain the natural resource base.

ECCs serve as an alternative to the individual marketing of basic grains through intermediaries. By joining to store and bring their crops to market, producers achieve economies of scale in distribution and transport, and manage supplies of key crops in local and regional markets, avoiding market gluts and responding to market shortages—and ultimately earning better prices.

ANEC came together in 1995, emerging from a series of demonstrations and producer mobilizations over the previous five years. In most cases these were local or regional responses to agricultural policies. Many got little government response; others were violently repressed. The situation demanded coordinated action, and the first opportunity came in April 1995, when several national and regional organizations came together for a meeting in Mexico City.

The gathering produced a set of policy proposals, which were presented to state governors and to the president. The main demand was that the government continue its agricultural support programs but with the active participation of producer organizations through their ECCs at the regional, state, and national levels. The participants agreed that only the creation and consolidation of these collective enterprises could give them the strength to negotiate within the market and with government institutions.

In August a national workshop on rural alternatives and the commercialization of basic grains highlighted nearly 200 local ECCs that had been created in the previous five years in twenty states, as well as the organization of ten centralized regional commercialization centers. While this represented significant progress in organization and in the training of leaders, managers, and advisors, there was still a need to strengthen coordination of member producers and to recruit more members. The goal was to respond to the needs of each ECC and region, increasing efficiency and competitiveness without turning into a private enterprise.

Thus, ANEC was inaugurated in September 1995, to respond to local and regional demands for coordination. ANEC defines itself as an autonomous and plural association, independent of any political party, farmers' union or private or public institution. Its stated goals are: the revaluation and modernization of peasant agriculture; the defense and promotion of food sovereignty; and the construction of an inclusive, equitable, and socially responsible food-producing industry. In practice, ANEC promotes the creation and consolidation of ECCs, providing training, advice, market information, and trade contacts at the local level as well as to regional, state, and interstate ECC networks.

ANEC now has a membership of 180,000 small- and medium-scale producers of basic grains and manages 220 ECCs in twenty Mexican states.[12] These ECCs run 135 collection centers and storage units with a storage capacity of nearly one million tons. Together these organizations collect and trade 600,000 tons of corn, 250,000 tons of sorghum, 80,000 tons of wheat, 20,000 tons of beans, and 7,500 tons of chickpeas for export. This represents approximately ten percent of Mexico's commercial production of these crops. ANEC estimates that producers' collective efforts earn a ten-to-fifteen percent price premium for its members.

Building Sustainable Farms and Markets

ANEC's main goal is to revalue peasant agriculture, which it sees as economically and socially viable, sustainable and critical to the country's food security and the protection of its biological and agricultural diversity.[13] This approach stands in stark contrast to the logic of globalization "from the top" which holds that national food security is an archaic myth, that monoculture farming of improved seeds is the countryside's future, and that the only legitimate development is narrowly economic, free of social and environmental concerns. For ANEC, small producers are not an anachronism but rather the protagonists of the only real development worthy of pursuit: equitable, humane, and inclusive.

This implies the creation of an alternative market for basic grains that, on the one hand, ensures the survival of producers who defend such social values and, on the other, meets the country's consumption needs and protects food security. One strategy that addresses both needs is the development of a "solidarity market." This innovative approach identifies regions in which there is a shortage of production, either due to chronic conditions or temporary problems such as flood or drought, and supplies produce directly to those markets from ANEC-affiliated ECCs in regions with a surplus. This has been particularly effective, for example, in supplying surplus corn from Chiapas, Chihuahua, Durango, and the state of Mexico to consumer organizations in Oaxaca dealing with shortfalls in production.

To break into the commercial market, ANEC needed to develop enough storage capacity to be able to warehouse grains prior to bringing them to market. With the divestment of Conasupo, some government facilities became available. ANEC acquired 110 collection centers with storage capacity of 800,000 tons.

To manage such a large infrastructure, ANEC created Integrated Storage and Commercialization Systems of Mexico (Siacomex), its own enterprise to coordinate commercialization at the national level for the ECCs.

This allowed ANEC to join with MINSA, the second largest corn flour producer in Mexico, to purchase Almacenes de Centro Occidente (ACO), one of three regional warehouses whose assets were sold by the government in 1996. ACO was the only state enterprise taken over by a private food company associated with producer organizations. It was also the only one with a business plan that called for modernizing internal agricultural markets rather than those based on imports. ANEC obtained the capital for the purchase from ECC contributions, short-term credit, and some risk capital from the government.

To strengthen local ECCs' ability to compete in the market and to meet the diverse needs of producer organizations, ANEC established services for training and specialized technical assistance. It also began publishing a weekly Internet bulletin with key market information, prices, and news related to the Mexican countryside. This bulletin, distributed since December 1995, provides an alternative to the public information services (ASERCA, SNIM, Sagar) and the private sources (Reuters, Mercader), which were not only inaccessible and expensive for most producer organizations, but also difficult to understand and not always reliable.

The training program became essential with the institutional void left by the government and the increase in international competition. ANEC set up a center to provide ECCs with leadership training, advice, and organizational and commercial support. ECC leaders receive training in planning and commercial strategy, grain storage and preservation, management of collection centers, project design and evaluation, staff training, and legal matters. This program is a critical part of ANEC's effort to create a new culture of participation and organization.

To build a broad-based movement, ANEC has developed extensive collaborations with other national networks of rural organizations, particularly the independent groups working with coffee farmers (CNOC), forestry (Red Mocaf), and credit (AMUCSS). The organization has also built ties with producer organizations from other countries, such as the National Farmers Union of Canada, the American Association of Corn Producers and the National Coalition of Family Farmers in the United States, and the Confederación Nacional de los Trabajadores en Agricultura (CONTAG) of Brazil. ANEC is an active member of several international peasant networks as well, including La Vía Campesina, the InterAmerican Agriculture and Democracy Network, and the Global Peasant Agriculture and Globalization Network.

ANEC's growing organizational power has allowed some farmers to survive the invasion of the transnational enterprises under conditions harsh enough to bring down not only peasant organizations but many large Mexican businesses and commercial banks. But survival is not ANEC's sole objective. While it is difficult to measure ANEC's impact on farmers' lives, its most important contribution may be its ability to give peasant farmers viable forms of resistance and survival, collective actions that allow its members to continue being peasant farmers but with their own competitive commercial enterprises. Under the new market conditions, it is no longer enough to simply produce; one must also be able to market agricultural products in a way that benefits the producers.

Changing Government Policy

ANEC was founded not just to market grains but to give producers more influence over the policy decisions affecting their lives and livelihoods. The goal is not only to combat destructive agricultural policies and proposals but also to empower producers to develop their own proposals. The country needs an alternative model for rural development, not just critiques of government liberalization policies. The viability of the peasant farming sector depends on its ability to develop new commercial relationships, new markets, and new internal organizational relationships—and these all require new government policies.

To promote its public-policy proposals, ANEC has organized public meetings, participated in broad coalitions, lobbied members of Congress, negotiated with government officials, organized mass demonstrations, and presented its positions in the media. ANEC has also developed an impressive array of its own policy proposals, dealing with food security, fair trade, sustainable agriculture, government budgets, agricultural subsidies, and the economic organization of producers.[14]

While ANEC has been unable to change the government's overall policies toward the countryside, it has had some important successes. ANEC helped win access to credit and inputs for corn farmers in 1996, from the farm-support program Procampo. The organization was also successful in lobbying to include producer organizations in the transfer of government assets, through the government's main rural program, the Alliance for the Countryside. By winning the demand that the divestment not create a private monopoly, ANEC convinced the government to transfer sixty-one of its seventy collection centers to local organizations at discounted prices of only ten to fifteen percent of market value.

Another important victory involved the 1999, agreement by the Agriculture and Interior Departments to create a new Alliance for the Countryside program to support commercializing enterprises. Through this program nearly one million dollars for organizational and commercial support were channeled to 220 ECCs in twenty states. The program's success forced the executive branch to extend the program into 2001, and broaden it to include coffee growers (in 2000) and bean producers (in 2001).

One of ANEC's strongest campaigns has been to change government policies related to grain imports, which have regularly allowed above-quota imports. The organization won its demand that corn imports be suspended for the last quarter of 1996, and the first quarter of 1997, which allowed producers to market their sorghum and corn harvests under more favorable market conditions. More important, as a result of years of campaigning ANEC convinced the government to charge tariffs on the above-quota imports of corn, beans, sorghum, and other products regulated by NAFTA. The commitment was included in legislation for 2000–2006. ANEC also won its five-year campaign to be included in the official Committee for the Assignment of Import Levels for Corn and Beans, the body associated with the Departments of Economy and Agriculture that determines the quantities of corn and beans that can be imported.

ANEC has been actively involved in budget negotiations, lobbying Congress for greater support for producers. It succeeded in defeating a Fox administration proposal for the lowest agricultural budget in six years, winning instead an increase of more than $400 million. The new budget gave bean producers some $70 million for commercialization as compensation for the loss of government price guarantees, Conasupo's disappearance, and the rise in imports from the United States.

ANEC has also been active on environmental policies, participating with other civil society groups in the effort to nullify the contract between the national university (UNAM) and Diversa corporation for bioprospecting and to establish a moratorium on bioprospecting contracts (see chapter 6). This is a result of ANEC's ongoing interest in preserving Mexico's biodiversity and keeping crop genetic diversity in the hands of the peasant farmers who have been the long-term custodians of this biological wealth.

A Difficult Road Ahead

ANEC faces formidable challenges, both in its own organizational development and in the context of accelerated economic integration. It has proven difficult to train new leaders and leadership remains overly concentrated, with the executive director and a few key activists providing the bulk of the direction. The constant pressure to respond to urgent demands makes it difficult to pay adequate attention to leadership development or to build technical capacity at the local level. This has also hampered the development of democratic, horizontal cooperation among local, state, and regional organizations.

Internal matters pale in comparison to the continued problems related to the liberalization of basic grains markets. While it was a breakthrough for ANEC to create alternative markets and self-managed commercial enterprises in the face of the economic crisis, this progress will bear little fruit without government policy changes and new international agreements. The organization's rural development strategy needs to be implemented as public policy.

Among the most important proposals is the renegotiation of NAFTA. Grains producers continue to face tremendous obstacles from the massive importation of U.S. grains, which compete with Mexican production based on an unfair set of advantages and asymmetries. They also continue to confront the Mexican government's unwillingness to comply with the original agreement and charge tariffs on above-quota imports.

At its Fifth Assembly, in 2001, ANEC's small- and medium-size producers passed a resolution calling for the renegotiation of the NAFTA agricultural clauses, pointing to "the inequality of conditions in the agreement, which only benefits agribusiness," and stating, "the import quotas should be set in accordance with national production levels in order to meet the needs of the country." Delegates called for the declaration of a state of emergency in Mexican agriculture and a three-year suspension of the tariff reductions called for under NAFTA. They also demanded that above-quota imports pay a minimum tariff of thirty percent and that Mexican producers be paid a premium price to recognize the high quality of locally produced grains.[15]

ANEC delegates agreed to push an antidumping claim against U.S. imports and demand damages and compensation in 2002. To ensure adequate consultation with its membership, ANEC held formal consultations with member groups regarding the proposals to renegotiate NAFTA and proposed that ANEC keep all members informed about NAFTA and WTO issues.[16]

ANEC's national plan coming out of this assembly called for continued lobbying of Congress's rural budget discussions and militant action to halt basic grain imports, particularly transgenic crops, including direct actions to prevent their processing and distribution in the country. Delegates vowed to build alliances with like-minded peasant organizations and demanded a revolving government fund to recognize the role of producer organizations and promote food security, in order to "promote and stimulate national agricultural production with the end goal of satisfying national demand and reducing dependence on the exterior."[17]

In Defense of the Peasant Farmer

For a decade, the designers of neoliberal agricultural policies have been handing down a death sentence for small-scale producers of basic grains in Mexico. Left without government support, technical capacity, financing, infrastructure, and economies of scale—and flooded by imports—small-scale producers seemed destined to fade into history, supplanted by large producers linked with transnational agribusiness.

Ten years later, however, they have not disappeared. They keep producing, feeding their families, their communities, and the country, and struggling to compete more effectively—on their own terms and according to their own conditions. They have learned how to combine social priorities with economic objectives and to adapt to the vicissitudes of the international market under adverse conditions.

By uniting to fight for alternative proposals, they have enhanced not only their economic capacity but also their social capital. They have insisted that the country "value the national capacity that we have as a country to produce healthy food in adequate supplies for everyone who lives in the country, and this speaks to the revaluation of indigenous peasant farmers, as well as sustainable, organic, and other alternative forms of production."[18] The organized resistance of small- and medium-scale producers, defending their cultures and their livelihoods, has taken them from the countryside to the streets, and from the streets to the desks, where they design the polices that most affect them. In the end, they have moved from protests to proposals in a struggle to defend the peasant economy and the production of basic grains.

Notes

1. By contrast, in the United States the average size of farms in the basic grains sector is 160 hectares.

2. U.S. participation in world exports of basic grains fell from seventy-one percent in 1979, its highest historical level, to thirty-eight percent, its low, in 1985–86. The European Union was the main winner in the global market, going from being a net importer of 26.6 million tons of grain in 1976 to becoming a net exporter of 28.6 million tons in 1991–92.

3. The United States called for the elimination of nontariff barriers over ten years, elimination of export subsidies within five years, reductions in state support for production, and establishment of clear rules for sanitary and phyto-sanitary measures.

4. The four administrations were: Miguel de la Madrid 1982–1988; Carlos Salinas Gortari 1988–1994; Ernesto Zedillo 1994–2000; and Vicente Fox 2000–2006.

5. Between 1965 and 1971, the government added price guarantees for rice, sorghum, soya, cottonseed, sesame, sunflower, barley, and several other products to those already established for corn, beans, and wheat.

6. In 1994, Conasupo accounted for 54.8 percent of corn purchases. In 1995, its share fell to 43.6 percent, then to 21.6 percent in 1996. It recovered slightly to 45.2 percent in 1997, then fell in its last year to only 22.9 percent.

7. Estimates vary on the number of indigenous groups currently active in Mexico.

8. Alejandro Nadal, *The Environmental and Social Impacts of Economic Liberalization on Corn Production in Mexico* (Oxford and Washington: Oxfam GB and WWF International, 2000), 4.

9. The initial quotas and tariffs set by NAFTA were, for the United States (and Canada in parentheses): Corn–2.5 million tons (Canada: 1,500 tons), with a 215 percent tariff; Beans–50,000 tons (1,500 tons for Canada), with a 138 percent tariff; Barley–120,000 tons (30,000 tons for Canada), with a 128 percent tariff.

10. U.S. Department of Agriculture Foreign Agriculture Service, "Grain: world markets and trade" February 1997. Available at http://www.fas.usda.gov/grain_arc.html.

11. Instituto Nacional de Estadística, Geogratia e Informática (INEGI), National Accounts, Mexico. Annual statistics compiled by Bancomex. The agricultural trade balance includes agriculture, forestry, hunting and fishing, beekeeping, as well as foodstuffs, beverages, and tobacco.

12. Chiapas, Chihuahua, Durango, Guanajuato, Guerrero, Hidalgo, Jalisco, Michoacan, Morelos, Nayarit, Nuevo Leon, Oaxaca, Veracruz, Puebla, Tlaxcala, Sinaloa, Sonora, Tamaulipas, San Luís Potosí, and Zacatecas.

13. Small corn producers in Mexico manage more than 300 varieties of corn that have been developed from the mother-strain known as *teocintle*, which is native to Mexico.

14. ANEC's list of policy proposals reads like a comprehensive agenda for the Mexican countryside: "For Inclusive, Unified, and Long-term Commercialization Policies;" "An Emerging Program for Basic Grains Production;" "The Transfer of Government Infrastructure to Producers;" "Demand for a Multi-year Agriculture Law;" "Policies for Fair, Unified, and Predictable Prices for Corn, Wheat,

Sorghum, and Beans;" "New Selective Subsidies for the Corn-Tortilla Production Chain;" "Sustainable Policies for Food Security;" "Toward a New Policy for the Countryside 2000–2006."

15. Minutes from ANEC's Fifth Assembly, Tuxtla Gutierrez, November 26–28, 2001. www.laneta.apc.org/anec.

16. ANEC Fifth Assembly.

17. ANEC Fifth Assembly.

18. From the speech by ANEC Executive Director Victor Suarez at the conference, "In Defense of Corn," Mexico City, October 2001.

8

Peasant Farmers in the Global Economy: The State Coalition of Coffee Producers of Oaxaca

Josefina Aranda Bezaury

MORE THAN TWO CENTURIES AGO, MEXICO BET MUCH OF ITS AGRICULTURAL FUTURE on plantations. Since then, the production of sugar cane, rubber, and coffee have played an important role in the economies of the Mexican south-southeast, coffee being the most important in social as well as economic terms. During that time, this region of the country and most of its residents have endured cycles of economic and social prosperity as well as crisis. These are rooted in the unique history of southern Mexico, where the wage laborers and peons from the coffee plantations became indigenous peasant coffee producers.

The process of economic globalization and the neoliberal policies developed by recent Mexican governments have created a profound crisis in the Mexican coffee industry. They have also provoked a creative and independent reaction. Emerging from a first stage of crisis in 1989, coffee-industry organizations have developed proposals to defend the coffee sector and promote a new model, not only for production but also for organization. Within a large national movement, the State Coalition of Coffee Producers of Oaxaca (CEPCO) has emerged as the largest and most developed statewide organization. CEPCO's experience highlights the difficulties and opportunities for small producers facing the vicissitudes of the international market.

Coffee Production in Oaxaca

Mexico is the world's fifth largest coffee producer. Along with vegetables, coffee is one of the principal agricultural sources of income in the Mexican

149

economy. Among Mexican states Oaxaca currently has the second highest acreage planted in coffee and ranks third in the number of families that depend directly upon the income generated by coffee production. The vast majority of Oaxacan coffee farmers are small-scale indigenous producers.

Oaxaca is not just a state; it is a world of diverse traditions and languages, featuring mountainous terrain and a people with a shared history of colonization and exploitation. Colonized by the Spanish more than five centuries ago, Oaxaca still bears the marks. As was the case in other parts of Mexico, the indigenous communities resisted the settlers, moving to the most remote and isolated parts of the state to avoid domination and to preserve their cultures.

Even though the Mexican government has developed countless policies to address indigenous issues, indigenous communities still suffer the worst incidence of poverty, the lowest indicators of development, and the greatest inequality. Manufacturing, communications systems, and other investments associated with development have all expanded in the northern, central, and western parts of Mexico, while the economies of the southern and southeastern states such as Oaxaca are still based on exports of raw materials—particularly tropical and forest products—and the emigration of the labor force.

Oaxaca's entrance into the world coffee scene came relatively late, toward the end of the nineteenth century. In various regions of the state, indigenous people were exposed to coffee cultivation as laborers on coffee plantations established by foreigners, much of it on land seized from indigenous communities by the government of Porfirio Diaz (1876–1911).

Indigenous people began to appropriate and extend coffee cultivation when, as indigenous leaders now tell it, "the elders saw that coffee was money."[1] They began to steal coffee plants from the plantations to sow in their towns and on land cleared for the purpose. By 1920, coffee production had developed a new identity, becoming not just a crop imposed by outsiders but a vital part of the rural economy and a source of local identity.

Table 8.1 shows the distribution of coffee production in Mexico and the number of producers and area devoted to coffee (one hectare=2.47 acres). Table 8.2 shows the distribution of Oaxacan coffee production by farm size. Together these figures illustrate the predominance of the southern states (Chiapas, Oaxaca, and Guerrero in particular) in Mexico's coffee production, as well as the predominance of small farms among Oaxacan coffee farmers.

Traditionally, coffee production in the southern states has been considered part of the so-called *rusticano* system—also known as mountain-grown or natural coffee farming. This label is based on the structure of the coffee farm, the production techniques used, and the productivity of the

Table 8.1 Distribution of Coffee Production in Mexico by State

State	Municipalities	Localities	Producers	Area (ha)	Production[a]
Chiapas	60	1,418	73,742	228,254	1,551
Veracruz	46	783	67,227	152,457	1,334
Oaxaca	76	771	55,291	173,765	624
Puebla	37	441	30,973	62,649	758
Guerrero	13	73	10,497	50,773	198
Hidalgo	18	473	25,630	42,404	120
San Luís Potosí	11	247	12,920	23,706	44
Nayarit	7	49	3,730	18,731	92
Jalisco	2	4	800	3,060	7
Tabasco	2	29	788	2,236	6
Colima	8	34	783	2,776	14
Querétaro	1	3	248	356	1
Total	281	4,325	282,629	761,165	4,750

Source: Data from Consejo Mexicano del Café (Mexican Coffee Council), with information from Inmecafe census of 1989 and 1992.
Note: a. Production information for 1998–1999, in thousands of 60kg bags.

Table 8.2 Distribution of Oaxaca Coffee Producers by Farm Size

Cultivated Area	Producers		Hectares	
2 hectares or less	34,487	59%	41,855	27%
2 to 5 hectares	17,150	29%	56,652	31%
5 to 10 hectares	5,759	10%	42,381	24%
10 hectares or more	1,264	2%	33,051	18%
Total	58,660	100%	180,329	100%

Source: Consejo Estatal del Café (State Coffee Council), Oaxaca, 1994.

farms. Here I will argue that this system should be considered an "indigenous system of coffee production."[2] There are four reasons for making such a distinction:

1. **Just over 80% of area in Mexico planted in coffee is farmed by indigenous producers who farm less than five hectares.** The unique relationship that southern producers have had with coffee is due largely to the particular characteristics of indigenous culture. Examples of this include the use of traditional technologies to maintain and preserve the coffee plantations, and non–chemical-intensive techniques that minimize the damage to ecosystems and water basins. Coffee in this region has been produced mainly according to indigenous customs that "guarantee the quality of the

soil (preventing erosion), the conservation of water, the retention of carbon dioxide, and a healthy environment free of agrochemical substances."[3]

2. **Coffee production takes place in the context of the peasant household economy.**[4] With an average of six people per family, coffee production fundamentally depends on the strength of the family workforce.[5] Family members are involved not only in the harvest but in initial processing, which transforms the ripe "cherry" coffee beans into dried "parchment" beans (or *pergamino* coffee), which are much easier to store and transport than the fresh coffee. This is important because most producer communities are quite remote. Coffee production takes place within the economic logic of the poor peasant, who cannot grow adequate supplies of basic foods and who relies on diverse sources of monetary income. Although coffee constitutes the main income-producing commercial crop, income is also supplemented by family members doing wage labor, remittances from migrant workers, government subsidies for agricultural production, and sales of homemade products.

3. **Coffee production takes place in communities and regions that lack services and basic infrastructure.** Mexico's coffee regions are also the country's most extreme zones of poverty. Consequently, coffee-producing families daily face multiple needs and shortages in nearly all areas—health, education, communication, and transportation—that impoverish their standards of living.

4. **Coffee growers possess a strong community spirit for work and organization.** One cannot understand coffee farmers' organizations without understanding their cultures and their ancestral forms of social organization. Cultural norms influence the distribution of responsibilities; the activities and work agreements among members of a local group or of a coffee industry organization; the way in which decisions are made; the traditional systems that govern how to elect and delegate authority and representation (*usos and costumbres*); and the strong collective identity that comes from being part of a specific group or association. All of these organizational features are based in community practices that have evolved over hundreds of years.

The Crisis of 1989

As a household, or as a group, coffee growers have learned to deal with capital. Only in their case financial gain is subordinated to sociocultural objectives; well-being supercedes profit. The patched and creaky economic

apparatus built by farmers may be imperfect, but it transcends the short-sightedness of private enterprise, a profit machine that may be efficient but is soulless.
—Armando Bartra, *Sobrevivientes, Historias de la Frontera*

In 1989, structural adjustment policies led the government to abandon the coffee sector. The withdrawal caused a serious imbalance in the sector because for forty-five years the agency in charge of coffee production and commercialization, the Mexican Coffee Institute (known as Inmecafe) played a critical role in coffee-growing communities. Its pervasive power in economic and social life derived not only from the production and trade of coffee but also from its role in organizing producers, building community infrastructure, providing training and agricultural extension services, and offering credit.

Inmecafe's withdrawal had a severe impact on coffee communities, not only because of its significant economic and social influence but because the withdrawal took place rapidly and inefficiently, without offering any alternative to small producers. It clearly demonstrated the government's lack of interest in this important branch of agricultural production and in its producers. As an associate of CEPCO in the Mazateca region remarked, "When Inmecafe left us orphaned, we had to look ahead in order to be able to continue, even though we knew nothing, because this father did not teach us anything, he only controlled and protected us a little by giving loans, buying our coffee, and giving a few odd jobs."[6]

Two specific characteristics of this period deserve emphasis. First, due to the inequity of Inmecafe's dismantling, all the costs associated with the transfer of its functions and assets to the various parties involved—whether the private sector or farmers' organizations—fell exclusively on the backs of those who were struggling to deal with the crisis by creating new forms of organization.[7] Second, as a consequence of trade liberalization policies reinforced by NAFTA, rapid commercial integration accelerated, allowing the dizzying arrival of large transnational companies that operate globally and compete directly with the coffee-producer organizations. In this way the new trade liberalization policies, the government's withdrawal, and the unequal transfer of assets and state functions presented producers with the challenge of creating their own alternatives, but without resources or support, and all under the threatening gaze of international capital, a scenario one commentator likened to "swimming with sharks."[8]

Finally, it is important to note that many of Inmecafe's functions were not taken over by other entities. For example, nothing was put in place for technical support and training, technology transfer, or research. It is telling that Inmecafe's specialized library on coffee, which was located in the institute's central offices in Jalapa, Veracruz, simply disappeared.

In June 1989, in conjunction with the application of these economic policies, other external factors brought on the crisis of 1989–1994, which "signal[ed] a drastic shift in the economic history of the coffee bean and a decisive turning point in our coffee culture."[9] A critical part of this crisis was the cancellation of the economic clauses and quota system of the International Coffee Organization, in which coffee-producing and coffee-consuming countries negotiated supplies, purchases, and prices.[10] Since 1976, the agreement had managed the supply and demand of coffee within a range of prices above farmers' production costs. In 1989, the agreement was broken, which completely liberalized the market. The failure to reach agreement drove down coffee prices to well below production costs.

To this global context we can add one local factor. The Oaxacan government created its own decentralized public entity—the State Coffee Council—which claimed to include all of those involved in the coffee production process but in fact excluded representatives from the independent organizations of small-scale coffee growers.[11]

The fight against exclusion from the organization, heightened by the farmers' demands related to Inmecafe's withdrawal and the drop in prices, brought with it a new organizing process. It united independent peasant organizations and brought together the majority of coffee-farmer groups that had previously been organized by the government through Inmecafe. These Economic Units for Production and Commercialization (known by their Spanish acronym, UEPC) had been controlled by the rural organizations of the ruling party, consistent with the prevailing corporatist practices of the Institutional Revolutionary Party (PRI).[12]

Just to Survive

Ever since the government abandoned us, we realized that the peasant farmer means nothing to them. We had to organize ourselves so that our product would have value, so that our children would have enough to eat and be able to study, and so we could find a way to survive.
—Ricardo Hernández, Mazateco farmer, leader of CEPCO

For producers, there was total crisis due to the government's withdrawal, low prices, and an organizational crisis within the sector. However, this complex economic situation, like all critical moments, presented a series of risks—because producers needed to fight for their survival—and opportunities—because the fight also implied dissolving old forms of subordination and government control.

The 1989 formation of the State Coalition of Coffee Producers of Oaxaca, which brought together 21,000 small coffee growers from across the state—with different organizational and ethnic backgrounds, but under equal conditions of poverty and crisis—also represented both risk and opportunity. There was great political risk in breaking with the traditional corporatist-*cacique* structures, but there was opportunity to get to know others in the same situation and to coordinate and mutually support one other. In particular, CEPCO's founding offered indigenous peasant coffee-farming communities the opportunity to face collectively the death sentence issued by the Mexican.

The organizational process from which CEPCO originated had two defining features. First, the organization resuscitated long-forgotten organizational forms, mainly at the municipal and regional levels, to provide the legal framework under which the new base groups came together. Second, CEPCO designed a new set of associations called UEPC Unions, which brought together some of the formerly government-controlled producer groups. Both features had a common element: the direct incorporation at the regional level of community representation by the producers in these "new/old" organizations. This promoted tremendous grassroots participation and gave producers an active role in the day-to-day construction of their new organization. "The existence of the indigenous community, with its cohesive power at a local level, also played a positive role. The social cohesion emanating from community practices was a key factor that explains, at least in part, the reconstitution of these producer organizations. Its strength comes from the vitality of these base organizations, as well as from its capacity to generate constructive responses to external economic changes and to give advice and support to its members and partners."[13]

CEPCO began as a movement demanding to be heard and proposing coordinated actions in the face of crisis. It quickly became, within six short months, an organization uniting numerous groups of small coffee producers from the entire state of Oaxaca. These groups "committed themselves to the creation of a social enterprise capable of managing the harvesting, processing, and sale of coffee for its members, the securing and administering of credit, the promotion of income-generating projects, the full participation of women farmers, the diversification of production, and the fight for indigenous rights."[14] Indeed, even though CEPCO began as an organization solely concerned with coffee-related issues, its work through the years has been multifaceted, playing an important role in the peasant movement.

Forty-six regional organizations currently participate in CEPCO as collective enterprises, and each forms part of daily life in the state's coffee regions. These organizations bring together families from one or more communities and form a regional organization that then affiliates with the statewide group. In this way, the organizational affiliation is not individual and local but collective and regional, with members generally sharing a geographical area and a language. For this reason, there is great variation in the size of the participating CEPCO groups and their organizational, economic, and political development. Groups share the same principles, practices, and programs, but they maintain the diversity and specific characteristics of each region.

Altogether, CEPCO has 21,191 members living in 423 communities, belonging to seventy-three municipalities of Oaxaca, and representing thirty-seven percent of Oaxaca's coffee-growing families. The organization includes ten of the state's indigenous groups, including Nahuas; Mazatecos; Chinantecos from both the mountains and the low-lying areas; Zapotecos from the mountains, the south, and the Isthmus of Tehuantepec; Mixtecos from the south and the coast; Chatinos; Mixes; Zoques; and Tacuates. Almost one-third of the members—about 6,000—are women who actively participate in production and service projects. The cultural and gender diversity of CEPCO's members makes the organization a complex, multiethnic group with representation from distinct cultural groups with their own languages, practices, and traditions.

Despite their cultural richness, CEPCO members count on few economic resources. They own very little land, and much of it is of poor quality. Most members grow basic grains for subsistence. The poverty index is very high, with ninety-eight percent of the municipalities in which coffee is produced considered "highly marginalized" by the state population agency.[15]

Recovering Lost Traditions

CEPCO's organizational structure is characterized by three defining features. First, it is based on the revaluation, recovery, and promotion of many aspects of indigenous community organization and life. Decisions are made in community-wide assemblies, for example, and the election and delegation of leaders is by consensus. This enriches the organization not only at the local level, but at the regional, state, and national levels.[16] Through this process, leaders are chosen through community consensus and are obliged to consult with their constituents and respond to community needs. Although this particular feature does not differ substantially from some other indigenous peasant organizations, CEPCO is unique in applying such practices in all levels of organizational functioning. Thus state and regional leadership has been established and maintained with an unprecedented degree of accountability to those who elected them.

Second, CEPCO put together a staff composed of regional leaders and technical advisors linked with the organization who offer assistance, training, and ongoing technical support to the members.[17] Since its inception, the group has relied on the active participation of leaders and advisors with prior experience in peasant-indigenous movements. These experienced activists helped strengthen and enrich the indigenous organizations that joined the statewide group. CEPCO's staff was also able to generate concrete proposals in response to the rapid policy changes emanating from the government.

Finally, CEPCO established a clear set of organizational principles: pluralism, democracy, autonomy, and administrative transparency (including regular presentation of financial reports to members). These principles structured the group's internal and external relations. They emerged as a response to persistent complaints about traditional corporatist organizations, and as such they represented an explicit rejection of the features members did not want the organization to have.

In practice, the principle of pluralism has meant a commitment to tolerance and respect for political, linguistic, religious, and cultural differences. Respecting pluralism has also allowed CEPCO to prevent differences from overwhelming the common interests and the collective struggle—a rare experience for peasant organizations and their leaders and for the majority of the country's political organizations.

The principle of democracy is understood to go well beyond electoral matters to encompass practices that should guide organizational life at the level of the family, the community, as well as regional and state organizations. Strict adherence to democratic practices has allowed horizontal decision-making by the members on a wide range of topics, a process that can be slow but that ensures full consultation and agreement in community, regional, and state assemblies.

The principle of organizational autonomy developed partly from the desire to ensure decision-making independent of outside influences such as political parties, social organizations, or other entities that have no direct relationship to the internal life of the organization. CEPCO also insists on autonomy within the organization itself. Not only does each regional organization have the autonomy to make independent decisions, but within regional organizations certain members, such as women's groups and organic coffee producers, can make their own decisions. Because they have a specific interest and maintain the support of their narrower constituency, their autonomy is respected.

Finally, CEPCO insists on the principle of administrative transparency, based on the established practice of regular financial reporting. From the beginning, leaders asserted the need to make all of the organization's accounting and financial activities transparent, despite—or perhaps because of—the urgency of finding resources to finance the whole process of harvesting, processing, and commercializing coffee. In practice, this led to two organizational institutions. One was the presentation in monthly assemblies of the organization's finances and sources of support, whether public (resources from the state or federal government) or private (from foundations). This prevented "the private uses of a social organization by its peasant leaders, which has been common in other organizations."[18] The second was a form of internal revolving loan fund, which came to be known as *la bolsota*, or "big purse," which members could tap for urgent needs. (*La bolsota* has now evolved into a credit union in which the regional organizations are the majority members.)

A Time to Learn:
Peasant Entrepreneurs and Entrepreneurial Peasants

"The crisis taught a lesson: that peasant survival strategies can be more effective than those that are purely business-oriented...[These organizations] jointly manage large agro-industries and are on top of daily international price fluctuations . . . many of these groups collectively manage powerful economic enterprises. . . . But they have learned the lesson: They are no longer trying to be businessmen so they can stop being peasants.
    —Armando Bartra, *El Aroma de la Historia Social del Café*

The leap from coordinating and running an organization to managing a large enterprise was dramatic for CEPCO. Establishing a powerful economic enterprise over the years has made it possible for members to add value to their product in the various stages of production and enjoy the benefits and profits from their organization.

Still, the process that has allowed CEPCO to take control of production and build a socioeconomic alternative has not been easy. During the early years, for example, producers did not realize that coffee was not exported directly as *café pergamino*—the dried "parchment coffee" processed from the freshly picked beans. As one of the members explained, "The government through Inmecafe was doing everything and we didn't know anything about the business, we were ignorant about almost everything and then the government abandoned us. . . . But these were not times to cry, they were times to think and dream of our future and work hard to get there."[19] In spite of the rapid dismantling of the government infrastructure, trust in farmers' own initiatives and abilities unleashed a struggle based on the search for immediate alternatives and the appropriation of the productive process.

Inmecafe's divestment of its productive assets mainly benefited the large industrial and export producers, but to a small and important extent emerging social organizations like CEPCO also took advantage of the transfer. Some of these assets, such as mechanical dryers, allowed the group to begin its own autonomous effort to produce, process, and market its coffee. For the most recent crop cycle, 2000–2001, CEPCO sold a total of 57,117 *quintales*[20]—about 5.8 million pounds—of its members' green coffee. For the growers, this is clear proof of the organization's capacity, fruits of the effort these small-scale indigenous Oaxacan producers undertook to organize themselves and take control of a process previously unknown to them.

The Marketing Strategy

Since its inception, CEPCO's principal strategy was directly exporting its coffee, which allowed it to establish relationships with several buyers and sell at better prices than most other organizations. Moreover, with the collaboration of some of Inmecafe's former workers, who joined the staff, CEPCO quickly developed needed experience in the production process and in training.[21]

To launch this strategy, CEPCO created a commercial enterprise, the *Comercializadora Agropecuaria del Estado de Oaxaca* (CAEO), whose primary role was to develop the capacity to market directly the coffee grown by members.[22] This strategy included planning for the annual coffee harvest, which provided CAEO with large quantities of marketable coffee; sorting the coffee by type and quality for different markets and buyers; negotiating contracts; using service agencies to make exporting possible; and billing and collecting.[23] These activities have allowed CEPCO to develop export skills and, more important, earned the organization respect among its clients as a serious and professional social enterprise with the ability to establish broad and lasting commercial relationships.

A critical part of this process was the work of the regional organizations that collected members' coffee. CEPCO currently has twenty coffee-collection centers, which are directly managed by regional organizations with the financial support the organizations get from the credit union and other sources.[24] The group's ability to collect and directly market its members' coffee gave it an important economic role in the coffee-growing regions of Oaxaca: regulating the price of coffee in the countryside in favor of the small producers.

Financial Self-Sufficiency

> *The fact that CEPCO from the beginning has been able to sell the harvests of its members at higher prices than those paid by local merchants and by Inmecafe gave the organization real prestige among producers, which strengthened the organization. Their commercial success was matched by other achievements in financing. Faced with insufficient capital for harvesting and marketing coffee, CEPCO decided to form a fund with the resources of its own member organizations, with the purpose of sharing the money. . . . The trust implied by such a venture is directly related to the horizontal, nonhierarchical relationships among its members.*
>
> —Fernando Rello, *La ocupación campesina de los espacios dejados por el Estado. El caso de la Coordinadora Estatal de Productores de Café de Oaxaca (CEPCO)*

CEPCO's success in appropriating the production process would not have been possible without financial self-sufficiency. In 1990 the aforementioned *bolsota* was formed. Although initially this revolving loan fund compensated for the shortage of capital by allowing access to bank credit for the coffee harvest, it soon became inadequate. Faced with the need for a financial intermediary with greater capacity to negotiate with the banking system, on February 20, 1995, the organization inaugurated its own credit union: UCEPCO. The Union's initial assets—$1,425,000 pesos (about $150,500 US)—came from transfers to the regional organizations by different Mexican government agencies.[25] When the regional organizations received these funds, many transferred the funds to UCEPCO.[26] By 1999 the credit union's capital had grown to 9 million pesos ($950,870 US).

CEPCO members constitute the majority (seventy-five percent) of UCEPCO's shareholders, with the rest coming from coffee producer groups from other states, and from other organizations and enterprises. To make savings programs available to credit union members, the organization created FidUCEPCO, a trust under the administration of UCEPCO that takes the small amounts of money saved by CEPCO members (and others) and earns relatively high interest rates. The group also manages several microcredit funds: *el banquito* (the little bank), a revolving fund for emergency situations (deaths, illness, school expenses); and a Women's

Loan Fund and Fund for Diversification of Production, which rely on capital from Fonaes, a Mexican government agency,[27] and the Inter-American Development Bank, respectively.

The balance sheet from these first years is positive. The credit union has capitalized its initial investment thanks to its administrative efficiency, competent management, and investment of capital. With capital of nearly seven million pesos (about $800,000), CEPCO wields a great deal of financial power and, with its own commercial enterprise (CAEO), it can support the gathering, processing, and marketing of its members' coffee.

The Promotion of Organic and Sustainable Coffee

CEPCO also promotes the production, processing, and commercialization of organic and sustainable coffee.[28] One goal is to eliminate the use of chemical inputs in coffee farm management, which can be achieved through organic coffee production. Another is to improve environmental conservation while expanding the market for "fair trade" coffee. Coffee sold to the fair-trade market earns a premium price. Organic coffee generally earns about fifteen cents per pound more than regular coffee, and organic *and* fairly traded coffee (incorporating environmental and social factors) can earn the producer as much as $1.41 per pound. This guarantees the producer a profit margin, something the regular international coffee market cannot do.

This strategy brings many advantages to the producers. In addition to earning a premium price for their product, it raises the production level per hectare and improves and preserves coffee quality. Because organic coffee production is more labor-intensive, it generates jobs and promotes the use of family labor. It also offers a range of environmental benefits, including reducing chemical pollution, promoting soil and water conservation, and preserving biodiversity.

CEPCO is currently Oaxaca's largest producer of organic coffee. Starting with 948 producers six years ago it now has 6,000 members certified as organic producers. The effort to transform cultivation practices has been slow because it involves changing cultural practices of long duration. It also requires elaborate record-keeping, because extensive documentation is required to gain certification as an organic producer and to sell on the organic coffee market.

The organization has established an impressive infrastructure for training and technical assistance and has a group of agricultural experts dedicated to organic conversion. These experts in turn train experts from each community, who are selected by the community's organic coffee group. After receiving training they serve as peasant inspectors for the certification of the product. This has allowed for better quality control of production and processing, which is clearly reflected in the market. Furthermore, it has allowed for new projects such as those related to sustainable coffee, which goes beyond organic production. Sustainable coffee is based on production that sustains environmental quality, the quality of the producers' lives, and the quality of the product itself. This process is supported by the fair trade market, made up of consumers willing to pay more not only for an organic product but to reinforce production systems that promote cultural diversity and community organization.

This approach also hopes to win greater recognition for the ecological services provided by coffee farmers. It has been documented, for instance, that shade-grown coffee as it is practiced in most of Oaxaca plays an important role in preserving an ecosystem needed by migratory birds.[29] Related to this is an ongoing effort to develop a digital map of organic coffee areas, for use in projects on environmental services and climate change.

Women Coffee Farmers

CEPCO's success also stems from an understanding that indigenous small-scale coffee production is essentially a peasant activity in which all members of a family take part. As such it is not an exclusively male activity—women's full participation is essential to the broader effort to overcome current levels of social inequality.

Since 1992, CEPCO has undertaken an innovative effort to promote the participation of women coffee-growers. The organizational work, which ultimately resulted in the current Women's Commission, began four years after the organization's founding in 1989. In those early years, a few women who attended assemblies and some staff began asking some simple questions: Who produces the coffee? Only men? Why don't women participate in the organization? Little by little, the organization began to acknowledge the valuable role that women play in coffee-growing families. The regional leaders began to gain interest in promoting women's participation, until finally, with the passing years, the profile of the membership has slowly shifted from small coffee producers to the more inclusive concept of coffee-grower families.

CEPCO began to promote the creation of women groups with a variety of objectives: to advance the organizing process of peasant women; to recognize the capabilities and participation of women; and to fight to improve the unfavorable living conditions peasant women suffer. It encouraged the integration of women into every type of meeting and assembly—whether local, municipal, or CEPCO-related—so their voices and opinions could be taken into account. The group also sought to support the family economy by promoting women's production projects, which generate needed income and savings.

Statewide as well as in regional groups, the structure for women's participation is innovative and creative. In addition to having a Women's Commission, CEPCO has a Women's Directorate, a leadership body elected by women. Currently more than 5,000 women from diverse backgrounds actively participate. They have production and service projects, such as coffee-seed nurseries, flower-farming, bakeries, and tortilla shops. They take part in technical training courses, in microfinance and savings programs, and they run food and supply programs as well as nutrition and health projects.

The participation of women has led to an explicit recognition of their contribution to the social life of their communities and their experience as producers, and it has strengthened the organizations' commitment to fight for the rights of indigenous peasant women. Men have also begun to recognize the value of women's domestic, production, and organizational work, and its importance in empowering women and promoting self-esteem. As women themselves noted at one women's assembly: ". . . Being organized helps us lose our fear." ". . . We are organized because we can learn more, we can be more valuable, and it makes us happy." ". . . We are no longer afraid to change ideas and we feel proud of ourselves, to know our rights as women."[30]

The Current Crisis

The production and sale of conventional coffee at 2001 prices was not sustainable. Producers faced selling prices that were lower than their production costs. December 2001 prices, for example, were just $46.84 per hundred pounds, while production costs in Mexico average $70 per hundred pounds. According to the analyses of CEPCO and its national affiliate, the National Coalition of Coffee Organizations (CNOC), the current crisis is much more serious than that of 1989, because the fall in prices is due to global overproduction—mainly of low-quality coffee—and the accumulation of inventories in the importing countries. The imbalance in the supply and demand of the last two growing cycles is almost ten million bags per cycle, and it is likely this will increase since Brazil, the world's largest producer, foresees a production increase. This would bring the market to the edge of total collapse.

Overproduction is largely the result of a global increase in coffee farming, according to CEPCO and CNOC. With the support of international financial institutions like the World Bank, several countries—including Vietnam, Brazil, India, Guatemala, Peru, and Mexico—encouraged expanded production. As Table 8.3 shows, Vietnam and Brazil are the most dramatic examples. Over the last ten years, Vietnam increased coffee production 1,130%; Brazil has not only increased total production but relocated many of its coffee plantations to areas less prone to damaging climatic events.

The impact of the price drop has been enormous. Figure 8.1 shows the downward trends. The prevailing prices of over $100 per hundred pounds fell in 1989, with the breakdown in the International Coffee Organization, reaching a low of about $50 in 1992. Prices rose sharply due to a frost in Brazil that dramatically reduced world supplies, but have declined precipitously since 1997, due to overproduction.

The present crisis can be resolved in two ways. There could be a full-scale commercial war among the producer countries, which would probably result in victory for the countries that produce low-quality and/or low-priced coffee—mainly Indonesia, Vietnam, and several African countries—and major losses for those with high production costs—especially

Figure 8.1 Average Monthly Price of Contract "C" Coffee on New York Exchange, 1988–2001 (dollars per 100 pounds)

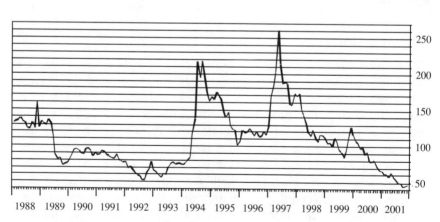

Source: Coffee, Sugar & Cacao Exchange (CSCE)

Table 8.3 World Coffee Production 1991–2000
(in thousands of 60kg bags)

	1991	1992	1993	1994	1995	1996	1997	1998	1999	2000
Brazil	27,297	25,972	26,787	29,688	15,784	27,664	22,756	34,547	32,343	32,000
Vietnam	1,308	2,340	3,020	3,532	3,938	5,705	6,915	6,947	11,648	14,775
Colombia	18,222	13,823	11,320	12,989	12,878	10,876	12,211	11,024	9,398	10,532
Indonesia	8,463	5,577	7,301	6,280	5,865	8,299	7,759	8,458	5,432	6,716
Mexico	**4,727**	**3,401**	**4,285**	**4,163**	**5,527**	**5,324**	**5,045**	**5,051**	**6,442**	**5,125**
India	3,000	2,818	3,448	2,984	3,727	3,469	4,729	4,372	5,457	4,853
Guatemala	3,496	4,318	3,536	3,787	4,002	4,524	4,219	4,892	5,201	4,700
Ivory Coast	4,129	2,246	2,293	3,007	2,532	4,528	3,682	2,042	5,899	3,974
Uganda	2,088	2,185	3,142	2,393	3,244	4,297	2,552	3,298	3,097	3,205
Ethiopia	3,061	1,794	2,865	2,537	2,860	3,270	2,916	2,745	3,505	2,768
Peru	1,200	1,812	665	1,179	1,871	1,806	1,922	2,022	2,506	2,539
Rest of the world	24,644	22,548	21,132	22,783	23,419	22,733	21,258	20,819	23,535	21,257
Total	101,635	88,834	89,794	95,322	85,647	102,495	95,964	106,217	114,463	112,444

Source: International Coffee Organization (ICO)

Colombia and Mexico, the latter of which also suffers negative balance-of-payments and an overvalued currency. Or, if producer countries can unite, they can define and implement concrete actions to rectify the current state of oversupply.

CEPCO and CNOC have proposed the following joint policies for producing countries:

1. Destroy at least five percent of the lowest quality coffee exports.
2. Enter negotiations with the United States and the European Union to establish stricter quality controls to prevent the entrance of poor-quality coffee into their markets.
3. Promote coffee consumption more actively.
4. Demand that the international financial institutions that supported global overproduction now support a gradual reduction, in agreement with the producer countries. (Vietnam proposed this at the World Coffee Conference in London in May 2001).

Storm Clouds and Hope

The map of rural poverty matches that of coffee production, and that of armed resistance and peasant uprisings in the country. The desperation is great.

—Luís Hernández Navarro,
Café: La pobreza de la riqueza, la riqueza de la pobreza

As a result of many of the factors surrounding CEPCO's founding—particularly Inmecafe's disappearance and the state government's formation of its own state coffee council—both CEPCO and CNOC have played an important role in the development of public policies for the sector. This role becomes particularly important in the current economic crisis. Independent coffee growers have struggled to make the Mexican government understand that its policies towards the small-holder coffee sector are based on the mistaken assumption that small producers are not economically viable. CEPCO and CNOC maintain that the problem with small producers is not simply low productivity, which has been a problem for a long time and remains one today. Rather, the problem also rests on the failure to free small producers from a debilitating system of intermediaries and on the government's failure to promote and develop the sector. With adequate support and the cooperation of other producer countries it would be possible to raise the quality of production and strengthen a sector bled dry by harmful policies.

CEPCO and CNOC's demands in recent years address these problems and propose steps to improve Mexican coffee farming.[31] First, the coffee-related institutions must be reformed. The national Mexican Coffee Council must be restructured and transformed into a national body that includes state and regional organizations in a more efficient, autonomous, and representative body capable of developing and directing strategic projects and managing the budgets for coffee activities. Second, Mexico needs an integrated coffee-promotion program with greater resources. The program must promote environmental sensitivity and sustainable-production practices: organic, shade-grown, and fair-trade coffee. It should also promote the domestic consumption of high-quality Mexican coffee, since the market for quality coffee in Mexico remains very undeveloped. Third, it is essential to establish mechanisms to stabilize prices. Over the last twenty-five years average prices have been high enough to be profitable. The main problem, especially in the last ten years, is the wild fluctuation in prices, not only because of the international market but also internal factors such as the overvaluation of the Mexican peso. Fourth, Mexico must cooperate with other producer and consumer countries. Social organizations must work together to demand such cooperation and to promote increased international consumption of coffee sold directly by small fair-trade coffee producers. Finally, CEPCO and CNOC have been building alliances with other independent peasant organizations to promote fair agricultural policies in Mexico. They have worked with the basic grains producers of ANEC, the forest coalition organized by the Mocaf Network, the credit unions that are part of AMUCSS, as well as other organizations that share the same vision of a revalued Mexican agriculture.[32]

Meanwhile, CEPCO continues to build its own destiny, making democratic decisions, confronting poverty with its own unique social and ecological perspective, and building more equitable gender relations. Despite the many challenges the organization's members face because of neoliberal government policies and globalization, their experience up to now leaves them optimistic about their future.

Notes

1. This sentence is frequently quoted by the elders in the Mazateca region of Oaxaca, home to the largest number of Oaxacan coffee producers.

2. V.H. Santoyo C. S. Diaz, and B. Rodriguez P. in *Sistema agroindustrial café en Mexico: diagnostico, problematica y alternativas* (México: Universidad Autónoma Chapingo, 1995).

3. Victor M. Toledo and Patricia Moguel, "En busca de un café sostenible en Mexico: la importancia de la diversidad biologica y cultural" (Morelia, Mexico:

Ecological Center, Universidad Nacional Autónoma de México, 1996), 9. Presentation at the First Congress on Sustainable Coffee, September 16–18, 1996.

4. Verena Stolcke, "The Labors of Coffee in Latin America: The Hidden Charm of Family Labor and Self-Provisioning," in *Coffee, Society and Power in Latin America*, ed. William Roseberry, Lowell Gudmundson and Mario Samper K. (Baltimore: Johns Hopkins University Press, 1995), 67. Stolcke states: "Many authors have regarded coffee as a monoculture whose expansion tended to displace subsistence agriculture, overlooking the fact that coffee has often been grown together with food crops. . . . Attention to forms of exploitation of family labor reveals . . . the frequent combination of coffee as a cash crop with food production for self-provisioning by family labor."

5. Theodore E. Downing, "A Macro-Organizational Analysis of the Mexican Coffee Industry, 1888–1977," in *The Hidden Crisis in Development: Development Bureaucracies*, ed. Philip Quarles van Ufford, Dirk Kruijt, and Theodore Downing (Amsterdam: Free University Press, 1988), 5. Downing describes coffee growers in a similar way: "Marginal producers own small parcels of land, with most holding less than two or three hectares. In contrast to the small producers, coffee is not the only crop planted. A higher proportion of their lands is cultivated with maize, beans and other subsistence crops, with coffee being an important petty-cash crop. For manpower, marginal coffee producers rely on domestic labor, and infrequently, upon unpaid reciprocal labor relations with extended-family members."

6. Ricardo Hernández J., Mazateco coffee producer, current Treasurer of CEPCO.

7. It is particularly noteworthy that the Mexican government did not provide support or training so that peasant social organizations could take on all the functions abandoned by Inmecafe.

8. Luís Hernández Navarro, "Nadando con los tiburones: la experiencia de la Coordinadora Nacional de Organizaciones Cafetaleras," in *Cafeteleros, la construccion de la autonomia; Cuadernos de desarrollo de base #3* (Mexico: National Coordinator of Coffee Organizations/Servicio de Apoyo Local A.C., 1991).

9. Armando Bartra, "El aroma de la historia social del café," in *La Jornada del Campo* (July 28, 1999): 4.

10. Benoit Daviron, "La crisis del mercado cafetalero internacional en una perspectiva a largo plazo," mimeo from CIRAD (Montpellier, 1990), 8. Daviron explains, "The agreement was based on an export-limit system. Each exporting country had a base quota determined by successive annual agreements. The Board of the OIC set a fixed global quota each year of exports for all the producer-country members based on the anticipated future imports by the consuming-country members. This global quota was distributed quarterly to insure a regular supply to the market throughout the year. . . . The agreements of 1976 and 1983 established a range of prices within which an indicator price—the average prices of the robust coffee and the other mild arabica coffees—had to be maintained (120–140 cents per pound since 1980)."

11. Fernando Celis, "Nuevas formas de asociacionismo en la cafeticultura mexicana: el caso de la CNOC," mimeo, Xalapa, Veracruz, August 2000, 22. Celis states: "With the liquidation of Inmecafe, [Oaxaca] Governor Ramirez saw the opportunity to create a state organization that would control this activity. He invited Fausto Cantu Pena, ex-director of Inmecafe, to develop the project. At the

beginning of 1989, a forum was organized to present the new project. This was attended by a small group associated with the independent organizations, which criticize the Cantu Pena project because it did not include independent producers and the state wanted to control the financing and marketing of the coffee."

12. This organizational approach was a majority because almost all (ninety percent) of the small producers were part of one of the 500 existing UEPCs in Oaxaca. With the support of Inmecafe, all of these producers were considered members of the State Union of Coffee Producers of the PRI-affiliated National Peasant Confederation (CNC). The mechanism by which this confederation ensured the representation of all the UEPC members was simple and identical to the other corporatist government structures: They were automatically affiliated to their local, municipal, regional, and state organizations, giving the CNC formal representation of all coffee producers.

13. Fernando Rello, "La occupacion campesina de los espacios dejados por el Estado. El caso de la Coordinadora Estatal de Productores de Café de Oaxaca," CEPAL undated mimeo, 4.

14. Rosario Cobo, "Huertas indias," mimeo, 1999, 28.

15. The indicators used to define the classification of high marginality are: the amount of housing without a sewage system, electric power, or plumbing, and with overcrowding and soil floors; and the proportion of the population with incomes less than two times the minimum wage.

16. CEPCO is a member of the National Coordinator of Coffee Organizations (CNOC), which brings together independent organizations of small producers from all over the country: Chiapas, Oaxaca, Hidalgo, Guerrero, Puebla, San Luís Potosí, and Veracruz. "The majority of the organizations that formed the CNOC came from movements to pressure and negotiate with Inmecafe in three different periods. The first came in 1982–1984 with strong mobilizations of groups from several states. Then in 1987 [. . .] the central motive was the demand for an increase in the liquidation price [. . .] The third period is in 1989, in Oaxaca, with the creation of a State coffee council following the withdrawal of Inmecafe at a national level. The goals in that case were to influence the new body so as to maintain support programs for the producers." Fernando Celis, 2000, 22.

17. The technical staff began as a part of a local nongovernmental organization, the Center to Support the Oaxacan Popular Movement, then became CEPCO. The staff has grown as new organizational needs have emerged, particularly in areas in which CEPCO has specialized: organic coffee production, organizing women coffee-growers, financing, and commercialization.

18. Fernando Rello, "La ocupación campesina," undated mimeo.

19. José Ramos, former President of CEPCO, leader from the Chinanteca region.

20. The *quintal* is the conventional measure used in Mexico for coffee production. Equivalents are: one quintal equals 57.5 kgs. (127 lbs.) of parchment coffee, or 46 kgs. (101 lbs.) of green coffee.

21. Celis, "Nuevas formas de asociacionismo," 59.

22. In 1995, the Secretary of the Interior and Public Credit (SHCP) established a legal entity called "Integrated Enterprises" to allow organizations to offer services to their members and to manage campaigns to increase the participation of micro, small, and medium enterprises. Presently CAEO is registered as an integrated enterprise. (CEPCO Evaluation, 1994–96, 39.)

23. CEPCO's production of parchment coffee has fluctuated over the years with conditions and prices. Between the 1990-91 growing cycle and the 1999–2000 cycle, volumes (in *quintales*) have been: 56,053; 66,117; 41,890; 39,998; 27,523; 28,868; 42,245; 62,891; and 57,357.

24. Among the other sources of credit: Banrural and Banco del Bajio, with the mediation of FIRA and Bancomex; Fondo Acción de Banamex and Fonaes.

25. These funds came mainly from Fidecafe and the National Indigenous Institute–Solidarity, from its program for gathering and commercialization of the 1993–94 harvest.

26. Regional organizations had the choice to invest their share of these funds in the credit union, and not all the organizations did. Some of them spent the money and others invested in the creation of regional funds, like savings accounts.

27. Fondo Nacional de Apoyo para las Empresas de Solidaridad.

28. To promote this alternative, CEPCO is a member of and participates actively in different forums such as Registro Unico del Mercado Justo (FLO), Comercio Justo Mexico, Consejo Civil para la Cafeticultura Sustentable en Mexico, Ecomex, etc. CEPCO's producers have also been involved in promoting fair trade coffee by visiting consumer groups and importers in the United States, Canada and Europe, to share their experience. Other related CEPCO projects include a program for crop diversification among coffee farmers, another for carbon sequestration, and one to better classify coffee lands.

29. Robert A. Rice and Justin R. Ward, *Coffee, Conservation and Commerce in the Western Hemisphere. How Individuals and Institutions Can Promote Ecologically Sound Farming and Forest Management in Northern Latin America* (Washington: Natural Resources Defense Council and Smithsonian Migratory Bird Center, 1996), 11.

30. CEPCO internal document, 1998, 91.

31. See Fernando Celis Callejas, "Un Horizonte para la Cafeticultura Mexicana," mimeo, August 2001.

32. Coordinadora Nacional de Organizaciones Cafeteleras (CNOC), a coalition of regional peasant coffee-growing organizations; Federación de organismos de base de uniones de crédito campesinas (AMUCSS), a coalition of thirty-two peasant farmers' credit unions; Red Mexicana de Organizaciones Campesinas Forestales (MOCAF), a community-based forestry coalition.

PART 3

EMPLOYMENT UNDER FREE TRADE: EXPLOITATION AND EXPULSION

9

The Struggle for Justice in the *Maquiladoras:* The Experience of the Autotrim Workers

Pastoral Juvenil Obrera

THE NORTH AMERICAN FREE TRADE AGREEMENT (NAFTA) GAVE A STRONG boost to the export manufacturing industry in Mexico. This sector, which has shown considerable growth in the past few years, stands at the core of the Mexican government's development strategy. Under the logic of comparative advantage, Mexico has bet a good part of its future—and the future of its workers—on maintaining low wages to attract foreign investment. This strategy in turn is intended to fuel the Mexican economy's lift-off to development. The cost of labor in Mexico is estimated to be only one-tenth the cost in the United States.

During the NAFTA negotiations, the opinions of unionists, environmentalists, and human rights activists from the United States, Canada, and Mexico were largely disregarded. These groups expressed concern that expanding the *maquiladora* export-processing sector would lead to an increase in worker exploitation and a severe deterioration in the environment, particularly on Mexico's northern border where much of the industry is concentrated. They also warned that the lack of guarantees for workers to freely exercise their rights would leave workers without effective democratic organizations to protect their wages and benefits. They saw NAFTA's labor side agreement as extremely limited because it ignores Mexican workers' most pressing need: the freedom to form independent unions.

The story presented in this chapter highlights the working conditions in the *maquiladora* industry in Matamoros, just across the border from Brownsville, Texas. Workers in Matamoros face low wages, deplorable health and safety conditions, persistent health problems, deterioration in the surrounding environment, and a denial of basic labor rights and the freedom to organize. The case focuses on the long struggle for health, safety, and labor rights at the Autotrim plant in Matamoros, a fight that involved new forms of cross-border solidarity, innovative local strategies to win basic representation, and a precedent-setting complaint under NAFTA's labor side agreement. The Autotrim workers' experience makes it clear that the deterioration of labor conditions in the *maquiladora* industry can be stopped only through international regulation of labor standards, and that these standards must form an integral part of any trade agreement.

The *Maquiladora* Industry and NAFTA

The *maquiladora* industry was not created by NAFTA. It began in 1965 with the passage of the Mexican government's Program for Border Industrialization, designed to address the migration problem created by chronic unemployment and economic stagnation in Mexico's northern states after the United States unilaterally discontinued the Bilateral Convention on Guest Workers, commonly known as the Bracero Program. Since then, the *maquiladora* sector has been growing steadily, with particularly fast growth in the 1980s and another spurt after NAFTA went into effect.

The *maquiladora* sector is a classic duty-free, export-processing zone. Foreign-owned companies can set up factories to produce for export and enjoy a wide range of benefits. The companies are exempt from income and property taxes, and exports are not subject to the value-added tax. They do not have to pay duties on the intermediate goods they import for assembly, and the government subsidizes many of the costs of doing business, including building infrastructure and offering electricity and water at low prices. The vast majority of *maquiladoras* are U.S. owned, producing auto parts, light machinery, clothing, and other goods, mostly for the U.S. market.

Interestingly, NAFTA contained provisions for converting the sector's preferential fiscal status to one more on a par with domestic firms. Starting in 2000, companies could cease being classified as export firms, with all the tax and tariff advantages, becoming permanent enterprises subject to income taxes. Unfortunately, every time the Mexican government attempts to implement such a change the multinational corporations balk, threatening to pull out of the country. As will be discussed later, this same threat allows *maquiladora* owners to avoid improving wages and working conditions and to deny workers their constitutional right to organize.

In the last two decades, the number of *maquiladora* enterprises grew seven-fold while employment in the sector jumped ten-fold. Since NAFTA, the number of factories and jobs has more than doubled (see Table 9.1.)

While the *maquiladora* industry remains concentrated in the border states, NAFTA helped accelerate its spread to other parts of Mexico. The Mexican government authorized the creation of *maquiladora* zones in the interior in 1972, but a decade later eighty-eight percent of the industry was still along the border, with only twelve percent in the interior. By 1993 that percentage had doubled to twenty-four, and by early 2002, nearly forty percent of *maquiladoras* were in the interior.

The growth and spread of the *maquiladora* sector means that it is no longer simply a response to the problems of migration along the border. It has become a model for industrialization. Under NAFTA, foreign capital has been able to take advantage of the *maquiladora* structure, deepening and extending it.

False Promises

The *maquiladora* sector's importance to the Mexican economy has also grown. In 1980 the sector brought in 16.1 percent of the total value of exports; in 1993, that percentage had increased to 42.9. By April 2001, the *maquiladoras* contributed 48.3 percent of Mexico's total export earnings.[1] There has been a related rise in the importance of the manufacturing sector as a whole. Between 1987 and 2000, the sector's share of gross domestic product grew from six percent to nearly thirty percent.[2]

Unfortunately, the export boom has not helped solve Mexico's national economic problems; rather, it has deepened them. The assumption that the

Table 9.1 Growth of the Maquiladora Sector, 1982–2002

	Border States		Nonborder States		Total	
	Firms	Jobs	Firms	Jobs	Firms	Jobs
1982	455	113,000	59	13,821	514	126,821
1993	1,574	388,000	472	152,797	2,046	540,797
2002[a]	2,054	653,744	1,313	417,966	3,367	1,071,710

Source: Alberto Arroyo and Alejandro Villamar, *Tratado de Libre Commercio (TLCAN): México, 7 años* (Mexico City: Mexican Free Trade Action Network (RMALC), April 2001), available at: http://www.rmalc.org.mx/.

Note: a. The data for 2002 are for January–April, from the monthly statistical summary of the National Council for the Export Maquiladora Industry.

Mexican economy would grow steadily and sustainably on the basis of manufacturing exports has not been borne out. "The overall tally of eighteen years of neoliberalism, and the seven years under NAFTA, is very slow growth," according to researcher Alberto Arroyo. From 1982 to 2000 Mexico saw real per capita growth of only 0.48 percent per year. Under NAFTA it has been only slightly better, at 1.74 percent.[3]

Export assembly industries have a very small effect on other areas of production, generating little indirect employment, and largely failing to stimulate the rest of the economy. In part this is because they use very few domestic inputs, aside from labor. Generally the *maquiladoras* get only two percent of their supplies from domestic sources (the maximum was just 3.1 percent in 2000), with imported goods accounting for ninety-eight percent.[4] "The majority of imports under NAFTA are intermediate goods (77.2%), principally primary materials," according to Arroyo. "These imports of intermediate goods represent a delinking of national production chains and employment losses due to the closing of enterprises that used to produce such goods. This is the other side of the denationalization of export manufacturing and the limited impact these enterprises have on the rest of the economy and on employment."[5]

Despite the expansion of the export industry, between 1994, and 2001 there has been a net loss of employment. In other words, while new jobs are created in the export manufacturing sector, a larger number are lost in other industries and sectors, primarily those producing for the domestic market. The recent economic slowdown in the U.S. economy has highlighted the export model's vulnerability due to its enormous dependence on the exterior. According to government sources, the *maquiladora* industry lost 235,435 jobs between October 2000, and November 2001, a drop of eighteen percent.[6]

While the export model promotes the *maquiladora* sector, it also contributes to the deindustrialization of the country. There has been a rise in bankruptcies in domestic industry and skyrocketing growth of the informal economy. In Mexico only one-third of the labor force has formal employment. From mid-1993, through mid-2000, the Mexican economy added approximately 6.2 million jobs, of which more than half (51.2 percent) were in the informal sector. Furthermore, sixty-two percent of the new jobs do not have benefits and seventeen percent pay less than minimum wage.[7]

Despite relatively strong growth in the *maquiladora* sector under NAFTA, the manufacturing sector as a whole has not prospered. The manufacturing sector achieved an impressive 43.8 percent increase in productivity in that time, yet net employment decreased 0.3 percent, the real cost of labor dropped by 29.9 percent, and manufacturing wages lost twelve percent of their buying power.[8] In other words, the export sector's dynamism came at the expense of employment, wages, and national industrial development.

Promoters of the export model argue that foreign investment will raise wages because transnational companies pay more than domestic companies. In Mexico the numbers show a different trend. The average wage in the *maquiladoras* is actually seventy-five to eighty percent of the average wage in domestic manufacturing.[9]

Environmental Costs

The environmental costs of export-led development have been high. Mexico offers lax environmental standards and easy evasion, which has permitted the *maquiladora* industry to become a serious source of pollution. The production and inadequate disposal of toxic wastes; the contamination of the water, air, and soil; and the inadequacy of urban hygienic infrastructure are the principal environmental problems associated with the establishment and functioning of the *maquiladoras.*

According to PROFEPA, the main government environmental enforcement agency, *maquiladoras* have made the states of Baja, California and Chihuahua the country's largest toxic waste producers. Thanks to the export industry around Tijuana, Baja, California, reports fifty-one percent of its factories dump toxic waste, while Chihuahua, with *maquiladora*-intensive Ciudad Juárez, reports twenty percent. According to government figures, 36.2 percent of *maquiladoras* generate solvents, thirteen percent oils and grease, 7.7 percent paint and varnish, eleven percent lead solder, tin, and resins. Overall, the *maquiladora* industry produces 52,148 tons of waste annually.[10]

Researchers have estimated that in El Paso and Ciudad Juárez, transnational firms are responsible for eighty-five percent of environmental pollution, including the discharge of toxic chemicals into the sewer systems and waterways and the disposal of chemical waste in garbage dumps. According to some estimates, in the last seven years some 8,000 tons of toxic waste have been dumped along the Mexican border.[11]

Capital Mobility

Such conditions persist because the labor market is nationally and internationally competitive, and residents have few alternatives. Two major factors make it difficult to improve wages and working conditions: the high mobility of the enterprises and the related obstacles to establishing unions. The general numbers about the growth of employment in the *maquiladora* sector also hide the fact that companies are constantly moving. Even though the number of jobs may be reported as stable, for the individual workers the experience is anything but. The constant closing and opening of firms means high turnover, little job security, and a prevalence of short-term contracts.

As a result, workers have limited opportunities for labor organizing and have great difficulty building seniority, which is often the only way to earn higher wages and benefits. The mobility of the *maquiladora* industry is a strong obstacle to unionization, since any attempt to organize is confronted with the threat of plant closings and the consequent loss of employment. As the Autotrim case shows, the labor force is controlled through official unions, which assure order while they combat independent worker initiatives for better pay or working conditions.

The Autotrim Workers

The struggle to improve the health, environmental, and wage conditions in the *maquiladoras* grew from a local struggle to an international campaign due to the practices of Autotrim de México, a car parts *maquiladora* located in Matamoros. Autotrim was established in Matamoros in 1985, as a subsidiary of the Canadian company Custom Trim. In April 1997, it was acquired by the U.S. consortium Breed Technologies, headquartered in Lakeland, Florida. Breed Technologies is one of the largest car-parts manufacturers in the world. It produces leather coverings for steering wheels and gearshift levers for General Motors, Ford, and Chrysler, among others. Currently Autotrim employs more than 1,400 workers.

In 1992, Autotrim workers began to organize to improve their living and working conditions. Their experience over more than eight years highlights some of the ways in which the *maquiladoras* promote the intensive use of labor and impose a double standard for wages and labor rights in the different countries where the parent companies operate, and how the *maquiladora* model promotes productivity at the cost of the physical and psychological integrity of the workers, without granting them fair compensation for their labor.

Autotrim workers began to see the connections among the various health problems many had suffered. The sewing work for the steering wheel covers and gearshift levers is done manually and requires many repetitive motions with significant force, which can cause serious damage to ligaments and muscles in the hands, arms, and neck. Production processes also involve glues and solvents, which, when used without adequate protective gear, can cause irritation in the throat and on the skin, respiratory problems, allergies, and harm pregnant women and their babies.

These conditions are not uncommon in the *maquiladora* industry, which has a long history in Matamoros, even before the industry's growth following NAFTA. The state of Tamaulipas is home to the third largest number of *maquiladora* jobs and plants, after Chihuahua and Baja, California. In recent years the industry has even expanded to rural communities, where municipal governments offer facilities and where salaries can be even lower.

In 1994, 293 plants were registered in Tamaulipas; the number grew twenty-eight percent by 2000 to 375. In the city of Matamoros growth was even more rapid, with the number of plants rising thirty-three percent, from 89 to 119. Statewide, *maquiladora* employment increased even more dramatically, from 100,027 in 1994 to 181,150 six years later, an increase of eighty-one percent. In Matamoros, employment growth was seventy-two percent, from 38,361 to 66,023.[12]

A Portrait of Exploitation

General concerns about the working conditions in the *maquiladora* industry in Matamoros prompted an investigation by the Metropolitan Autonomous University (UAM), which carried out a detailed survey of the industry and its workers. Its report paints a dismal picture of the city's *maquiladoras* and shows that the conditions confronted by Autotrim workers were quite typical of the industry.[13]

The UAM study documents the changes in the labor force that have accompanied the expansion of the *maquiladora* sector. With few alternative sources of employment, the *maquiladoras* are among the limited options available to the families of Matamoros. According to the survey, fifty-nine percent of the families in Matamoros have between two and five family members working in a *maquiladora*.

The workforce is made up mostly of women, a characteristic of the industry that only recently has begun to change. The industry explanation for this phenomenon is that women are more suited for the meticulous work involved in the assembly process. In practice, the reasons may be more related to the fact that employing women allows the industry to pay lower wages, offer few, if any, benefits, and give no job security. This has changed little with the recent trend toward hiring more men. The electrical industry in Matamoros, for example, used to employ more than ninety percent women; by 1992, this percentage had been reduced to seventy percent, and recent statistics show it to be down to sixty-one percent. This has not brought up wages, however, but rather has kept wages low due to the increasing labor market competition between men and women. With Mexico's economic restructuring, men are willing to accept lower wages, while wage discrimination against women continues. The result is deterioration in wages and working conditions for both genders. Adding to the labor market competition is the industry preference for younger workers. The UAM study shows that more than forty percent of the *maquiladora* labor force in Matamoros is made up of workers between eighteen and twenty-five years of age. The glut of workers has allowed companies to raise the academic requirements to apply for jobs, with many jobs requiring a high school diploma, even for entry-level positions.

Low wages leave many full-time workers living in poverty. The UAM study showed that only twenty percent of Matamoros's *maquiladora* workers earn wages higher than Mexico's official poverty line, set at twice the minimum wage (around $90 per month). These figures translate into harsh daily realities for *maquiladora* workers, forcing them to cut back on necessities, extend the work day, put more family members to work, or look for alternative income. The UAM study included revealing testimony from Matamoros workers such as Antonia:

> I work in Modern Technology. My husband abandoned me. I have six daughters, and the oldest one is thirteen. My work week is forty hours. My net pay is 396.50 pesos a week [about $45]. I have to make the monthly payments for my land, so I save 112.50 [pesos] each week. . . . My daughters are alone the whole day, they don't go to school, and the eldest takes care of them. When I have the opportunity I buy them shoes and used clothes. I have hardly any furniture, just a stove, a bed, and a small table. We never have enough food. The only way I can buy milk, a little fruit, and sometimes meat is when I work Saturdays, Sundays, and overtime during the week, but because I work so much, I leave my children very unattended. Sometimes I despair—I don't know what to do to get out of this situation.[14]

Working conditions are particularly hard for women. The industry commonly administers pregnancy tests to female job applicants, and this has not changed under NAFTA even though it is against the law. Women who became pregnant during their initial probationary period often are fired without receiving their maternity pay or medical attention, both of which they are entitled to under Mexican law.[15]

Sexual harassment of women is also illegal, though plant managers and their allies in the pro-company labor unions continue to treat it as a personal problem and not a labor issue. Most companies have no code of conduct to identify, investigate, and resolve sexual harassment complaints; the official unions won't file claims in most cases.

Women suffer harassment from other workers as well as supervisors and administrative personnel. It is now deeply ingrained in the industry culture. Some women respond with open or hidden prostitution, which helps them compensate for low wages. For example, in one company, some male employees—mainly administrators and some workers—hold a weekly raffle, selling tickets to male employees with the winner earning the right to have sexual relations with a female employee who has agreed to be raffled off. The woman sometimes earns as much as $275 for one night, about fifty times the minimum wage. Of course, the ticket price depends on the beauty and age of the woman in question.

There are few services for mothers and fathers. Day-care services are limited, with waiting lists of two years or more. Many mothers leave their children in private day care, or in informal day-care arrangements with few formal qualifications; these can cost ten to fifteen dollars per week. Women's incorporation into the labor market does not exempt them from their domestic activities, which they carry out when they get home, basically working a double shift. Their wages are too low to allow them to hire domestic help, and few men contribute to this type of work. It is also common to find *maquiladora* workers carrying out informal activities to make more money, such as selling used clothes and other articles in stands and flea markets on the weekends, or selling cosmetics or domestic articles during work breaks.

Living Conditions in Matamoros: Squatter Communities

The growth of the *maquiladora* industry was badly planned, and the arrival of new workers from impoverished rural Mexico has resulted in a severe housing shortage in Matamoros. According to the UAM study, only thirty-three percent of the city's *maquiladora* workforce is from Matamoros. The rest come from the interior of the state of Tamaulipas or from the center and the south of the country, many from the states of Veracruz, San Luís Potosí, and Chiapas. The new arrivals pushed the city's population growth rate to 3.2 percent per year in the 1990s, higher than the statewide rate of

2.1 percent and the national average of 1.9 percent. Most new arrivals live on abandoned land they have taken over to form improvised settlements. In the last six years, more than thirty such settlements have been established on the outskirts of Matamoros. This kind of unorganized growth is hard on both people and the environment, particularly when public investment is directed toward infrastructure for foreign companies rather than urban public services. The industry's irresponsible management of industrial waste magnifies the problem.

Working Conditions: Faster, Dirtier, and Less Secure

With the recent trends toward "flexible" work organization, the quantity, quality, and pace of work have intensified in the *maquiladoras*. The state of Tamaulipas was one of the first to implement the so-called new work culture, which involves replacing guaranteed social benefits (such as life insurance, savings clubs, loans, and scholarships for workers and their children) with cash bonuses based on attendance, productivity, and work quality. Productivity is based on very high work quotas, which earn workers weekly bonuses of two to five dollars but which are very demanding. So-called continuous improvement programs to raise productivity and quality establish production and cost-reduction goals. To meet these goals, workers often have to work at a much quicker pace, work more hours per day, reduce their break time, and even take work home.

At Autotrim, for example, a production line for steering-wheel covers used to be staffed by six people, who were organized to each sew full covers with a production quota of twenty per person, or 120 pieces per line per day. Now the same six people carry out more specialized operations and the line has to produce 152 pieces a day, an increase of almost twenty-seven percent.

The work day in the *maquiladoras* has grown longer over time. The work week has been extended from forty to forty-eight hours, and there is mandatory overtime. Another recent innovation is the creation of the fourth and fifth shifts, with new forty-hour shifts that begin with four hours on Thursday, and then include twelve hours daily on Friday, Saturday, and Sunday. This allows the company to avoid paying overtime and keeps the factories running twenty-four hours a day. These shifts violate Mexican law, which places fairly strict limits on working hours, but they attract workers, particularly young people who can combine school and work.

There is typically very high turnover in the *maquiladoras*.[16] In Matamoros, the formal turnover rate is lower than in some other cities, but the prevalence of the short-term contracts (typically three months) with consecutive renewals prevents workers from earning seniority, which in turn leaves them with little job security.[17]

Safety and health conditions and pollution problems have generated the most organized resistance in the *maquiladoras*. The UAM survey documents this situation. In Matamoros, some 85,000 people work in industries that present some health risk. Fifty-three percent of the people surveyed reported that they use toxic chemicals such as solvents, glues, paint, thinners, degreasers, and solder. The remaining forty-seven percent said they did not even know if the products they work with are toxic. Sixty percent of those surveyed work with noise, dust, smoke, and fumes in their environment. Eighty-three percent reported that they receive some minimal safety gear but consider it insufficient to protect their health. Ninety-two percent report that their company has a formal Joint Health and Safety Committee, but that it does not function well. Sixty percent of the workers reported suffering health problems related to their work. Industry practices make it difficult to find official information on the health problems associated with *maquiladora* work, leaving most work-related problems underreported. The doctors at many public health clinics refuse to certify the health problems as work-related because companies refuse to pay the costs of evaluation or treatment.

The Struggle at Autotrim

Activism among Autotrim workers was first catalyzed by such health issues. Several workers individually took their health complaints to administrators. Getting no response after several months, workers organized a committee to discuss the problems directly with management. Management denied that the health problems had anything to do with working conditions. Workers responded with committees to demand basic information about the chemicals being used in production. They also requested reduced production quotas. Management fired the most vocal workers shortly afterward. The threat of dismissal is management's most effective tool to keep workers from organizing.

In 1993, a group of twenty workers forced the company and Mexico's social security agency (IMSS) to recognize that their injuries were work-related. Workers were granted disability for work accidents, with compensation of ten to sixty percent of the maximum legal benefit. This set a precedent by recognizing that working conditions had caused the reported health problems. By 1994, more than 150 workers had demonstrated injuries to their hands. More worrisome, there were many cases of birth defects in workers' children. The company and IMSS refused to grant any further disability claims, medical attention, or compensation. An anonymous testimony from the UAM study highlights the continued health problems in the Autotrim plant:

> "I worked for two years in the sewing area, I hurt my hand and was incapacitated for one year. Now I'm in the finishing area, cleaning the steering wheel with a rag drenched in Barsol to get rid of the rubber stains. I apply heat with a pistol to get rid of wrinkles. My production quota is sixty-five steering wheels a shift, but I can only do forty-five. I feel pain when I stretch out my hand to grab the wheel, my fingers often go numb, my whole right arm hurts, and so do my neck and back. I have to take pills, sometimes every four hours. I can't complete my household chores, I drop things all the time, I can't do laundry, nor can I carry heavy things. I come home in a bad mood, I feel so useless. I'm very depressed to be like that. I cry a lot."[18]

Corporatist Unions and Independent Organizing

The commissions that the Autotrim workers organized had no formal authority because workers were officially represented by the CTM, the largest union federation in the country for the last six decades. The CTM, together with other union federations like the Revolutionary Confederation of Workers and Peasants (CROC) and the Revolutionary Confederation of Mexican Workers (CROM), controls the majority of unions in the *maquiladora* sector. These union federations operate much like company unions elsewhere, with the added feature that the unions are closely tied to the former ruling political party—the Institutional Revolutionary Party, or PRI—as part of the broad corporatist structure in the country. In the *maquiladoras*, the official unions typically sign a collective bargaining contract before the plant even opens, without consulting the workers. In general these contracts establish the minimum standards required by law. This system has proven very effective in preventing the emergence of independent workers' organizations. The existence of an official contract recognized by government authorities forces workers to dispute the validity of the official representation by asking for a public vote to decertify the official union and establish their own union. This means confronting not only the power of the companies but also the might of the official union federations and the complacency of government labor authorities.

The official union system rules in Matamoros. In January 1998, for example, labor authorities, the business organization, and the CTM-affiliated

Union of Industrial and Day Laborers of Matamoros and the Maquiladora Industry signed a pact behind workers' backs establishing a two-tier pay scale. The agreement set an upper limit of fifty pesos a day (about $4.50) for newly hired personnel. Because the wage differential between new hires and workers with highest seniority runs as high as sixty-eight percent, companies have responded by firing high-seniority workers in favor of workers earning the restricted minimum wage. The benefit to employers is obvious.

At Autotrim, the independent workers' group tried to get the backing of the local CTM union representative, but without success. The workers decided to replace him and name one of their own members as the representative within the formal structure of the CTM. Between 1994, and 1995, five workers' representatives were fired, one after the other, after demanding medical attention, disability payments, and a reduction in production quotas. In 1995, the workers managed to get a meeting with Fidel Velázquez, the national leader of the CTM, who promised to solve the problem. He sent a doctor to the plant to examine the affected workers. After examining only a few workers, his diagnosis was the same as that of the company doctors: the workers were faking injuries to avoid work and had psychological problems. Backed by this diagnosis, the executive committee of the official union went along with the company's demand that the affected workers return to work and make their production quotas. They would face dismissal if they did not comply.

"The plant hired a doctor to check all the people with hand injuries," one worker explained. "When I was with the doctor, he asked me to write my name on a piece of paper with my injured hand, he asked me to show him how I put on my watch, and he started to ask me a lot of questions which made me very angry, questions like: 'When you comb your hair, how do you do it? How do you wash yourself? When you put on your underwear, how do you do it?' And other questions like that, designed to humiliate me. In the end, his answer was the following: 'What you should do is return to work; you should protect your job. Think of your children.'"[19]

With the failure to resolve the labor conflict through the official union, workers began to organize independently. During 1996, the strategy consisted of organizing secret meetings, to build a nucleus inside the factory while avoiding firings. The activists began working with a church-affiliated workers support center, the Pastoral Juvenil Obrera (or Young Pastoral Workers). This helped establish a more systematic organizing process based on research and worker education. Workers learned about federal labor laws and their current collective bargaining agreement. They organized legal defense for fired workers so they could win full compensation.

They collected information about toxic materials in the plant. And they researched the company, studying its markets, clients, and the location of its parent company and its other subsidiaries.

National and International Alliances

In October 1996, the Autotrim workers were invited to the annual meeting of the Coalition for Justice in Maquiladoras (Coalición Pro Justicia en las Maquiladoras, or CJM), a trinational organization bringing together U.S., Mexican, and Canadian activists and experts, including health and safety experts, religious organizations, local and national unions, NGOs, and organized nuclei of *maquiladoras* workers. These new international connections gave the Autotrim organizers a range of new information sources and support. They got help from the health departments at the University of California campuses in Los Angeles and Berkeley in analyzing the chemicals used in the production process. They researched subsidiary plants of Autotrim in other cities in Tamaulipas: Valle Hermoso, Control Ramírez, and Ciudad Victoria. They contacted workers from Custom Trim Valle Hermoso, which was owned by the same company, and began a network linking the two sets of workers. Exchanging information, they realized that the health and safety problems were similar in both plants.

With the mediation of CJM, Autotrim workers also established contact with Local 1090 of the Canadian Steelworkers Union of Ontario, Canada, which represents workers at the company's main plant. In December 1996, the Canadian union leaders visited Mexico and met with workers from Autotrim, Custom Trim Valle Hermoso, and Control Ramírez. The information exchange showed similarities and differences with respect to working conditions in the two countries. The Canadian unionists informed their Mexican counterparts that the Canadian plant had lost about sixty percent of its jobs due to the expansion in Mexico. The Canadian workers realized through the visit that the pace of production was much slower in Canada, and that they received wages twenty times higher than their Mexican counterparts. The Canadian workers reported they were generally given safety equipment and that their injuries on the job were usually treated as work-related. In contrast, Autotrim workers reported on their four-year struggle for company recognition of work risks and accidents.

Work Stoppages and Repression

The renegotiation of the collective bargaining agreements at Autotrim and Custom Trim opened new possibilities for joint action. In 1997, workers from the two enterprises met periodically to discuss contract issues. In addition to wage and benefits increases, they proposed contract changes to improve safety and health, oblige the company to inform workers about the chemical products in the plant, and guarantee the availability of safety equipment. The independent activists at Custom Trim managed to convince the official union representative to include them in the negotiations and to propose their contract demands. When the company did not take the demands seriously, the workers asked the union to declare a strike. When the union refused, the activists initiated their own five-day work stoppage. The company responded by suing the leaders of the stoppage for $75,000 in damages and losses. This forced the strikers to offer to end the stoppage if the company withdrew the lawsuit. The company refused, keeping the striking workers locked in the factory's patio. Meanwhile, Autotrim workers carried out their own stoppage in solidarity with Custom Trim workers.

The conflict came to a head when Mexican labor authorities and the leaders of the CTM intervened. The CTM had signed the contract behind the workers' backs. Striking workers were ordered to return to work, and twenty-eight organizers were fired. The Canadian Steelworkers Union set up a humanitarian fund for the fired workers, who sued under Mexican labor law. Despite the loss, the conflict was widely publicized through CJM, earning workers support from a large number of organizations.

Out of this international cooperation came a new cross-border campaign called Jobs with Justice. The campaign's goals were to get the fired workers reinstated, to publicize the health and safety problems in the Mexican plants, and to support the Canadian workers' demands to keep their jobs and prevent the company from moving the work to Mexico. As part of the campaign, a group of workers from Custom Trim and Autotrim traveled to Canada, where they demonstrated outside the Ontario plant, held press conferences, and met with members of Parliament.

The international campaign provoked new reactions from the company, in both countries. In Mexico, those who went to Canada were harassed, and some even received death threats. The Canadian subsidiary fired the workers who participated in the campaign and, a few months later, closed the Ontario plant and moved the entire operation to Mexico. This was carried out through the sale of the company to the U.S. corporation Breed Technologies. The move was devastating, putting an end to the new campaign for international workers' solidarity, defeating the Canadian workers' efforts to keep their jobs, and weakening independent labor activism among Mexican workers at Autotrim and Custom Trim.

The Safety and Health Committees:
An Alternative Form of Organization

Even with extensive international alliances, Custom Trim and Autotrim workers were unable to overcome the political and economic power of transnational capital, with its easy mobility inhibiting workers' attempts to organize. Still, in the Mexican plants, workers' social networks of solidarity and friendship allowed them to maintain a cohesive nucleus. These workers were also marked profoundly by death. Two children of workers died after being born with spina bifida. Another seven children of workers died at birth from respiratory problems and other ailments. For the workers, the connection between these deaths and the working conditions inside the plant was beyond doubt.[20] These tragedies prompted the worker-organizers to reinitiate organizing around health and safety issues.

> Before I was not that conscious about what was happening in the factory, but a year ago, my second child was born with anencephaly and died," tells the mother of one of the victims. "I got very angry. I was asking myself: What is happening? Fifteen days later, another girl was born with the same problem. In the last year there have been six cases, two of anencephaly, one of hydrocephalus, and three with respiratory problems. There have also been more than ten cases of miscarriage. After that, I have been talking to my coworkers, telling them about what is happening. I'm furious with the injustices that they are doing to me and to the others. I want to do something to prevent them from harming more people. Somebody has to stop this.[21]

The workers' strategy was to join the existing Joint Safety and Health Committees, learn how they worked, and influence company policy. On the committee, the workers were able to get the company to substitute a water-based material for toxic rubber, and this small victory gave the committee greater negotiating power.

In 1998, seventy-six workers with hand injuries were removed from their jobs with full compensation; fifty of these were members of the organizing group. Despite this setback, the health and safety activities continued. The group held training sessions on ergonomics, toxicology, and popular education, training a team of workers who then trained other workers, both inside the plant and in their communities and church groups. Outside the factory, the organizers and their advisors and supporters worked to avoid dismissals and address workers' fears of company reprisals. The work with safety and health experts allowed the workers to combine technical training on toxic substances, their effects on health, the laws and regulations about sanitation, and the role of governmental institutions, with content on ethical values, humanization of work, and the right to a dignified and healthy workplace. The health and safety organizing has produced only limited improvements in the working conditions in the *maquiladora*, but it has been effective in maintaining workers' cohesion outside and inside the factory.

Testing NAFTA's Side Agreement

In May 1999, workers decided to prepare a lawsuit against the company for damages to workers' health, to be presented to the Local Conciliation and Arbitration Board. The suit had to be based on medical evaluations that certified the health of every person that worked in the plant, the individual level of contact with toxic materials, and details on each of the toxic materials. These studies, lawyers' fees, and other payments proved prohibitively expensive for the workers, so they abandoned the plan. As an alternative, they decided to file a complaint with the National Administrative Office (NAO), the body created by NAFTA's labor side agreement, the Parallel Agreement on Labor Cooperation. With help from the Human Rights Clinic of St. Mary's University in Texas, workers began working intensively to prepare a formal complaint on behalf of the workers of Custom Trim de Valle Hermoso. In July 2000, workers submitted the complaint to NAO with endorsements from twenty-two organizations in Mexico, the United States, and Canada.

The action was not received well by the business sector and the official unions, which responded with a campaign to discredit and intimidate the workers who signed the complaint and their families. Among the criticisms was the charge that the workers were at the service of foreign interests because they were supported by groups from the United States and Canada. This was certainly a surprising accusation from a transnational company, particularly directed against workers demanding compliance with the law before an institution established under a trinational agreement. The workers tried to neutralize the smear campaign by using the means at their disposal: flyers, press releases, and Internet campaigns. They won sympathy and support within local communities, but their campaign had little impact within Mexico's official unions, which (along with their international union supporters) clearly do not consider the *maquiladora* sector important, and in any case do not have the power to confront international capital.

In August 2000, through the mediation of the Coalition for Justice in the Maquiladoras, the workers gained support from the president of the

National Union of Workers (UNT), one of the most powerful independent union federations in Mexico. In December the hearings took place in the NAO office in San Antonio, Texas. Workers, accompanied by their advisors, presented their testimonies. The company and the government were not present at the hearings, but the company handed a thousand-page report to the NAO. NAO carried out a site visit to verify the working conditions. In advance of the visit, the company carried out several repairs, gave out safety equipment to the workers, hid some chemicals, and intimidated workers to prevent them from voicing complaints during the visit. NAO also met with union leaders and local government officials.

On April 6, 2001, NAO issued its report. The investigation found deficiencies in the inspections and verifications of health and safety carried out by the Mexican government in the Autotrim and Custom Trim factories. They found that the company failed to carry out pertinent tests and monitoring, committed errors in the way the inspections were carried out, ignored ergonomic problems, and showed anomalies in the diagnosis of work-related diseases, physical injuries, and psychological problems. The report also confirmed the Mexican government's failure to respond to worker requests for inspection and its inconsistent compliance with the Parallel Agreement on Labor Cooperation. The report found reasonable cause for applying economic sanctions against the Mexican government, in accordance with the parallel accord, if the health and safety violations persisted.

For the workers at Custom Trim and Autotrim, the NAO finding was welcome news, because it showed that their claims were well-founded. The NAO decision mainly carries political weight since it challenges the company to recognize and attend to its health and safety problems. It also mandates ongoing monitoring of the problem and leaves the door open for future intervention, including economic sanctions, if the company and the Mexican government fail to comply with the laws.

Still, the NAO decision is only a partial victory, because it does not address workers' right to organize, and in so doing, gain the legal recognition that could allow them to defend their rights. At Autotrim, each effort by workers to apply the law resulted in their leaders being fired, necessitating a new organizational effort. If the NAO resolution sets an important precedent in the use of the legal instruments inscribed in the parallel agreement, it also highlights the extreme limits of these instruments. The side agreement's mandate is limited to three areas: child labor, minimum wage, and health and safety. With its scope so restricted, the labor agreement is clearly insufficient to rein in the abusive behavior of transnational capital. In a global context, the Autotrim workers' small victory with NAO will create no systemic changes.

Conclusion

The *maquiladora* industry has transformed itself into Mexico's model for industrialization, and the Fox administration has placed it at the core of its economic strategy. There is no doubt that the sector has expanded considerably with Mexico's neoliberal policies, despite the downturn caused by the recession in the United States. Nevertheless, the industry's spectacular growth has not translated into higher wages or increased buying power for workers. The jobs that have been created are precarious and of low quality, and many offer poor working conditions. The regions, cities, and localities where the new industries have been installed face grave environmental and social problems. Regional economies have not been reactivated, and the production and commercial links that could be associated with industry have not been strengthened.

The experience of the Autotrim workers presents the human side of many of these problems. It clearly shows the prevalence of difficult—and sometimes dangerous—working conditions. It also shows the tremendous obstacles workers face when they try to defend themselves through collective action. At the hands of the company, they suffer firings, hostilities, and threats. From the official union leaders, they face corruption and collusion with the company. From government authorities in charge of applying labor laws, there is little enforcement of worker protections and, on occasion, complicity with illegal corporate actions.

The case also highlights the limitations of NAFTA's Parallel Agreement on Labor Cooperation. Even though NAO issued a ruling in favor of the Autotrim and Custom Trim workers, this has had little impact on working conditions in these plants and has done little to promote respect for the rights of workers in Mexico. The case suggests that many of the warnings of NAFTA's opponents were correct. The agreement has had a negative impact on working conditions in all three countries: the loss of high-wage jobs in the United States and Canada; the creation of precarious and low-quality jobs in Mexico; and little or no stimulus to the Mexican economy as a whole.

To counteract these tendencies, different policies are required at the national and international levels. In Mexico a thorough reform of union practices and labor laws is essential. Currently these laws maintain a corporatist regime that favors corrupt unions and abusive corporate practices. International agreements must establish labor standards that guarantee the collective rights of workers and that promote a "harmonization upwards" in working conditions. Transnational companies also need to be held to performance requirements, preventing corporate double-standards that seek the most lenient rules. If trade agreements are to improve the economies of the member countries, the workers' living conditions have to be taken into account in their design. The expected standards must be laid out, clear measures to achieve them have to be detailed, and the regulatory mechanisms and sanctions to guarantee their compliance strengthened. Economic sanctions should be applied directly to the companies that violate the law, not just to governments. Eight years of NAFTA have shown that labor and environmental issues are not side issues but are a substantial part of member countries' economic relations and, as such, have to be addressed within the text of trade agreements.

Facing future trade agreements, particularly the Free Trade Area of the Americas, the great mobility of capital has to be recognized as an enormous obstacle to workers' efforts to achieve better living and working conditions. Capital mobility undermines workers as they seek to counterbalance the power of the companies and enforce the laws designed to protect their interests. Any new agreements must take steps to recognize this imbalance.

This case study also shows that the movement for labor rights has begun its own process of globalization, a phenomenon now seen in many areas of social activism. The cooperation between Mexican workers and their Canadian counterparts may not have produced the desired results, but it represented a new way to pressure transnational enterprises and pointed the way forward in strategies to establish such international alliances. Better coordination among unions is the only effective response to capital mobility. The Coalition for Justice in the Maquiladoras, a trinational alliance, gave the local struggle at Autotrim international publicity, which provided it with important solidarity and support.

For the Latin American countries now discussing possible entry into the Free Trade Area of the Americas, the Autotrim experience and the history of *maquiladoras* in Mexico offer important warnings and lessons. The *maquiladora* export industry should not be seen as a desirable means of generating economic growth and employment. It does not promote regional development, it does not create economic linkages, it does not stimulate economic activity in the country as a whole, and the employment it generates is unstable and of low quality. If the task is to improve living standards for the majority of the population, a different model of industrialization is needed. To achieve this, workers' collective power must be strengthened as a counterweight to the growing power of transnational corporations.

Notes

Pastoral Juvenil Obrera (or Young Pastoral Workers) is a church-affiliated support group for *maquiladora* workers. This chapter was written as a collaborative effort by several members of the group who participated in supporting the organizing efforts at Autotrim. Due to fears of reprisal from company and official union representatives, the names of the individual authors are being withheld.

1. Alberto Arroyo P., ed., "El TLCAN 7 años después. Contenido, resultados y propuestas," México, D.F., 2001, mimeo.

2. Banco de México, http://www.banxico.org.mx/

3. Alberto Arroyo P., "Economía en crecimiento?" in *Resultados del Tratado de Libre Comercio de América del Norte en México: Lecciones para la negociación del Acuerdo de Libre Comercio para las Américas,* ed. Alberto Arroyo P. (México City: RMALC, 2001), 15.

4. Alberto Arroyo P., "Mitos y realidades de México como potencia exportadora," in Arroyo (ed.) *Resultados,* 39-48.

5. Arroyo, "Mitos y realidades," 46.

6. Instituto Nacional de Estadística, Geografía e Informática (INEGI), "Personal Ocupado en la Industria Maquiladora de Exportación (Número de Personas)," January 2002. Available at http://dgcnesyp.inegi.gob.mx/pubcoy/coyunt/empleo/poimaq.html.

7. Arroyo, "Empleo y salario," in *Resultados,* 67–77.

8. Arroyo, "Empleo y salario," 71–73.

9. Teresa Rendón and Carlos Salas, "La Evolución del Empleo," in *Trabajo y Trabajadores en el México Contemporáneo,* ed. Arturo Alcalde, et al. (México City: Miguel Ángel Porrúa, 2001), 70.

10. Centro de Estudios Regionales y Comunicación Alternativa (CERCA), Frontera Norte, *Impactos de la maquila y el medio ambiente de Ciudad Juárez* (México City: Habitat International Coalition, Ciudad Juárez, 1992), cited by Miriam Alfie C. in *Y el Desierto se Volvío Verde: Movimientos Ambiéntales Binacionales* (México City: UAM-Azcapotzaldo, 1998).

11. Miriam Alfie C., *Y el desierto se volvió verde.*

12. INEGI, "Aspectos económicos de Tamaulipas. Características de la Industria Maquiladora de Exportación," http/www.inegi.gob.mx.

13. Miriam Alfie C. and Luis H. Méndez B., *Maquilas y Movimientos Ambientalistas: Exámen de un Riesgo Compartido* (México City: Conacyt, Editorial Eón, 2000). See Chapter 5, "Maquila, Medio Ambiente y Salud." Research project funded by the Universidad Autónoma Metropolitana-Azcapotzalco and the Consejo Nacional de Ciencia y Tecnología.

14. Alfie and Méndez, *Maquilas y Movimientos Ambientalistas.*

15. Human Rights Watch, "A Job or Your Rights: Continued Sex Discrimination in Mexico's Maquiladora Sector," *Human Rights Watch Report,* December 1998. Available at http://www.hrw.org/reports98/women2/

16. Andrés Peñaloza, et al. "Ensambladas a su mundo: las maquilas en la base geopolitica y económica de dominación" (México City, 2001), mimeo.

17. As the testimony of Marisela, a *maquiladora* worker, shows, the instability of employment has economic and psychological consequences for the workers, who find it impossible to plan their lives, in addition to living under constant stress and tension: "I was working for seven months at Sunbeam Oster, a *maquiladora* that produces controls for electric blankets and thermal cushions. When I started working, they told me that I had to pass a probation period of twenty-nine days. During this time I forced myself to be on time and comply with production quotas and respect the breaks. Afterwards they gave me a contract for three months. When the contract was about to run out, I couldn't sleep for a week;

the job wasn't good but I needed it a lot. Previously I had worked at Autotrim and I had hurt my hand; I didn't dare go to the doctor to get disability, because I knew that if the company found out, they would fire me. I put up with all I could. When the three months were up, they told me that they would renew my contract for another three months. Afterwards I had one absence and one report because I arrived three minutes late from a break, and when the second contract was up, they fired me. All they told me was that they didn't need me anymore and that my contract had run out. Another trip to the union and starting out again at another *maquiladora*." (Alfie and Méndez, *Maquilas y Movimientos Ambientalistas.*)

18. Alfie and Méndez, *Maquilas y Movimientos Ambientalistas.*

19. Alfie and Méndez, *Maquilas y Movimientos Ambientalistas.*

20. The danger of the toxic materials at the Autotrim plant, and the relationship between them and the tragedies suffered by workers and their children, are documented in the official complaint before the NAO: US NAO Public Submission 2000–01, June 30, 2000. Available at http://www.dol.gov/dol/ilab/public/media/reports/nao/Sub2000-01pt1.htm.

21. US NAO Public Submission 2000–01.

10

The Migrant Club El Remolino: A Binational Community Experience

Miguel Moctezuma Longoria

ONE OUT OF FIVE MEXICAN HOUSEHOLDS DEPENDS ON REMITTANCES FROM migrant workers in the United States. The economic impact of this export of labor is tremendous. Mexico receives on average $17 million a day in currency sent by its nationals abroad, and the phenomenon now extends to nearly all parts of the country. This flow of money constitutes not only the principal source of income for many families (the only source for forty percent of them), but also a structural part of the Mexican economy. In 2000, remittances reached $6.5 billion, making them the third largest source of foreign currency for the country.[1] According to the government, remittances lowered the deficit in the balance payments for the same year by twenty-seven percent. Mexican Central Bank figures suggest that remittances increased to nearly $9 billion in 2001. Compared to highly fluctuating sources of foreign currency, such as income from oil sales, remittances represent a relatively constant flow of net income.

While remittances are seen as a survival strategy by most recipients, especially in rural areas, for some migrant groups abroad they are part of a strategy for community development. This case study focuses on migrant organizations from the central state of Zacatecas that are channeling a variety of social investments into their communities of origin in Mexico. Through their activities, these organizations are generating two new social processes: the construction of the "collective migrant" as a new social subject, and the use of pooled remittances for binational investment in productive infrastructure. These processes are just getting underway, but they

195

have strong implications for both local economies and cultural identities. While recognizing these initiatives' limitations, and the difficult economic context in which they take place, this study assesses the potential of this new strategy by migrant organizations to stimulate development in Mexican communities.

Zacatecas Migration:
Economic Crisis and Social Networks

Emigration from Zacatecas to the United States began at the end of the nineteenth century and grew steadily[2] as the social networks of Zacatecan migrant communities in the United States proliferated.[3] The exodus increased with the economic crisis in the 1980s, exacerbated by the Mexican government's neoliberal policies.[4]

The impacts have been particularly severe in the agricultural sector. Farmers who grow basic grains have been hurt by low prices and rising imports, and fruit growers have yet to find stable commercial outlets for their *guayabas* or their peaches, important crops in some of the areas that have seen the most intense out-migration. Farmers have also seen high interest rates, declining government subsidies, and high costs for inputs such as machinery and electricity. A persistent drought over the last decade has imposed further hardships, particularly on bean and corn farmers, who are important national producers. Demographic studies document that in the last two decades the flow of migrants has become generalized throughout the state, increasingly affecting the north and northeast municipalities which are heavy bean producers and which previously registered only moderate rates of out-migration.[5]

The Zacatecas economy has not generated significant new employment to make up for the agricultural downturn. In fact, Zacatecas has the country's third lowest rate of labor market participation. The proportion of workers who work less than thirty-five hours a week is the fourth highest in the nation, and of the working population, only thirty-six percent receives a formal salary. With a per capita GDP of only $2,791, Zacatecas is among the poorest states in the country.[6] Only thirty percent of the working population earns more than two minimum wages (about $8.00 US a day).[7]

The state government has recognized the depth of the employment crisis: "As a result of the growth of the working age population, every year 8,000 to 12,000 additional jobs are needed just to absorb the young people who enter the labor market each year. Meanwhile, jobs are lost every year in the majority of the productive sectors, while in the most dynamic one, the manufacturing sector, only about 1,000 additional jobs have been created annually."[8] Between 1985, and 1999, Zacatecas showed no overall GDP growth. It is one of the ten states that during this period experienced a decrease in its relative contribution to the national economy, which is currently only 0.6 percent of the national GDP.[9]

All of this has resulted in high emigration rates. Zacatecas has the highest out-migration in the country, expelling five percent of its population annually, compared with a national rate of 1.7 percent. Between 1980 and 1990, twenty-one of the state's fifty-seven municipalities registered a negative rate of population growth—a key measure of migration. An average of 22,000 inhabitants left the state each year. Between 1990, and 1995, the number of municipalities with negative population growth rose from twenty-one to twenty-nine, with annual emigration of 26,000 people. By the end of the decade thirty-four municipalities showed negative population growth rates. More restrictive U.S. immigration policies, particularly the increase in border patrols, have exacerbated the depopulation problem in Zacatecas. While there is still a seasonal flow of migrants who leave and return, the dominant tendency since 1986, has been the settlement of the migrants in the United States. As it becomes harder to leave and re-enter the country, migrants now stay away from home longer or migrate with their partners and children. Since many of the migrants are young, a rising proportion of their children are born in the United States.[10]

The El Remolino Community

El Remolino is a small community that belongs to the municipality of Juchipila, Zacatecas. It is located about 200 kilometers southwest of the capital city, in the area of the state with historically the highest international emigration rates. The community has potable water, a public sewer system and electricity, as well as a primary school and a health clinic. El Remolino remains quite rural. Despite its proximity to the Zacatecas-Guadalajara highway, the road to the community is unpaved and in very poor condition. The town's streets are dirt. They do not have names. The houses are made of adobe brick, though one can find an occasional two-story concrete home, usually built recently by a migrant planning to return home.

The town has been losing population steadily. In 1990, El Remolino had 1,022 inhabitants, which by 1995, had been reduced to 911 and in 2000 dwindled to 865.[11] In other words, during the first half of the decade, the community presented an average population growth rate of –2.27 percent, and –1.03 percent during the second half. Because young men predominantly migrate, for every 100 women in El Remolino there were seventy-five men in 1990, and eighty-one in 2000.

The increase in female migration over the decade indicates the rising proportion of family-wide migration. This is also a general characteristic in the state.[12] Residents of El Remolino perceive this shift, pointing out that previously there were more young people of both sexes. Today males and females often depart for the United States as soon as they reach age eighteen. There are few jobs, and those that exist pay wages much lower than what migrants can earn in the United States. Some industrial assembly plants opened in the mid-nineties only to close for lack of workers willing to work for the prevailing wages.

The "Collective Migrant"

For almost two decades Zacatecan migrants in the United States have been organizing themselves in so-called migrant clubs. These are initially constituted by members of one sister community, that is, by those Zacatecans who share the same community of origin.[13] Over time, the fabric of such sister communities has become much more complex. Some social clubs are formed from various sister communities, while others remain smaller and more autonomous even as they engage in joint activities. The clubs have evolved from their predecessors in the 1960s, which emphasized civic and philanthropic activities, and whose relations were essentially communitarian and based in solidarity. The current clubs engage in social and political activities. They feature extensive links with the community of origin, engage in direct negotiations with representatives of the national governments involved, and, in recent years, began entering into agreements with their state and municipal elected officials in Mexico. The clubs' role in improving the hometown economy and influencing hometown politics is a recent phenomenon, which increasingly involves the clubs in the definition of public policy, both on a state and national level.

The current clubs represent a higher level of organization than simple sister communities, with clubs assuming political and economic obligations directly from their original communities. This in turn creates a new entity: the collective migrant. These are migrants who act according to interests defined by their status as members of a Mexican community of origin, taking advantage of the contributions they can make as migrants and as workers in the United States.[14] In practice, the collective migrant goes beyond family and individual ties, overcoming the individual isolation of the first migrants and opening a new binational form of interaction and social participation. These new collective migrants count on unprecedented levels of social capital,[15] bonds of trust that enable them to transcend parochial approaches and take on new challenges.

What is unique about the collective migrants is their capacity, through their clubs, to develop and use their social capital across borders, regardless of the migrants' physical separation from Mexican social networks.[16] Their social capital springs from the cultural heritage from their communities of origin, but it further develops abroad through the community activities of the clubs themselves, which extend social ties and obligations beyond the immediate community of origin, creating new tasks and obligations related to the club itself.

Over time the migrant clubs have developed more stable social and political relationships, creating associations at various levels. First, various clubs that come from the same community join together. Then migrant clubs from the same state in Mexico form. Federations then emerge in various U.S. states that can include hundreds of these organizations. Finally, multiple alliances emerge between various migrant club organizations from different Mexican states or even the whole country. The result is a complex social framework in which organizations are evolving simultaneously at all levels and in multiple directions. The organizations generally maintain clearly defined roles. For example, the migrant clubs of Zacatecas understand very well that they are engaged in community politics, and that party politics is the work of other structures. This has led to the creation of the Zacatecan Civic Front with its headquarters in Los Angeles, whose current task is an initiative to reform the constitution of the state of Zacatecas so that migrants have the right to hold elective office.

The extraterritorial Zacatecano migrant organizations go back to the 1960s when the social club Guadalupe Victoria from the municipality Jalpa was founded in Illinois by Gregorio Casillas, who headed it up for twenty years (1962–1982). This was followed by the Fresnillo Social Club, the Latin Brotherhood Social Club of migrants from the municipality of Jerez, and the Momax Social Club, which was founded in 1968. The clubs are now part of an elaborate structure. At the national level in the United States is the Federation of Mexican Clubs, made up largely of federations of migrant clubs organized by their states of origin. [17] Every federation includes migrant organizations that have adopted the denomination of their communities of origin.[18] Among the more significant are the Federation of

United Zacatecano Clubs of Southern California (FCZUSC), the Federation of Jaliscience Clubs, the Brotherhood of Sinaloa, the Association of Nayaritas, and the Regional Organization of Oaxaca.

According to Manuel de la Cruz, representative of the Zacatecas state government in the United States, there are about 250 Zacatecan social clubs in the United States. One-third can be found in Southern California, mainly Los Angeles, with the next largest concentration in Illinois, and many in Chicago. Significant numbers of clubs are also found in: Dallas and Houston, Texas; Santa Ana, Orange, Sacramento, and Oxnard, in California; and the states of Oklahoma, Arizona, Florida, Nevada, Wisconsin, Georgia, and North Carolina. Due to this high level of activity, the Zacatecan migrant clubs can boast the most extensive set of social and political organizations that Mexicans have created abroad. These organizations give life and dynamism to the phenomenon of collective remittances.[19]

The current Federation of Zacatecano Clubs of Southern California emerged in 1986. By the 1990s there was already a presence in nearly ten U.S. states. Currently there are Zacatecan clubs in fourteen states. Many are involved in community development. Between 1993, and 1996, the Zacatecano Clubs carried out 116 projects, concentrating mainly on improving potable water systems, repairing or constructing schools, fixing sewer systems, constructing and paving roads, and supporting local sports and recreation activities. Some of the projects received financial support from government matching programs in Mexico, first the "Two for One" program—with state and federal matches of the clubs' initial investments—and later the "Three for One" program, which added municipal funds to the matching pool.

The Peasant Club El Remolino

The Club El Remolino was organized in 1995, in California. Its first works included rehabilitating the primary school, buying equipment for the health clinic, and several other social projects. The Club El Remolino was one of the first clubs to go beyond such social and community projects to undertake productive investment—not in public goods and services but to stimulate private economic activity. The interest was sparked by members' desire to improve agricultural output by building a small dam for irrigation. This new orientation toward production created new issues for the club in terms of organization, fundraising, and the destination of funds. Until then, the objective had been the satisfaction of basic needs in services and social infrastructure, and the beneficiaries included the whole community of origin. Productive investments, on the other hand, support projects with limited partners and generally benefit primarily the families of those who invest. The club addressed the issue organizationally by creating a subgroup for productive investments, the Peasant Club El Remolino, leaving the larger group responsible for community investments.[20]

The dam project began in 1998. Initially the idea for the project came about when some of the migrants returned to the community.[21] Seeing the need for irrigation, they looked at the land and chose a construction site surrounded by flat and fertile agricultural land. The land belongs to brothers Glafira and Cutberto Rodríguez, who graze cattle there and who were amenable to the plan. Forty partners formed the new Peasant Club El Remolino, mainly those with family members raising cattle and farming land in the area of the proposed dam.[22] The project represents an investment in agriculture and livestock, as it will irrigate both croplands and forage for cattle. Its goal was to address the depletion of the local aquifer, caused mainly by the planting of *guayaba* and peach orchards, which also limited the land available for cattle grazing.[23]

For the construction, the club counted on the investment of its forty partners and matching funds from the Two for One and later the Three for One programs. The club hired an administrator in the community, Encarnación Luna, who had overseen previous social works financed by the migrants. The construction began during the first months of 1998. By May 10 of that year, the foundation had been laid to a depth of five meters, with the dam reaching four meters above the surface, creating a capacity of 1,773 cubic meters. The cost for this initial phase was 1,150,000 pesos (approximately $130,000).

The club had hoped to carry out the next phase of construction before the rainy season, which would have reduced costs, but there were endless problems with the state government. Government officials inexplicably removed Encarnación Luna as the administrator, taking over his functions themselves, with terrible results. [24] Thus the second phase cost more— 1,159,000 pesos—but added only 980 cubic meters of capacity to the dam, 793 cubic meters less than the previous phase.

The club's protests forced a number of changes. Although the club did not regain direct management of the project, the state government had to put the third-phase construction out to bid. In a questionable competition, the bid was awarded to the Loddi company, which immediately subcontracted the work to another contractor. This drew strong objections from club members in Los Angeles. Ultimately, 920 cubic meters of capacity were completed at a cost of 720,000 pesos. The fourth and final phase of the project remains—the construction of the canals and piping systems so the water can be used for irrigation. Despite the delays and conflicts, the migrants remain optimistic about project completion.[25]

The drawbacks in the project highlight some of the difficulties of managing such an enterprise from afar. The migrants, however, kept insisting on their right to make decisions in the execution of their project, making them an important counterweight to the arbitrary decisions of the state bureaucracy. The club maintains permanent oversight of the project, through site visits when they are back home, through telephone reports, and through direct communication with community members.[26] They have even used video to monitor the project, periodically filming the work and interviewing the project engineer, who explains for the viewers what has been completed and what remains to be done.

The Peasant Club El Remolino represents of a new evolution of collective remittances, combining the collective-social essence of traditional migrant clubs with a collective but private focus on investment. This reflects the club's composition as an association of migrant savers and their interest in collective investment in productive infrastructure.

The Collective Migrant and Public Policy

The Three for One program, with its matching funds for investments in public works, is well-suited to the communal nature and purpose of traditional migrant organizations. However, this case demonstrates some of the program's limitations when it comes to productive investments, which have been well documented in other studies.[27] Migrant savers—or migrant entrepreneurs—who pool their resources for productive investments need a new program with fewer restraints than the current program.

Such investments hold tremendous potential. Currently, small private investment projects are financed by a small elite of migrant entrepreneurs from metropolitan Los Angeles and Chicago, some of whom have been elected leaders of the Zacatecano clubs in California.[28] Nevertheless, these tend to be modest, individual, and dispersed investments in discrete projects such as hotels, gas stations, chile dehydration plants, salsa processing, and feed lots. Their potential lies in their ability to generate associative ventures with other migrant entrepreneurs, or with investors from the locality, region, country, or even foreigners. Such ventures will be feasible only if they are supported by incentive programs that go beyond community infrastructure.

The Peasant Club El Remolino is one of the few migrant clubs to invest in productive infrastructure through the Two for One program, which in 1988, became the Three for One program.[29] The Two for One program was started in 1993, with the idea that for every peso invested by migrants the state and federal government would contribute equal parts. The government's goal in setting up the program was to provide incentives for migrants to channel their remittances toward public works and projects that could combat poverty and promote regional development. Through this program, 219 projects benefiting twenty-eight municipalities were carried out between 1993, and 1998, with a total investment of 33.7 million pesos (about $3.7 million), of which one-third was contributed by migrants.

The Three for One program, in which municipal governments participate as well, began in 1999. That year the program supported ninety-four projects with a joint investment of 48.2 million pesos (about $5.4 million). In 2000, there were more than one hundred projects with a total investment of 60 million pesos ($6.7 million) benefiting thirty-one municipalities.[30] According to official sources, the 2001 investment through the Three for One program will amount to 72 million pesos in 130 projects in thirty municipalities. The Federation of Zacatecano Clubs of Southern California has been one of the most active participants in the program, accounting for about eighty percent of the Three for One projects.

Looking more closely at the uses of the program's funds for 2000, only five percent was devoted to productive infrastructure (dams, irrigation ditches, and wells). Seventy-one percent, by contrast, went for public services (electrification, pavement, drainage, potable water, etc.), with another thirteen percent supporting recreational facilities (parks, sports areas, horse parks, etc.) and eleven percent devoted to public buildings (schools, churches, libraries, clinics, etc.).

Migrant groups have pressured the Mexican government to make it easier to invest remittances in productive projects. In 2001, migrants won an increase in the federal financial ceiling of the program, which will allow larger projects to be funded.[31] The Zacatecan clubs hope that the government will create new options for preferential support for such investments, such as the Four for One program that incorporates additional government funds. Still, migrant groups often find that state and federal officials do not fully appreciate the distinction between social and productive investment. This is part of a more generalized perception on the part of migrants that officials do not understand their motivations. Most invest in public works such as paving a road not because they want to drive on that road themselves but because it promotes community development. In interviews, migrants repeatedly stress that their main motivation is their love for their hometown communities.[32]

Programs for migrant entrepreneurs, built on the social capital of the migrant clubs, can provide incentives for productive investment. For Zacatecas, one can start with the Three for One program, enhancing the program so it matches a wider range of projects and guarantees the matching funds at the three levels of government. Such projects should include those with access to broader financing from national and international organizations, provided the projects are sufficiently developed and the association of migrant investors is formalized and well established.

Six general points are worth considering in designing a package to promote productive investment projects like that of the Peasant Club El Remolino:

1. create a special package of fiscal incentives;
2. foment the development of pilot projects in highly marginalized zones;
3. count on the participation of the migrant community;
4. prioritize projects that are reproducible and can become self-sufficient;
5. ensure that projects contemplate all the different phases of the production process;
6. evaluate the projects from the perspective of integral development.

Globalization and International Migration

International migration in Mexico has been described as an escape valve for a low-combustion economy. The persistence of labor expulsion from Mexico demonstrates clearly the costs of the asymmetries that persist between the two economies: danger and death at the border, the abandonment of entire communities, the atrophy of local economies, and the loss of human resources. Contrary to the promises of economic integration, the exodus has not slowed.

The social responses to economic integration, certainly in regard to organized migrants from Zacatecas, challenge many established theories about migration in the United States, among them the notion that migrants are assimilated once they enter the country and rapidly lose their identities. Of this is true then how does one explain the persistence and recreation of hometown identities—such as Zacatecan, Mexican, and even peasant in the case studied here—among migrants established in the United States? To what can one attribute the emergence of the collective migrant, who joins with others to share resources toward a common end, in a society marked by individualism?

The answers to these questions rest on three subjects that the author has developed in other works and that reflect new theoretical work in the social sciences about the definitions of community, residence, migrant membership, and extraterritorial political participation.[33] First, a large part of the social and the symbolic in the peasant-migrant environment is constructed directly by the same agents, and to some degree independently from the state and from capitalist production relations. Second, in the rural environment the networks of migrants, among themselves and in relation to the members of their communities of origin, play a critical role, responding to primary necessities and filling vacuums that prevailing political and economic institutions cannot fill. Third, as peasants, migrants such as those from El Remolino construct their identities extraterritorially. Their *ethos matrio*[34] is transformed as they act binationally, sharing a common communitarian practice. Even as they adapt to new social circumstances in the United States, migrants maintain their links and commitments to their communities of origin. Because of this, the family, the *barrio,* and the "territorial belonging" constitute the keys to understanding how these two worlds are combined, making possible an authentically shared communitarian life, which in turn evolves abroad into innovative forms of social organization.[35]

Some researchers have suggested that in recent years, as globalization erodes national identities, Mexican migrants in the United States are having more difficulty maintaining their identities as Mexicans. Recent fieldwork on migrant clubs, however, challenges this view, suggesting that the organization of such clubs plays a strong role in reinforcing migrants' identities as members of a nation, a state, and a community of origin. The club in turn becomes a platform from which migrants maintain and nurture such ties. Alliances among migrant groups today are more and more frequent, with the objectives of overcoming isolation and taking collective action. In one sense, migrants start to re-appropriate their individual and collective identities as they view themselves as agents of change. Explicit political action contributes to this process. Most Mexican migrant clubs maintain that they are not political organizations, but there is no denying that they play an important role in many of the decisions made about their communities. Many, for example, have developed the capacity to negotiate with different levels of government. The growing participation of migrant groups represents an interesting contribution to democratic trends supported by civil society.[36]

Political activity aside, many have noted the marked increase in migrant involvement in the hometown projects carried out by their clubs.[37] These trends have been confirmed in focus groups with migrants. Zacatecan club leaders as well as the those of the Casas Guanajuato living in Los Angeles and Chicago openly vow never to "lose their roots" as they prepare "to face the transgenerational challenge" of connecting younger generations with their home towns. Through the clubs, they promote community service and the reaffirmation of migrants' roots. They assert that "the next generation is already secured."[38]

Their confidence is based on the experience and training the new leaders get through the clubs.[39] Already, some of the principal leaders of the Zacatecan migrant clubs are university-educated young people born in the United States.[40] Recently children of first-generation migrants formed the Zacatecan Youth Alliance of Chicago to support the overall objectives of the clubs.[41] Such involvement is promoted through the media. The radio program "Zacatecas in Los Angeles" airs every Sunday, and many clubs now have an increasing presence on the Internet. *Imágen* newspaper in Zacatecas even carries a regular column—"Saludos Paisanos"—by binational youth. Currently there is a proposal to establish telecenters to increase electronic communication between hometown residents and those who have migrated.

These are conscious attempts by migrant communities to work to maintain ties in the face of economic globalization, and these experiences directly address questions of identity and of the need for social networks and political participation. Facing life abroad, emigrants need a larger dose of energy and creativity to affirm Mexican national identity. And even for the many born in the United States, the least anonymous and closest identity is the one reconstructed from the *matria,* the community of origin.

Conclusion

Expressed in cultural terms, migrants strive to reconfigure their identities based on community belonging.[42] Far from home, migrants are conscious that their natural community is not made up of U.S. citizens but of Mexicans who share their place of origin. For Zacatecan migrants, such connections make it possible to maintain, recover, and in some cases reconstruct relations with hometown communities.

Migrants have become aware of the enormous economic power of collective remittances, which, with a great effort, they save and send home. The state government recognized this potential as well and is actively developing programs to channel resources. Recent research indicates that even though collective remittances represent only a small fraction of total remittances, and many cannot be easily quantified, they represent a quality resource for community development in conjunction with family remittances, most of which are used to fulfill the subsistence needs of individual families.[43] Family remittances have an important economic impact, but only collective remittances have the capacity to unite binational organizational efforts in regional development projects and to influence public policy. Their potential depends on the migrants' ability to save for new collective investments, as well as the ability of government to promote such investment. Currently, the two El Remolino Clubs plan to carry out seven more works in the immediate future: drilling a deep well for potable water, digging a chain pump well, paving two streets, the third phase of renovating the primary school, construction of the walls and electrification of the cemetery, installing meters for potable water use, and the fourth phase of dam construction.

The collective migrant is now a key binational actor with the ability to influence everything from the local economy in his or her home town to the design of national public policies. Migrants' collective investment, which is a product of the repatriation of their human resources and social capital, is emerging as a powerful engine for regional economic development in Mexico.

Notes

1. Raúl Delgado Wise, "Los Dilemas de la Migración Internacional Mexicana de Cara al Siglo XXI" in *Boletín de la Unidad Regional de México*, 2001. The same author indicates that in terms of net contribution of each sector, remittances are the second largest source of foreign currency, below oil sales but above the *maquiladora* manufacturing sector.

2. Miguel Moctezuma L. and Raúl Delgado Wise, "Metamorfosis migratoria y evolución de la estructura productiva de Zacatecas: 1893–1950," *Revista Regiones*, Centro de Investigaciones Sociales y Administrativas, Universidad de Guanajuato, April–June, 1993.

3. For more on the migratory population circuit see among others Jorge Durand, "Circuitos migratorios," in *Movimientos de población en México,* ed. Tomás Calva y Gustavo López Castro (Zamora: El Colegio de Michoacán, 1988); Roger Rouse, "Mexican Migration and the Social Space of Postmodernism," *Diaspora* 1 (1994).

4. Durand, "Circuitos migratorios;" Rouse, "Mexican Migration;" Moctezuma and Delgado Wise, "Metamorfosis migratoria."

5. Durand, "Circuitos migratorios;" Rouse, "Mexican Migration;" Moctezuma and Delgado Wise, "Metamorfosis migratoria."

6. Instituto Nacional de Estadística Geografía Informática (INEGI), *Sistema de Cuentas Nacionales de México; XII Censo Nacional de Población y Vivienda, 2000.*

7. Zacatecas State Government, *Plan Estatal de Desarrollo 1999–2004* (Zacatecas: State Government of Zacatecas, 1999).

8. Zacatecas State Government, *Plan Estatal de Desarrollo 1999–2004.*

9. Francisco Arroyo García, "Dinámica del PIB de las entidades federativas de México, 1980–1999," *Comercio Exterior* 51, no. 7 (July 2001): 585, 595.

10. Miguel Moctezuma L., "La transición hacia un nuevo patrón migratorio internacional en Zacatecas," in *Memorias de migración,* ed. Miguel Moctezuma L. (México City: Conacyt-Sivilla, 2000).

11. Instituto Nacional de Estadística Geografía e Informática (INEGI), *Censo General de Población y Vivienda de Zacatecas* (Aguascalientes: INEGI, 1990), 13; INEGI, *Conteo de Población y Vivienda 1995* (Aguascalientes, INEGI, 1996), 323, 2000.

12. Moctezuma L., "La transición."

13. Luís González, "Suave matria," *Nexos* 108, December (1986).

14. Miguel Moctezuma L. "Redes sociales, comunidades filiales, familias y clubes de migrantes. El circuito migrante San Alto, Zac.-Oakland, Calif." El Colegio de la Frontera Norte, doctoral thesis, December 1999.

15. Social capital is a concept that refers to the diversity of the relationships that are possessed as a product of individual, family and social history, which can be drawn upon in a determined moment.

16. M. Patricia Fernández Kelly, "Social and Cultural Capital in the Ghetto: Implications of the Economic Sociology of Immigration, in *The Economic Sociology of Immigration. Essays on Networks, Ethnicity, and Entrepreneurship,* ed. Alejandro Portes (New York: Russell Sage Foundation, 1995).

17. Luin Goldring, "El Estado mexicano y las organizaciones transmigrantes: ¿reconfigurando la nación, ciudadanía y las relaciones entre Estado y sociedad civil?" in *xix Coloquio de Antropología e Historias Regionales* (Michoacán, Mex.: El Colegio de Michoacán, 1997).

18. Douglas Massey, Rafael Alarcón, Jorge Durand, and Humberto González, *Los ausentes: El proceso social de la migración internacional en el occidente de México* (Mexico City: Consejo Nacional para la Cultura y las Artes/Alianza Editorial, Colección los Noventa, 1991).

19. Goldring, "El Estado mexicano."

20. Author's interview with Augustín Bañuelos, in Inglewood, CA, April 27, 2001. He served as FCZUSC president in 1998–1999 and was project secretary in 1999–2000. As of this writing he is president of his migrant club.

21. Author's interview with Simón Haro, El Remolino, Juchipila, Zac., July 4, 2000.

22. Author's interview with Encarnación Luna, El Remolino, Juchipila, Zac. July 4, 2000.

23. Author's interview with Encarnación Luna, El Remolino, Juchipila, Zac. July 4, 2000.

24. Interview with Encarnación Luna, El Remolino, Juchipila, July 4, 2000. According to Luna, the migrants protested the government intervention: "I told the brothers in the United States that people from the government had come here and had removed me without explanation, and that they had asked me to send the money to Zacatecas. I told them: 'Here is the documentation for the money I turned over.' They told me: 'We have you there so you work for us, you're our representative and nobody can remove you.'"

25. Interview with Encarnación Luna, El Remolino, Juchipila, July 4, 2000.

26. Interview with Encarnación Luna, El Remolino, Juchipila, July 4, 2000. "The migrants follow the construction work . . . When the partners come to the rancho, they go to see the dam. I tell them, here is what has been spent and also the notes for the gasoline of my truck. They go, look, and have to go talk to the engineer, Sergio Cabral, in order to know how many cubic meters have been constructed. . . . "

27. Miguel Moctezuma L. and Héctor Rodríguez R., "Programas Tres por Uno y Mi Comunidad, evaluación con migrantes zacatecanos y guanajuatenses radicados en Chicago, Ill. y Los Ángeles, Calif.," in *Informe de Investigación* (Unidad de Postrado en Ciencia Política, Universidad Autónoma de Zacatecas, October 2001).

28. Among them, Bernardino Bugarín (1993–94, 1995–96, 1996–97 and 1997–98), Ernesto Rojas (1997–98 and 1998–99), Rigoberto Castañeda (1997–98), and Felipe Delgado.

29. Other clubs that have invested in productive infrastructure are Club Social Chacuiloca, Tepechitlán (dam project); the Club Boquilla de Abajo, Cañitas de Felipe Pescador (dam), and Club El Tuiche, Nochistlán (deep well for irrigation).

30. Zacatecas State Government, *Programa Tres por Uno* (Zacatecas: State Government, 2001).

31. Author's interview with Guadalupe Gómez, President of Federación de Clubes Unidos del Sur de California, Los Angeles, Calif., March 10, 2002.

32. Author's interview with Rosalva Ruíz, President of the Federación de Zacatecanos Unidos en Illinois, Chicago, Ill., October 2000.

33. Luin Goldring, "La migración México-EUA y la transnacionalización del espacio político y social: perspectivas desde el México rural," *Estudios Sociológicos* X, no. 29 (mayo–agosto 1992); Goldring, "El Estado mexicano"; Robert Smith, "Los Ausentes Siempre Presentes: The Imagining, Making and Politics of a Transnational Migrant Community Between Ticuany, Puebla, Mexico and New York City," submitted in partial fulfillment of the requirements for the Ph.D., Columbia University, 1995; Robert Smith, "The Transnational Practice of Migrant Politics and Membership: an analysis of the Mexican case with some comparative and practical reflections," in *Impacto de la migración y las remesas en el crecimiento económico regional,* ed. Miguel Moctezuma L. and Héctor Rodríguez Ramírez (Mexico City: Senado de la República, 1999).

34. In cases like the migrants from El Remolino, daily life of a village is much like a *matria* (motherland). This concept refers to the small locality or the village, where, as González writes in "Suave matria:" (52–53) " . . . The radius of each of the mini-societies can extend only as far as one can see, or for a day's walk. . . . The people in each of the two thousand smallest Mexican municipalities tend to be related and know each other. They call each other by their first

names, their last names and their nicknames. Academics say that in these small human groups the direct interpersonal knowledge is a constant presence."

35. Rouse, "Mexican Migration," 14.

36. One interesting example of migrant political activity is the case of Andrés Bermúdez Viramontes, who as a migrant won election to the municipal presidency in his home town of Jerez, Zacatecas. He developed an effective strategy to unify migrants, their organizations, and residents in Jerez. In the end he was kept from taking office by the Federal Judicial Tribunal, which ruled his candidacy unconstitutional. Still, his bid stimulated a proposal to reform the state constitution to recognize binational or dual residence for holders of state offices.

37. José Itzigsohn, "Immigration and the Boundaries of Citizenship: the Institutions of Immigrants' Political Transnationalism," *International Migration Review* XXXIV, no. 4 (Winter 2000).

38. Martha Elva Real and Rafael Barajas, Marcos Reyes and Rosalva Ruíz, Focus Group interviews, Los Angeles, Calif. and Chicago, Ill., October 2000.

39. Focus Groups, Chicago. Ill., October 2000.

40. Some examples of this new generation of leadership are: Reina Reyes (Club Zacatecano Emiliano Zapata), Martha Jiménez (Club Hermandad Las Ánimas), and Ramón Zelázquez (Club Social Tayahua). This generation is characterized by a high level of gender equity, in addition to its training, educational level, and commitment to its parents' communities of origin.

41. Federation of United Zacateno Clubs of Southern California (FCZUSC), *Revista,* 1999–2000, 39, and 2000–2001, 63.

42. Gilberto Jiménez Montiel, "Apuntes para una teoría de la identidad nacional," *Sociológica*, no. 21, Universidad Autónoma Metropolitana, México, January–April (1993), 24.

43. Federico Torres, *Uso productivo de las remesas en El Salvador, Guatemala, Honduras y Nicaragua* (Mexico City: Comisión Económica para América Latina y el Caribe, 1998); and "Uso productivo de las remesas en México, Centroamérica y República Dominicana: Experiencias recientes," *Simposio sobre Migración Internacional en las Américas* (Organización Internacional para las Migraciones/Comisión Económica para América Latina y el Caribe, San José, Costa Rica, September 4–6, 2000).

PART 4

CONCLUSION

11

Lessons Learned: Civil Society Strategies in the Face of Economic Integration

Timothy A. Wise, Hilda Salazar, & Laura Carlsen

WHAT HAS GLOBALIZATION MEANT FOR MEXICO, FOR ITS PEOPLE, ITS COMMUNI-ties, its environment? The case studies presented in this volume offer a variety of recent experiences with economic integration. They touch on many sectors of Mexican society, and address diverse issues—labor, agriculture, the environment, the role of the state, and the impact of international trade agreements. Despite their diversity these cases, taken together, offer important lessons about the impacts of the current integration process in Mexico, and offer the visions and dreams of Mexican people about what it would take to structure that process in a way that fosters sustainable human development. Many of those lessons go beyond Mexico and North America. They are immediately relevant to current debates over the proposed Free Trade Area of the Americas and the new round of negotiations in the World Trade Organization. As a group these case studies paint a clear but troubling picture. The present model negatively impacts the more vulnerable members of Mexican society and the environment. The case studies paint a picture, not of helpless victims but rather a series of vivid portraits of civil society organizations defending their communities and livelihoods while fighting for policies and practices based on deeply held values and traditions. Their initiatives are creating important new models for resisting neoliberal economic policies and the further opening of the economy to transnational corporations. But the case studies also make clear that such organizational initiatives are not enough. International agreements, government policy, and corporate practices need to be structured differently for collective or community initiatives to succeed.

The experiences studied in this book demonstrate the need to empower both national governments and local communities to manage the process of economic integration. On the one hand that means allowing local communities to participate in setting the terms for—and limits to—transnational investment in their lands. On the other, it means enabling the state to play a critical role in guiding and regulating economic integration so that it furthers national development goals. The cases reveal many of the ways in which international trade agreements, particularly NAFTA, have undermined the state's and local communities' ability to play those roles. At the same time, they have accelerated many of the socially and environmentally destructive practices that make a strong developmental state necessary.

An enormous distance remains between the visions of the government and multilateral development institutions, on the one hand, and the communities and organizations described in the cases studied here. For the latter, no development can proceed without taking them into account. They have tired of trickle-down approaches that never reach them. Instead, they propose self-generated projects that address the new realities of economic integration while meeting the needs of the affected communities. They show no fear in stating that their cultures and communities are more important than "the liberation of the productive potential" of their lands. Their experiences offer lessons beyond adaptation to the global market; in fact, in most of these cases such adaptation is not currently feasible. Rather, they speak of "the moral economy," described by Mexican commentator Armando Bartra as "an economy of the subject and not the object, an economy that addresses human needs and potential, not only goods. . . ."[1] In other words, they speak of an economic integration in which everyone belongs.

This chapter begins with a synthesis of the most salient lessons from the civil-society strategies reviewed in the case studies. It then examines the implications for the role of the state, and concludes with lessons for future trade agreements.

Civil Society Strategies
in the Face of Economic Integration

The wealth of organizational experiences represented in the cases studied here provides rich material for those interested in assessing the effectiveness of strategies used by civil society groups in adaptating to and confronting neoliberalism and economic integration. Despite the diversity of the experiences, the cases present some common themes, strategies, and implications.

Social and environmental issues must be addressed explicitly and integrally, along with economic issues, if economic integration is to benefit the poor and the environment. While this sounds obvious, it is not the prevailing approach to international economic integration, at least in the language or structure of trade agreements. (NAFTA, remember, enshrined the separation of labor and environment by addressing the issues in separate side agreements.) Despite widespread evidence to the contrary, it continues to be an article of faith that trade expansion will stimulate economic growth, and that economic growth will naturally lead to improved living standards and environmental practices.

These case studies reinforce the growing body of evidence that the benefits of trade will extend to the poor and to the environment only if explicit steps are taken at all levels to ensure social and environmental improvements. Job growth in the *maquiladora* sector has not brought a significant increase in either living standards or basic labor rights. Instead, as the Autotrim case study shows, it has exerted downward pressure on wages, benefits, and labor rights. The case study demonstrates the need to protect communities and workers from the effects of unregulated market expansion.

Nor has integration naturally stimulated improved environmental standards in Mexico. In fact, what little progress we've seen has been the result of direct intervention by groups like the North American Development Bank and the North American Commission for Environmental Cooperation. Mexico's one clear environmental success story—dramatic reductions in lead and carbon monoxide emissions in Mexico City—is the product not of market forces but of strict regulation by governments.[2]

The case studies also show the importance of linking social and environmental concerns. Many of the organizations studied in this book demonstrate a profound understanding of social and environmental integration, based on the recognition that ecosystems are inhabited and maintained by the communities that have evolved within them. Small-scale basic grains production provides employment and sustenance to thousands of Mexican peasants, who act as the guardians of Mexico's rich biodiversity in corn. Collecting and storing germplasm is no substitute for making biodiverse small-holder corn production viable. Similarly, the many environmental benefits of shade coffee depend on the economic viability of the indigenous coffee economy. Biological corridors may preserve land and biodiversity, but they will be short-lived if they exclude the communities that have cultivated that biodiversity. El Balcón's success in managing local forestry resources—in a way that both protects the forests and provides sustainable livelihoods to the community—demonstrates the inextricable link between socioeconomic and environmental sustainability.

The only effective way to respond to economic integration is with large, democratic, and multifunctional civil society organizations. As ANEC's Victor Suarez pointed out at the August 2001 conference on these case studies, the days of individual production and marketing in agriculture are over. Only as part of a larger organization, with greater capital, expertise, and market power, can the individual producer hope to survive in today's competitive market. In productive spheres, such organizations have adopted what Luís Hernández referred to as a strategy based on "the construction of autonomies that promote the appropriation of the process of production and capitalization."[3] The CEPCO and ANEC cases illustrate evolving organizational structures and practices to adapt collectively to the open economy. The cases also show that these new structures can be successful, delivering significant tangible benefits to the organizations' members. Similarly, in El Balcón, vertically integrated production under close professional management has allowed community forestry to succeed from both an economic and an environmental perspective.

These structures are also flexible and multifunctional, in large part because organizations are filling the void left by the state's withdrawal. Hernández called this new type of grassroots organization an "animal with four legs," combining four relatively new features: 1) peasant enterprises to manage marketing; 2) independent political advocacy for members' needs and rights; 3) in-house technical staff; and 4) elements of a development agency to address broader social issues.[4] Such producer organizations face tremendous obstacles, and they remain relatively weak given the challenges. They lack strong national representation and articulation, and their local and regional structures are rarely as strong as those of ANEC or CEPCO. But they have grown and are learning to confront the challenges of globalization without losing their commitment to grassroots democracy and social equity. Perhaps most important, while they draw on a rich tradition of collective action in Mexico, they are free of traditional corporatist dependence on the state or any ruling party.

While CEPCO and ANEC are large organizations, smaller organizations have shown themselves capable of effective collective action as well, particularly as part of larger networks and coalitions. The indigenous movement in Mexico is an excellent example of the diversity of collective action with a united purpose at a national level. So, too, are the growing numbers of migrant organizations, such as those studied in the El Remolino case, dedicated to collective action to benefit their communities of origin.

Community-based management of natural resources represents a viable alternative to the current model of overexploitation of natural resources. Many of these cases provide strong evidence that the people best equipped to manage scarce natural resources sustainably are those who depend on such resources for their livelihoods. This comes as no surprise to those studying rural development and sustainable resource use. It has been widely accepted that community-based resource management can be the most viable long-term solution to resource degradation.[5]

This is not the orientation, however, in the current rush to free trade. The present model promotes the privatization of land and natural resources, allowing the market to determine prices. It also discourages—or even outlaws—imposing performance requirements on multinational corporations engaged in resource extraction, preventing local and national governments from sustainably managing their own resources. The two case studies of community forestry in Guerrero are striking examples of this clash, and they offer several important conclusions about preconditions for the success of community-based resource management.

First, corporate responsibility and community power to negotiate effectively with transnational corporations play key roles in achieving sustainable resource extraction for export. In the case of the Organization of Peasant Ecologists of the Sierra of Petatlán and Coyuca de Catalán, Boise Corporation promoted unsustainable forest clear-cutting to meet its short-term economic goals. In contrast, Westwood Lumber worked with the community in El Balcón to improve technology, enhance local skills, improve quality, and establish a stable international market for lumber that did not require the overexploitation of local forests. The El Balcón *ejido* was able to achieve this because it controlled its own forest resources and was united enough to effectively negotiate beneficial contracts with Westwood. Under the present model, Westwood must be seen as the exception to the corporate rule, but El Balcón's power to negotiate reasonable terms for such foreign investment points the way forward to more responsible corporate practices.

Second, a stable, democratic society, ruled by law and not violence, must prevail if civil-society groups are to play an effective role in determining how local resources are used. The instability of the Petatlán region, exacerbated by environmental destruction, led to serious human rights violations and the withdrawal of investment, while the experience of El Balcón clearly shows that where stable community relations exist, groups can make significant progress in managing resource use according to long-term plans that directly benefit the local population.

Finally, one of the fundamental lessons of the Guerrero cases is the importance of social property as a key factor promoting socially and environmentally sustainable rural production. In El Balcón, the success of the project depended on community ownership of the forest resources, community ownership of the logging and sawmill operations, and community management of the project. As an *ejido*, El Balcón retained collective property rights to the lands and the forests. As the authors of the case study point out, this was enhanced by the *ejido* winning the formal logging concession from the government. Collective ownership and the effective exercise of collective control over community resources ensured that responsibilities for and benefits from sustainable logging would be shared.

The persistence of community property in rural Mexico, in the form of *ejidos* and communal lands, as well as small property owners in the so-called social sector, a legacy of the Mexican Revolution, presents a challenge to the free-trade model. Especially since the Salinas Administration (1988–94), successive Mexican governments have tried to chip away at the revolutionary reforms while avoiding the high political costs of explicitly abolishing the social sector. The controversial 1992 reform to Article 27 of the constitution allowed the privatization of *ejido* and communal lands by agreement of the members. This has stimulated little apparent modernization in the countryside, but it has put increasing pressure on marginalized farmers to sell or rent their lands. While community property rankles free-traders, our case studies suggest that it can be an essential component of community-based development. CEPCO's membership is organized largely within *ejidos* and communal lands. This has facilitated the socialization of profits (and losses) and the adoption of more sustainable practices, such as organic production. Similarly, ANEC's members are largely *ejidatarios*.

The case studies also suggest that the value of community-based management extends beyond traditional definitions of natural resources. Forests fall within those definitions, but corn and coffee do not. Yet the case studies on ANEC and CEPCO make clear that small farmers in these sectors are the stewards of important natural resources as well. Corn farmers, and many others who grow basic grains, manage Mexico's rich natural wealth of genetic diversity in grains. Their careful cultivation methods over previous generations are responsible for the existence of that wealth in the first place, and their ongoing cultivation practices preserve that wealth for future generations. Similarly, indigenous coffee farmers are providing an important environmental service. Hillside cultivation of shade coffee provides several important ecological benefits. In addition to conserving biodiversity, it has been proven to offer essential shade trees for migratory birds. It also serves as a key barrier to further soil erosion and desertification in badly eroded mountainous areas, such as one finds in Oaxaca. Undermining the small-farming sector in basic grains will do irreparable harm to Mexico's stocks of genetic wealth, just as displacing Mexico's indigenous coffee farmers will cause untold damage to local soil conditions and to international migratory bird populations.

These ecological contributions have come to be known as environmental services. At present, they remain largely unvalued in the marketplace, externalities that do not factor into market-based calculations of efficiency and profitability. It is unlikely such services will be given any monetary value soon, but the case studies make clear that such environmental services, and the traditional practices and values from which they derive, have tremendous value for the community and the culture. If such environmental services are important to the nation—and to the international community, which depends on Mexico as a source of biodiversity and natural resources—nonmarket mechanisms will have to be developed to help stabilize and reinforce the traditional peasant economy on which they depend.

Neither the market nor international trade regimes are likely to internalize such costs. It therefore remains the province of government policy to determine the value of such environmental services and costs and to take appropriate action. ANEC has demanded that the Mexican government respect NAFTA timetables for the phase-out of tariff protection and consider renewed tariff protection for basic-grains farmers in Mexico. This would involve a renegotiation of NAFTA. It seems clear from these cases that such action is warranted as part of a larger set of policies to revalue such essential environmental services.

The external orientation of the Mexican economy must not preclude the development and strengthening of the internal market and regional markets. Adopting an export-oriented development strategy weakens internal markets in fundamental ways. The governmental sector becomes less of an employer and purchaser. As employers, including the state, seek to compete on the basis of inexpensive labor, wages and producer prices decline, driving down purchasing power. Declines follow in small and medium-size national firms in markets for internationally competitive goods and services. In the absence of compensatory measures in NAFTA to address the asymmetries between the U.S. and Mexican economies, Mexican firms have seen a wave of bankruptcies. Although these case studies do not deal directly with the issue, Mexico has experienced tremendous job loss among small and medium-size national enterprises, which have been driven out of business by foreign competition and by the 1995 peso crash and credit crisis. This unemployment fuels migration, both to the United States and to the export industrial sector.

In the cases dealing with productive enterprises, the weakness of the internal market undercuts many of the organizational efforts to commercialize their products. The rural economy is particularly weak, with many sectors hit hard by foreign competition, credit problems, and weak labor demand. The case studies deal with farmers of coffee and basic grains, but other farmers are in crisis as well. Rice, pineapple and sugar growers have faced bankruptcy.

Interestingly, some of the organizations studied here have shown great creativity in market construction. Coffee farmers are working to strengthen a weak internal market for quality coffee, including direct sales of high-quality coffee within Mexico. They have also successfully broken into the fair trade market, earning a premium price for their organic and shade-grown coffees. ANEC has promoted the development of regional markets, linking surplus producers in one state with regions seeing a deficit in that product. While these are valiant—and productive—initiatives, they cannot substitute for policies that stimulate domestic demand by promoting rising incomes for the lower and middle classes.

Cultural cohesion can be an important source of resistance and alternative models in the face of globalization. Many of the cases illustrate the strength of cultural ties in Mexico. In indigenous communities, culture is a resilient glue binding people together despite intense forces working to pull them apart. CEPCO calls its form of coffee production indigenous because the culture is so tightly bound with the productive activity. Likewise, Chiapan communities have rejected bioprospecting contracts in defense of their traditional collective knowledge and resources. But cultural cohesion binds nonindigenous communities as well. How else to explain the connections between long-time emigrants to the United States and their communities of origin in Zacatecas? Or the unwillingness of basic grains producers to abandon corn farming?

Globalization exerts new pressures on these cultures. The current model for economic integration weakens cultural diversity, substituting individualism and a mass consumer culture for traditional cultures and values. It forces the physical dispersal of the community, through migration, breaking the traditional link between indigenous people and the land. While migratory patterns from Mexico to the United States are long-standing in states like Zacatecas, they are of more recent origin in Oaxaca, where rural declines associated with economic integration have pushed marginal producers from local to U.S. fields. It is worth noting that one of the less-discussed negative consequences of increased U.S. border patrols is that migrants are now far more likely to stay in the United States once they get through, whereas before they would routinely cross the border for seasonal work and return home in the off-season. The new pattern makes it more difficult to maintain family and community ties although, as we've seen, these bonds are far stronger than one might imagine.

Many of the case-study authors speak to the importance of cultural practices, norms, and values as critical to community resistance. Indigenous peoples' way of defining the environment as the sacred heritage of the community stands as a significant obstacle to the imposition of a market-based intellectual property regime and the privatization of nature. The importance of corn in Mexican culture, as well as the economy, is partly responsible for the persistence of corn farmers under pressure from U.S. corn exports to Mexico. And while the Mexican government and its multilateral financial institution advisors are fully prepared to declare Mexico's significant rural social property sector—*ejidos* and communal lands—an anachronism, *ejidatarios* and *comuneros* still consider such lands the hard-won fruits of the Mexican Revolution. Culture remains a formidable economic force in the process of economic restructuring in Mexico.

There is urgent need for a clearer set of laws and institutions to regulate the use of genetic material. The cases on bioprospecting present this issue in all its stark complexity. The contracts studied cover a wide range, from callously exploitative to debatably equitable. On one end of the spectrum is the yellow bean patent, in which a U.S. businessman took a readily available Mexican product and, by winning patent rights to its DNA, won control of the market for the product. On the other end of the spectrum is the Uzachi case from Oaxaca, in which an indigenous community organization contracted with researchers and a multinational pharmaceutical company to find medicinal uses for native mushroom varieties, with the organization retaining rights to some of the profits from such discoveries.

Who owns the rights to Mexico's rich biodiversity in plant germ-plasm? The question remains difficult to answer. As the case studies on the U.S. patent for a Sinaloan yellow bean and the four bioprospecting cases make clear, under the current intellectual property regime such rights belong to the entity that identifies the DNA from a particular material and files for patent protection. Behind each of the contracts studied in these cases stood a corporate partner who would gain monetarily from bio-prospecting in Mexico. Current and emerging law on intellectual property clearly grants ownership rights to the owner of the patent, usually the "dis-coverer" of the DNA. The injustice of this system, in the many forms in which it is represented in the case studies, resulted in the call for a national moratorium on such bioprospecting contracts in Mexico.

Recognition of national sovereignty over genetic wealth under the Convention on Biodiversity only partially addresses the problem. Under the Diversa–UNAM bioprospecting contract the government ceded bio-prospecting rights in federally owned Natural Protected Areas without local consultation. The proposed Mesoamerican Biological Corridor leaves open the possibility that the federal government could sell off bio-prospecting rights in the corridor to foreign companies.

Recognizing a community's rights to sell patent rights to local plant genetic material offers its own pitfalls. This argument is based on the com-munity's undeniable role in developing and maintaining the ecosystem that supports potentially valuable genetic material and its ownership of the land, and generally includes terms of benefit-sharing. Among the bio-prospecting contracts studied here, the one between the Union of Zapote-can and Chinantecan Forestry Communities (Uzachi) and the transnational pharmaceutical firm Sandoz provides an example. But as regional and national groups opposing the contract have pointed out, serious questions emerge: *Which* community holds those rights? Is it fair for Uzachi to profit when the patent rights cover genetic material found not only on Uzachi members' lands but on neighboring lands, or, for that matter, on lands in other parts of Mexico or other parts of the world?

Such contradictions only become more acute as technology becomes more advanced and as globalization brings more land and people within the domain of those who control that technology. These case studies high-light the need for international laws and institutions that can clarify such issues without leaving it to the market. "In the absence of regulatory mech-anisms that truly protect the rights and interests of peasants, indigenous peoples, and local communities," wrote the Action Group on Erosion, Technology and Concentration, "equitable bioprospecting is a myth."[6]

The current proposals in the World Trade Organization and other international bodies to extend intellectual property rights to living things under prevailing property regimes fall short of this standard. Others have proposed defining a regime in which life forms belong to humanity and therefore cannot be patented. Clearly, there is a need for a wide and democratic debate on the issue, driven not by the interests of private firms but by the long-term interests of a more representative cross-section of humanity.

Mexico needs both jobs and foreign investment, but the present export-oriented model offers limited benefits, with high costs. The economic strategy revealed in these case studies has two related consequences for workers: exploitation and expulsion.

The Autotrim case focuses on the difficulty of independent union organizing in one plant, but the backdrop is the sprawling *maquiladora* export industrial zone along Mexico's border with the United States. The case study itself highlights the environmental and labor problems endemic to the sector. It is worth dwelling on some other generalized observations regarding the limitations of the *maquiladora* model.

First, the employment gains from the sector, while large, fall dramatically short of Mexico's most basic employment needs. The *maquiladora* sector currently has roughly one million jobs, and the total has grown significantly with NAFTA. Certainly no other sector of the economy has experienced faster growth under the neoliberal model. Yet the sector is falling short of the country's needs if it is to be the engine of Mexico's economic development. By most estimates, Mexico needs one million new jobs *per year* just to accommodate those entering the work force, leaving aside those who have lost their jobs in the economic restructuring process. In other words, just to accommodate new workers the country needs the equivalent of a new *maquiladora* sector every year, not just one at the end of more than three decades of development.

The sector's dependence on the U.S. market also makes it vulnerable to precipitous decline. The sector's recent expansion came during the longest sustained period of economic growth in U.S. history. In 2001, when the U.S. economy softened, the sector lost 171,000 jobs.[7] Further declines are predicted as other countries (particularly China) join the world trading system, offering even lower wages than Mexico can.

The *maquiladora* case study notes other limits of Mexico's model of low-wage, export-oriented industrial development. With most of the inputs coming from the United States, backward linkages are weak, stimulating relatively few sustainable industries. Forward linkages are also lacking, as most final products return to the United States. The prevalence of low wages limits internal market stimulation. The employment of women provides a source of income for women laborers but the *maquiladoras* take advantage of women's relative lack of power to impose working conditions with low salaries, mandatory overtime, lack of legal protections, and insecurity. Finally, the short-term nature of the foreign investments creates high economic instability. Limited benefits are offset by very high costs—both to the environment and to social and cultural cohesion.

The other significant cost is the expulsion of large numbers of people from their communities and, in the absence of viable employment in other sectors of the economy, their country. The current model for liberalization is particularly cruel for these workers. While goods and capital travel ever more freely across borders, restrictions on Mexican migration to the United States become more severe.

Although the *maquiladora* model makes a poor engine for development, one can imagine such a sector playing a more limited role in Mexico's economic progress. Export orientation is not in itself the problem if the export sector is being developed strategically as part of a national strategy. Interestingly many local organizations, such as CEPCO, recognize the need for jobs and have taken independent initiatives to build the export sector, including their own community-run *maquiladoras*. That approach is very different, however, from depending exclusively on export-oriented industrial development. It seems clear that the *maquiladora* sector will not absorb the surplus labor generated from other sectors by economic restructuring. In an economy with significant labor surplus, it makes far more sense to promote policies that maintain current sources of livelihood. Agriculture still employs eight times more people than the *maquiladora* sector. As noted in the previous discussion, there are significant models of dynamic, forward-looking entrepreneurship in the Mexican countryside on which to build.

Cross-border collaboration among civil society groups is one of the clear positive features of globalization. Perhaps the only area in which one could claim consensus about a positive effect of economic integration is the rise in international linkages. For some, these new openings are commercial. El Balcón and CEPCO have developed more equitable international commercial partnerships, which would have been much more difficult prior to economic integration.

Local issues are more often finding their way into international campaigns. In this context, the peasant ecologists' campaign for the release of their jailed leaders serves as a prime example. The Metalclad case is also an excellent model. Local activists physically stopped the trucks from unloading drums of toxic waste, the municipal government refused a permit, and Greenpeace-Mexico brought the case to international attention. All of this ultimately led to the defense of the Metalclad shutdown by the Mexican federal government. Such international cooperation, with each party respectfully playing its appropriate role, is a promising new development. Similar cross-border cooperation is taking place in the efforts of *maquiladora* workers to win the right to independent unions, as seen in the Autotrim case. U.S., Canadian, and Mexican unions have also begun to coordinate organizing drives across borders to deter the kind of runaway shops characteristic of globalization. Such coordinated campaigns by allied national unions can go a long way toward confronting the unilateral power of transnational firms to relocate production.

The Role of the State

As we noted earlier, the free trade program involves much more than the trade in goods. It includes what has come to be known in much of the world as neoliberalism—a coherent set of policies designed not only to reduce barriers to foreign goods but to open avenues for foreign capital while reducing the state's direct role in the economy. This package of reforms, often referred to as the Washington Consensus because of its active promotion by U.S. and multilateral financial institutions, includes an end to capital controls, privatization of state-owned enterprises, elimination of price supports, and reductions in publicly funded services to meet strict budget constraints.

One of the overarching conclusions that emerges from the case studies in this book is that the state needs to play a proactive role for economic integration to benefit the majority. This should come as no surprise to economic historians. As economist Alice Amsden has shown in her recent book, *The Rise of the Rest*, only two countries can claim to have developed relatively modern economies via free trade: Hong Kong and Switzerland. These exceptions, which owe their good fortune to unique locations in the evolving systems of world trade, only highlight the rule that active state involvement in directing the economy is critical to successful economic development, under virtually any economic model.[8]

An interventionist state is not necessarily at odds with an export-oriented, open-economy model. The so-called East Asian miracle was the product of just such an approach. But it is at odds with the Washington Consensus, which is promoted (and enforced) by the strict and punitive policies of the multilateral financial institutions. As these case studies on Mexico show, Mexico's approach has hewed to the neoliberal line enshrined in NAFTA and advocated in Washington. On the one hand, we see clear cases in which the Mexican state has abdicated its role in promoting development. Basic grains producers not only saw their products lose tariff protection because of NAFTA, they then saw the Mexican government allow NAFTA's import quotas to be surpassed without applying the agreed-upon tariffs. They also saw the state withdraw producer-price supports, reduce its involvement in marketing and technical assistance, and limit its role in providing credit for small farmers. The story is much the same in coffee, where the government withdrew its promotion of international supply management under the International Coffee Agreement, then withdrew from its central role in marketing, credit, and extension services.

As noted earlier, the Mexican government's abandonment of the small-farming sector was very much by design, the goal being to eliminate inefficient producers from the newly competitive marketplace. In that sense, this is not an example of a government seeking to develop an economic sector via neoliberalism but failing. Rather it is an example of a government trying to destroy an economic sector—and failing.

That failure, at least up to now, is striking. Perhaps the most impressive aspect of the ANEC and CEPCO cases is the resilience and resourcefulness of the farmers under attack by such policies. In both cases, farmer organizations exhibited precisely the kind of self-reliant collective entrepreneurship that development specialists dream of. ANEC and CEPCO adapted to the harsh new market conditions; evolved new, more powerful forms of organization; achieved economies of scale; took advantage of new opportunities afforded by liberalization; capitalized their operations through well-considered acquisitions of state production facilities; and created new markets under changing conditions. By all accounts, these efforts were (and are) exemplary. They also are clearly inadequate, absent a stronger state role in promoting the sectors' development.

Related to this point, the cases show that governments at different levels still need to maintain the sovereign right to manage their economies and societies according to their own priorities. In that regard, they need to develop (or maintain) the capacity to regulate effectively, decide the appropriate role for the public sector, and meet basic needs. As several cases show, Mexico has lost or given up the capacity to have the government play such a role.

The Metalclad case is explicitly about sovereignty, and whether an international tribunal under NAFTA can override the decisions of elected local governments based on their legitimate health and environmental concerns. In the Guerrero cases we see two vastly different experiences, one leading to widespread deforestation, the other to sustainable forestry practices. Are such outcomes to be determined by the deregulated market and the contest between citizen groups and local power-brokers? Or does the Mexican government play an important role in determining the extent to which the nation's natural resources are exploited for private gain?

As noted earlier, the state also has a crucial role to play in ensuring democracy, transparency, and the rule of law. This necessarily involves strengthening the state, particularly in a period of rapid economic integration where institutions need to withstand not just local or national pressures but also new international forces. Many of these case studies show the institutional underdevelopment of the Mexican state. In some cases, organizations have been able to fill the institutional void left by the state, and many now have their own autonomous and democratic institutions. However, these cannot be expected to replace the state's essential role in promoting, regulating and financing development. Guaranteeing basic rights is also part of this institutional role, but it is not the only one. Transparency is essential as well, but the Mexican state still lacks much institutional development in this area.

Institutional development is also needed in constructing new laws to address emerging issues brought on by economic globalization. The study of bioprospecting highlights the underdeveloped nature of Mexican laws and institutions regarding intellectual property and indigenous rights. This should not be surprising, as this complicated new area has been thrust into the spotlight by recent technological developments, corporate practices, and an evolving body of international law and trade regulations. It urgently needs attention.

The Mexican state cannot abdicate its role in designing a coherent, national development strategy for the country and actively promoting policies that can achieve national goals. The prevailing conformity to the Washington Consensus, which leaves important development decisions to the whims of the market or the interests of multinational corporations, will not produce sustained or sustainable economic development for Mexico. Until there is some acceptance that a strong state is required to implement policies and develop clear priorities based on the concerns and needs of a broader set of citizens, Mexico will remain a nation mired in poverty and social inequality.

As the case studies suggest, civil society organizations have a unique capacity to bring about changes in public policies. This implies improving forms of representation, advancing the reform of the State, opening avenues for citizen participation and consultation, and ending the many forms of discrimination against indigenous people, women, homosexuals, the disabled, and other groups whose full exercise of citizenship is limited. One thing remains clear: the democratic transition in Mexico cannot come from above but only from constant pressure from below.

For the economy, democratization implies changing the State to be more responsive to the needs of the Mexican people and less to the prescriptions of multilateral institutions. To elaborate a national development plan based on sovereignty, equity, and sustainability, the State will have to work closely with social organizations, learning from them the values that guide their actions and the practical lessons that spring from their own rich experiences.

Implications for Trade Agreements

What does all this mean for trade agreements? The case studies make clear that while NAFTA was by no means the sole cause of the issues community groups are dealing with, it was a significant one in every case. NAFTA did not initiate the process of economic integration, but the agreement set the ground rules by which economic integration would take place. NAFTA also made it much more difficult for the Mexican government to diverge from the neoliberal path. With the Free Trade Area of the Americas—a NAFTA for the Western Hemisphere—now being negotiated, it is worth considering briefly what these case studies imply.

1. **No investor-state provisions should allow multinational firms to undermine governments' efforts to protect the health and well-being of their citizens.** NAFTA's Chapter 11, so clearly exposed in the Metalclad case study, has become the boilerplate for other trade agreements, including the proposals for the Free Trade Area of the Americas (FTAA). Foreign investors' rights to fair treatment can be guaranteed without rescinding governments' right to set policies. Chapter 11 effectively extends international law on "takings" well beyond U.S. law, granting corporations undue power to limit government policies. Such provisions should be eliminated so as to restore to governments their sovereign rights to legislate in the

interests of their constituencies. While the Metalclad case deals with health and the environment, the investor-state provision has broader implications related to restoring government sovereignty over a wider range of areas, including economic policy.

2. **Performance requirements should be allowed as a lever to encourage the upward harmonization of standards.** The case studies show that foreign direct investment does not, of its own accord, bring social and environmental benefits. While some areas do benefit, the neoliberal model generally encourages the depression of wage levels and the overexploitation of natural resources. It also depresses the internal market by emphasizing export-oriented production with few forward or backward linkages. In the past, governments could address such limitations by imposing performance requirements on foreign investors, insisting, for example, that a certain percentage of manufacturing inputs must be purchased domestically, or that foreign investors make specific infrastructure investments to protect the environment. Under NAFTA and the proposed FTAA, such performance requirements are considered unfair barriers to trade. Performance requirements have proven critical to ensuring that foreign investment supports long-term national development.[9]

3. **Trade agreements must respect nations' rights to food sovereignty—the ability to limit dependence on food imports and support its farmers.** Agriculture remains a contentious issue in international trade negotiations, and Mexico's experience under NAFTA illustrates why. As the ANEC case shows, the deregulation of trade in basic grains has dramatically affected those who produce the majority of Mexico's food crops. This not only impacts those producers directly, it also affects rural communities as a whole. The U.S. government maintains a policy of ensuring its own food sovereignty. Mexico and other developing countries must be allowed to maintain such policies as well. For Mexico that will undoubtedly mean continued tariff protection for many basic grains, limiting U.S. exports of its farm surplus to Mexico.

4. **Negotiate labor and environmental issues within the core of trade agreements, not as side agreements, as they were under NAFTA.** NAFTA's side agreements have proven inadequate for meeting the goals of protecting labor rights and ecosystems. It is striking that, among these diverse case studies, there is not a single example in which the side agreements played a significant role. Labor and the environment need to be considered within the text of

the trade agreements themselves, as many citizens' groups have proposed. Many provisions within these wide-ranging agreements have important implications that must be evaluated on their own. Any measures to address labor and environment must be backed by the same kind of commitment and enforcement power seen in other parts of the agreements, such as NAFTA's Chapter 11. Agreements must include minimum global standards, consistent with ILO commitments, to promote freedom of association and respect for basic human rights.

5. **Trade agreements must explicitly address migration, negotiating further liberalization so that labor mobility can increase as capital mobility increases.** By all accounts, migration was not meaningfully on the table when NAFTA was negotiated, as it was vetoed outright by U.S. negotiators. Mexico's experience with the economic integration process has shown quite clearly that too few jobs are being created in Mexico to accommodate new entries into the work force and those who have been displaced through economic restructuring. With an increasingly militarized border with the United States, Mexicans find labor markets less free than ever. One cannot help but be dismayed that one of the most productive rational choices open to the poor in Mexico in a period of liberalization remains illegal, notwithstanding its consistency with free-trade principles. Mexican President Vicente Fox has called for a transition to more open borders, but negotiations with Washington have stalled. Significant increases in workers' rights to migrate must be part of any trade agreement.

6. **Trade agreements must directly address asymmetries between trading partners by funding significant investment in less developed regions.** Free trade favors the large and powerful. If economic competition in a more open economy is to be fair, it must include provisions to bring the least developed regions up to a minimum level of development so they too can compete. This approach has been proven to work in the European Union, where large investments in less developed countries have stimulated economic development, which has allowed them to compete and begin to catch up to their more developed trading partners. NAFTA joined even more unequal economies, yet funded only small initiatives— for example, the North American Development Bank and the Fund for Environmental Cooperation—to address those disparities. Such investments cannot be left to the private sector or expected from the governments of less developed countries.

7. **Support international efforts to manage the supply of commodities and promote fairly traded products.** As the CEPCO case shows, commodity prices for products such as coffee will tend downward without some sort of international supply management. This is particularly true when development organizations like the World Bank actively promote production in many parts of the world at the same time, thus exacerbating the oversupply. International supply management is barred by the OECD, of which Mexico is a member, so such steps would represent a radical departure from the free-trade norm. Efforts to promote the growing fair trade market, such as in lumber and coffee, can help encourage more sustainable markets and practices, but they are no substitute for international supply agreements. CEPCO's farmers, for example, can expect only a small percentage of their sales to go to the fair-trade market, even if it expands dramatically.

Outlines of an Alternative

Although the present course and structure of global integration is often presented as inevitable and immutable, there are alternatives, many of which recognize and accept the world's growing economic integration while seeking more just and sustainable structures. These case studies offer living proof that citizens' organizations are not seeking to turn back the clock to the days of protectionism and import substitution. While many would suggest that the poor are worse off now than they were under that model, few would argue it served well either the poor or the environment. Instead, civil society groups such as those studied here seek an alternative approach to managing globalization in a way that promotes sustainable development.

The case studies in this book demonstrate some of the strengths of a society organized to promote productive capacities, develop new markets, and design integrated alternatives that combine self-sufficiency, culture, care of the environment, and production for the market. These are initiatives from below that come from the same marginalized sectors that the State and the market see as inefficient anachronisms in a modern Mexico. What they have achieved goes well beyond mere survival, difficult in itself. These initiatives offer a different model altogether. Where the State imposes welfare programs, civil society groups test self-management. Where the market favors the rich, these organizations attend to the needs of the poor. Where government officials issue dubious claims that they are protecting the environment, peasant farmers and others implement sustainable practices. In their daily work, these civil-society groups advance the age-old struggle to end discrimination against women and defend the rights of indigenous people to self-determination. In most cases, this is done without government support and often in the face of unfavorable social and economic policies.

Many see in these efforts—still incipient and weak—the embryo of an alternative economic model, one based on new relations with the global market, which now constitutes an inescapable framework for economic relations. The groups that work in self-management, fair trade, collective investment, stewardship of the environment, and dignified work accept some of these rules of the game, but they reserve the right to reject others. In the course of constructing new forms of economic integration, they defend the larger project of converting into comparative advantages non-market-based human values such as sustainability, dignity, and equity.

It is beyond the scope of this book to present a comprehensive alternative approach for managing economic integration, but some civil society groups in Mexico have begun the process. In anticipation of the Free Trade Area of the Americas, a broad range of organizations from across the Western Hemisphere began meeting in 1998, to resist the push to base the FTAA on NAFTA. Now known as the Hemispheric Social Alliance, this network has crafted one of the more comprehensive alternative frameworks for economic integration. Their joint document, "Alternatives for the Americas," highlights that they are not—as prevailing characterizations would paint them—"globophobes":

> We are not opposed to the establishment of rules for regional or international trade and investment. Nor does our criticism of the dominant, externally imposed form of globalization imply a wish to return to the past, to close our economies and establish protectionist barriers, or to press for isolationist trade policies. But the current rules have not helped our countries overcome, nor even reduce, our economic problems. We propose alternative rules to regulate the global and hemispheric economies based on a different economic logic: that trade and investment should not be ends in themselves, but rather the instruments for achieving just and sustainable development.[10]

The document goes on to outline a comprehensive set of principles and policies, including chapters on human rights, labor, environment, the role of the state, immigration, foreign investment, international finance, intellectual property rights, sustainable energy development, agriculture, access to markets, and enforcement and dispute resolution. These are not necessarily the only, final or best answers in the search for a coherent, workable, alternative approach to economic integration.[11] The mere existence of such a document, however, is a sign of a broad disposition to manage economic integration, not just resist it, and that civil society groups directly involved with people most affected by current policies are actively engaged in designing that alternative. By the thousands people have taken to the streets to back such proposals, declaring that "another world is possible." It is significant, too, that for the FTAA this alternative vision has developed outside of official circles, largely in Peoples' Summits run parallel to the Summits of the Americas in which FTAA proposals have been advanced.

These alternative models break decisively with the orthodoxy of the free trade model. They value not just the market but also subsistence economies. They promote not just international commerce but regional trade. They counterpose the impersonal imposition of faceless market forces with widespread participation and transparency. Ultimately they attempt to define, from the experiences of resistance and self-reliance of those at the base of the economic structure, sustainable forms of production and equitable forms of development, based on human values that go beyond market efficiency, productivity, and competition.

The case studies presented in this book, and the analysis of their lessons, suggest that the time has come to bring such alternative proposals into official discussions of economic integration. Mexico's experience, and in particular that of the organized communities studied here, paints a clear picture of some of the ways in which the present model is not working, as well as some ways in which a different approach could. Hopefully such perspectives can be welcomed in the effort to manage globalization for the benefit of the majority.

Notes

1. Armando Bartra, *Mesoamérica: Los Ríos Profundos* (Mexico City, Mexico: Instituto Maya, A.C., 2001) 49.

2. Mario J. Molina and Luisa T. Molina, *Integrated Strategy for Air Quality Management in the Mexico City Metropolitan Area. Report No. 7* (Cambridge: Massachusetts Institute of Technology, 2000).

3. From formal commentary by Luís Hernández Navarro on the case studies on CEPCO and ANEC at the August 23, 2001, conference at El Colegio de México, "La Respuesta de las Organizaciones Civiles y Sociales Mexicanas ante la Integración Económica: Estudios de Casos."

4. Hernández, commentary.

5. See, for example, Sheldon Annis, ed. *Poverty, Natural Resources, and Public Policy in Central America* (New Brunswick, N.J.: Transaction Publishers for the Overseas Development Council, 1992); or Robin Broad, "The Poor and the Environment: Friends or Foes?" *World Development* 22:6 (June 1994), 811–822.

6. Action Group on Erosion, Technology and Concentration (formerly Rural Advancement Foundation International), "Biopiracy Project in Mexico Definitively Canceled," press release, November 9, 2001.

7. Rolando González, Consejo Nacional de la Industria Maquiladora, cited in *La Jornada*, December 8, 2001.

8. Alice Amsden, *The Rise of the Rest: Challenges to the West from Late-Industrializing Economies* (New York: Oxford University Press, 2001).

9. See Amsden, *The Rise of the Rest*, which argues that the imposition of performance requirements has been critical to virtually every successful attempt to stimulate economic development via export-oriented industry.

10. Hemispheric Social Alliance, *Alternatives for the Americas: General Principles*, available at http://www.web.net/comfront/alts4americas/eng/eng.html.

11. See, for example, Robin Broad, *Global Backlash: Citizen Initiatives for a Just World Economy* (New York: Rowman & Littlefield Publishers, 2002) for a survey of such civil society proposals.

About the Contributors

Olivia Acuña Rodarte is currently director of the seminar on agrarian issues at the National School of Professional Studies—Acatlán, of the Universidad Nacional Autónoma de México (UNAM). With a master's degree in Rural Development, she has collaborated with coffee-grower organizations from Chiapas and Oaxaca and has contributed to various research efforts on rural problems.

Josefina Aranda Bezaury is a researcher in the Instituto de Investigaciones Sociológicas de la Universidad Autónoma Benito Juárez de Oaxaca, where she researches issues related to rural peasant women and public policy. An anthropologist by training, she also is an advisor to the State Coalition of Coffee Producers of Oaxaca (CEPCO).

Andrés Barreda is a professor of economics at UNAM and a researcher with the Center for Social Analysis, Information, and Popular Education (CASIFOP). He has written extensively on issues of globalization and the environment, including research on the Plan Puebla-Panama development project and on bioprospecting in Mexico.

Fernando Bejarano González is the founder and current coordinator of the Mexican Action Network on Alternatives to Pesticides (RAPAM) and the main contact in Mexico for the International Persistent Organic Pollutants Elimination Network (IPEN). From 1993–96, he was coordinator of

Greenpeace-Mexico's Program on Toxic Waste, during which time he participated in the campaign to prevent Metalclad Corporation from reopening a toxic waste site in Guadalcázar, San Luís Potosí.

David Barton Bray is Coordinator and Associate Professor of the Environmental Studies Department at Florida International University in Miami. From 1986–97 he worked for the Inter-American Foundation, serving as a Mexico representative from 1989–97. He has been collaborating with the Ford and Hewlett Foundations on a research project on community forestry in Mexico.

Laura Carlsen is a researcher and journalist in Mexico, where she has lived since 1986. She is a member of the Environmental Commission of the Mexican Action Network on Free Trade (RMALC) and collaborates with the Center for the Study of Change in Mexican Countryside. She has written several articles and publications in English and Spanish on political, economic, and environmental topics.

Enrique Cienfuegos is an independent journalist in Mexico. With a degree in Communications from the Universidad Autónoma Metropolitana, he wrote a thesis on the Organization of Peasant Ecologists of the Sierra of Petatlan and Coyuca de Catalan (OCESP).

Leticia Merino is a Professor and Researcher at the Social Studies Institute in the Ecology Institute of UNAM. She has worked for twelve years on the forestry sector, particularly on themes related to community organization and resource use, including work in the Mayan Zone of Quintana Roo, the region of the Biosphere Reserve of the Monarch Butterfly, the State of Guerrero, and the Northern Sierra of Oaxaca.

Pastoral Juvenil Obrera is a nongovernmental organization in Matamoros, Tamaulipas, founded by Christian workers from the *maquiladoras*. A member of the Coalition for Justice in the Maquiladoras, the group was actively involved in the Autotrim organizing effort. For security reasons, the individual authors of the chapter on that campaign remain anonymous.

Hilda Salazar is Director of the Mexican nongovernmental organization, Women and Environment, and founder of the Women and Environment Network. She is a member of the Environment Commission and the Coordinating Commission of the Mexican Action Network for Free Trade

(RMALC), working on the analysis of the impacts of free trade agreements and economic integration on the environment and on women.

Timothy A. Wise is Deputy Director and Researcher with the Global Development and Environment Institute at Tufts University. He is the former executive director of Grassroots International, a Boston-based international aid organization, and co-editor of *A Survey of Sustainable Development: Social and Economic Dimensions.*

Index

239

Also from Kumarian Press...

Global Issues

Going Global: Transforming Relief and Development NGOs
Marc Lindenberg and Coralie Bryant

Inequity in the Global Village: Recycled Rhetoric and Disposable People
Jan Knippers Black

Running Out of Control: Dilemmas of Globalization
R. Alan Hedley

Sustainable Livelihoods: Building on the Wealth of the Poor
Kristin Helmore and Naresh Singh

Trapped: Modern-Day Slavery in the Brazilian Amazon
Binka Le Breton

Where Corruption Lives
Edited by Gerald E. Caiden, O.P. Dwivedi and Joseph Jabbra

Conflict Resolution, Environment, Gender Studies, Globalization,
International Development, Microfinance, Political Economy

Better Governance and Public Policy: Capacity Building and Democratic Renewal
in Africa
Edited by Dele Olowu and Soumana Sako

The Humanitarian Enterprise: Dilemmas and Discoveries
Larry Minear

Pathways Out of Poverty: Innovations in Microfinance for the Poorest Families
Edited by Sam Daley-Harris

Protecting the Future: HIV Prevention, Care and Support Among Displaced and
War-Affected Populations
Wendy Holmes for The International Rescue Committee

War and Intervention: Issues for Contemporary Peace Operations
Michael V. Bhatia

War's Offensive on Women
The Humanitarian Challenge in Bosnia, Kosovo, and Afghanistan
Julie A. Mertus for the Humanitarianism and War Project

Visit Kumarian Press at **www.kpbooks.com** or
call **toll free 800.289.2664** for a complete catalog.

Kumarian Press, located in Bloomfield, Connecticut, is a forward-looking, scholarly press that promotes active international engagement and an awareness of global connectedness.